TAMALES

TAMALES

Mark Miller, Stephan Pyles, *and* John Sedlar

with John Harrisson

PHOTOS BY LOIS ELLEN FRANK

MACMILLAN•USA

To the wonderful women of Teotitlán de Vialle, who taught us to make the best tamales in the world.
—Mark Miller, Stephan Pyles, and John Sedlar

MACMILLAN
A Simon & Schuster Macmillan Company
1633 Broadway
New York, NY 10019-6785

Macmillan Publishing books may be purchased for business or sales promotional use. For information please write:
Special Markets Department, Macmillan Publishing USA, 1633 Broadway, New York, NY 10019.

Library of Congress Cataloging-in-Publication Data

Miller, Mark Charles, 1949–
Tamales / Mark Miller, Stephan Pyles, John Sedlar, with John Harrisson.
    p. cm.
    Includes index.
    ISBN 0-02-861327-9
    1. Stuffed foods (Cookery) 1. Pyles, Stephan. II. Sedlar, John, 1954– . III. Title
TX836.M55 1997   97-38971
641.8—dc21   CIP

Manufactured in the United States of America

10 9 8 7 6 5 4

Book design by Nick Anderson

Table of Contents

Acknowledgments

*Thanks to Patricia Quintana for exposing me to the myriad tamales in Mexico,
and to Michael Chmar and Geoffrey Meeker, who have become the "Tamale Kings" of Star Canyon.*
— STEPHAN PYLES

To Helena Brandes, for assistance with recipe editing.

*To Ron Cooper and Dr. Howard-Yana Shapiro, for arranging our unforgettable research trip to Oaxaca,
and to Margarita Wynne for translating proceedings so adeptly.*

To Jennifer Griffin, our patient editor at Macmillan, who shared our collective vision.

— MARK MILLER, STEPHAN PYLES, AND JOHN SEDLAR

Introduction

Tamales are treasures. These fragrant, wrapped packages filled with warm corn dough and flavorful fillings are treats for all the senses. Tamales are a timeless food. They have existed in the culinary repertoire of Central and South America for centuries; the name itself is derived from *tamalli*, a word in the Nahuatl language spoken by the Aztecs, which referred to a wrapped food very similar to the tamales we enjoy today. In pre-Hispanic times, tamales of many different shapes, colors, and sizes were not only enjoyed as a dietary staple, but were also made as ritual and sacred offerings to the deities. They were documented as being an important element in feasts, fiestas, and all kinds of celebrations, and this is as true today in Mexico as ever. For example, when the Day of the Dead—a fascinating marriage of indigenous pre-Columbian and Christian belief systems—is celebrated in Mexico at Halloween time, tamales are still the main culinary offering placed on domestic altars and cemetery graves to sustain the spirits of the departed. (They are also enjoyed with abandon by the living who keep vigil during this holiday.) It is usually the favorite tamales of the dead that are offered or eaten. There are special tamales to mark nearly every holiday and celebration, including weddings, Christmas, New Year's, and even family reunions.

Travel to most countries in Latin America and you will discover infinite regional variations when it comes to tamales. Although they sometimes go by different names— *tamal* in Cuba and parts of Central and South America, *humita* in Bolivia and Ecuador, *bollo* in Colombia, *corunda* in the Mexican state of Michoacán, *zacahuil* in Veracruz (another Mexican state), and *hallaca* in Venezuela—all can be found prominently displayed in markets, street vendors' stalls, snack bar counters, and cafés and restaurants, where they steam enticingly and aromatically, wrapped in corn husks or banana leaves. Usually tamales are filled with a corn dough called masa, although sometimes ground or whole rice, mashed beans, or a wheat dough is substituted for the masa. Combined with the masa inside the tamale is a filling of meat or vegetables or other more unusual ingredients. Sometimes, too, different colored corn—blue, purple, or red—is used to make the masa. Occasionally, tamales consist of a wrapper surrounding a filling of meat, vegetables, or seafood with no masa at all. In most of Latin America, it is common to enjoy tamales at market or roadside stands with a small pot or *olla* filled with *atole*, the traditional corn-based drink, or hot chocolate.

Fresh tamales, properly made, are a far cry from the gluey, heavy examples of the craft all too often found in Mexican and Tex-Mex restaurants in the United States. You will find that the recipes in this book will yield light, tender, and deliciously fragrant tamales that melt in the mouth. Tamales are incredibly versatile. They can be served at parties as hors d'oeuvres or buffet finger food and at the table as appetizers, lunch or brunch main courses, accompaniments to dinner entrées, or dessert. They hold their shape and freeze well, making

TAMALES ARE TO MEXICO AND THE SOUTHWEST WHAT SANDWICHES ARE TO NORTH AMERICA and Europe. They are a wonderful culinary idea that allows for infinite variation, requiring only simple ingredients and equipment. All you need is some corn masa dough, a wrapper, a few flavors, your hands, and your imagination. Tamales may seem a little daunting to make at first, but once you get the hang of the technique you'll find them as easy as sandwiches and much more rewarding. For me, tamales provide the opportunity to create new and marvelous flavor combinations, using ingredients I wouldn't normally put together. It's a chance to meld complementary flavors and to create dynamic, more interesting taste profiles. I love "playing" with the masa dough and the other ingredients, using them as a stage upon which to build. From the moment, as a child, I first bit into what to me was an exotic, mysterious, and intensely flavored tamale at the legendary Fonda del Sol restaurant in New York City, I was hooked.

(MARK MILLER)

them ideal items to prepare ahead of time.

In Mexico and other countries in Latin America, tamales are often an excuse for family members to get together and join in the preparation process, especially when a fiesta or forthcoming celebration demands production on a large scale. In preparing this book, we were invited to visit a family in rural Oaxaca in southern Mexico to observe and experience firsthand the process of authentic tamale making in a family setting.

There, in the verdant village of Teotitlán del Valle, as guests of Don Cosmé Martinez, we watched as the Don Cosmé's Zapotec family prepared tamales in the traditional manner, based on more than three thousand years of culinary practice. As dawn broke on the first day of our visit, we accompanied the gracious Señoras Asuncion Martinez, Agustina Alavez, Agripina Bautista, Ernestina Martinez, Tomasa Chavez, and Señorita Ofelia Sosa on their daily walk

through the village. Walking with dried, soaked tamale corn placed in decorative baskets that balanced easily on their heads, the women walked toward the small local mill, where they ground the corn into masa. Returning to their house, the women set to the task of further grinding the masa into a finer paste on their stone *metates*, large, heavy, flat-surfaced grinding stones made of lava rock measuring about 15 inches wide and 24 inches long, standing on sturdy legs

SOME OF MY FIRST MEMORIES OF FOOD INVOLVE TAMALES. COMING FROM A SMALL TOWN IN west Texas, the Hispanic cultural and culinary influence was immense. The thing I remember most about my early encounters with tamales was that they were fun to eat. The fact that they came in their special little "gift wrappings" was not lost on an innocent and impressionable youth! Forty years or so later, they still have not lost their unique celebratory appeal. I have always had a particular interest in nontraditional tamales ever since I was 10: a cook in one of my father's restaurants brought in some tamales she had made at home. The stewed meat filling came from wild rabbit her husband had hunted locally, and it was at this point that I ceased thinking of tamales as a generic product.

(STEPHAN PYLES)

a few inches above the ground. Kneeling in front of the *metates*, each woman used a *mano*, a flattened cylinder of lava rock resembling a rolling pin, tapered at each end, to work the corn backward and forward until it reached the proper fine consistency. They scooped this freshly ground masa into a bowl placed at the far end of each *metate* before grinding more of the corn. Decades of grinding had left their mark even on the incredibly hard *metates*, which were all well worn with use.

Next, a rich, dark traditional mole sauce was prepared by the three older women of the family, Asuncion, Agripina, and Agustina, with toasted dried chiles, toasted seeds and nuts, and herbs and spices. Each ingredient was ground carefully on the *metate* and then mixed together. As is the case in many parts of rural Oaxaca, the preparation and cooking of food is done not in the house itself but in an adjacent outbuilding, which serves as *la cocina*. In Don Cosmé's house, cooking is done under a *palapa*, or covered shelter, over a wood fire on a *comal,* or clay griddle. Everything is prepared intricately and immaculately by hand, and because the process is labor intensive—there is no electricity, gas, or running water in the "kitchen" area—the meticulous skill of the women, who worked seamlessly and busily together while enjoying conversation about family, friends, and cooking (and joking about the assembled onlookers) represented an impressive art form in itself.

Next, a fresh turkey was cooked over the wood fire for the filling (Don Cosmé raises his own birds on his property) and the various tamale wrappers and flavorings were prepared—dried corn husks were rehydrated, fresh corn leaves selected and cleaned, banana leaves heated and softened, and avocado leaves picked from a tree in the yard. The tamales were then assembled; some with the ground corn masa spread inside the wrappers, the mole sauce ladled carefully over the corn, and the cooked fresh turkey placed on top of the sauce; others made with dried masa or beans; and still others made with fresh corn and herbs. The wrappers were folded into exquisite rectangular packages and tied neatly. A large clay *olla*, or cooking pot, was placed over a wood fire. A large pile of twigs was set over boiling water in the bottom of the pot, and the tamales were placed on top of the twigs, well above the water. The pot was then covered to let the tamales steam as we all waited in great anticipation.

Finally, it was time for our own Fiesta de Tamales to commence. As we sat down together for an open-air lunch with the whole family—the accomplished women cooks, Don Cosmé, his son, Pancho, and Pancho's children—at a large table in Don Cosmé's garden, the assorted tamales were brought steaming and fragrant to the table. We opened the beautiful tamales and could scarcely believe the lightness and ethereal quality of the corn masa and the intense flavors of the filling. Even the experienced and much-traveled chefs in attendance realized they were tasting probably the best, most perfect tamales of their lives. We hope, in this book, to bring to you a little of the spirit and soul of those precious moments spent in Oaxaca, as well as the knowledge and experience of a subject very close to our hearts.

(J O H N   S E D L A R)

IT WOULD PROBABLY SURPRISE MOST PEOPLE JUST HOW ACCESSIBLE TAMALES ARE, AND HOW easily both traditional and out-of-the-ordinary tamales can be made in the home kitchen. A multitude of fillings and wrappings, combined with innumerable salsas and toppings, make this food one of my all-time favorites. Tamales are surely one of the most satisfying and versatile of dishes. From classic to modern, from regional to international, tamales can be savory or sweet; hot, warm, or cold; they can contain stuffings of meat, fish, poultry, vegetables, fruit, cheese, nuts, spices, herbs, and seasonings. The wrappers may run the gamut from dried and fresh corn husks to banana, palm, grape, or avocado leaves; from foil to plastic wrap. They may even be enclosed within crab or lobster shells or even giant clam shells. Tamales have got it all—everything I know I have ever wanted in a simple little package.

Notes on Preparing Tamales

Tamales traditionally contain a corn dough—*masa* in Spanish—wrapped inside a dried corn husk, which is tied and then cooked by steaming. Occasionally the corn masa base is replaced by another ingredient, such as potatoes, grains, or vegetables. Sometimes the masa is flavored, and often a plain masa or flavored masa encloses a flavored filling. Certain regions of Mexico and Central and South America favor wrapping tamales in banana leaves rather than corn husks; in some places, such as Baja California and Bolivia, fresh corn husks are sometimes used as an alternative to dried. Now and again other leaves such as avocado or the large-leaved herb *hoja santa* are used as the tamale wrapper. The combinations and permutations are endless, which is one of the attractions of the tamale, but, ultimately, all tamales are made along much the same lines.

Here, then, are the basic pointers you need to know about making tamales:

MASA DOUGH

Most tamales, and most of the recipes in this book, use masa harina (also called masa seca) as the base for the dough. Masa harina is made from a special type of large-kernel corn, grown (as is hominy) specifically for this purpose; it is then dried and cooked in a mixture of water and calcium oxide (lime-water). The corn is then drained, dried, and ground into flour. Ready-made (or "fresh") unflavored masa dough can also be bought from tortilla factories. It not only provides a shortcut if you happen to live in a neighborhood with a tortilla factory, but the quality of the corn used and the large quantities usually made give the masa an attractively different, light texture and stronger flavor.

Alternative ingredients used in this book as the tamale base (instead of the masa dough) include rice, fresh sweet corn, potatoes, polenta, and spinach. Many of the innovative dessert tamales substitute fruit and other sweet ingredients for masa.

The essential elements of plain masa dough, in addition to the masa harina, are some kind of liquid—usually water but sometimes a stock, sauce, or milk—and a type of fat—butter, some type of oil, vegetable shortening, or some combination. Traditionally, tamales are made with lard, and there are many who swear by its superior flavor, but in today's more health-conscious environment, we have long since used lighter alternatives. Usually, there is no alternative to making tamales with fat of some kind; without it they will become dry and cakey and lack flavor. Finally, masa dough almost always contains a little salt and, usually, baking powder.

As you will see in the recipes that follow, each of us has a slightly different technique for mixing masa dough. We all use electric mixers to do the heavy work of forming the dough, and we like to let the dough rest at some point so the dry ingredients can thoroughly absorb the moist ones. As a general rule of thumb, you can test for masa dough doneness by dropping a little dough into a bowl of water. If it floats, it is light and ready to use; if it sinks, mix some more. To test whether the dough is too wet or too dry, make the following observation: if the dough all sticks to the paddle attachment of the mixer, it is too dry; if it all sticks to the side of the bowl, it is too moist. Ideally, it should stick a little to both. Then, if you press down lightly on a patty of dough, it should not crack at the edges, also indicating the perfect ratio of dry ingredients to fat and water.

The dough is best made 30 to 60 minutes before preparing the tamales, and no less; the dough will absorb the moisture while it is resting, making it the right airy consistency—not heavy. Wrap the dough in plastic wrap and leave at room temperature for this time (30 to 60 minutes), or for up to 2 hours. Then, put in the refrigerator, if necessary, for up to 2 days; after that, it will ferment and turn "sour."

The dough is best used fresh, rather than frozen. However, it can be frozen, like tamales, in an airtight container or double bag, and kept (ideally) for no more than 1 month.

Plain corn tamales make wonderful side dishes, but their true beauty is in the infinite variety of flavorings they typically carry. (This would be a distinctly thin volume unless the plain corn masa was flavored, or unless it contained a flavored filling of some kind.)

MASA DOUGH FLAVORINGS

As the recipes that follow show, Mark typically flavors the masa dough, while Stephan and John prefer to showcase plain masa with a flavored filling. Sometimes the masa flavoring is a liquid ingredient, such as a stock or a barbecue sauce, in which case the other liquids in the dough are reduced accordingly; other times a dry ingredient is added, such as herbs, spices, nuts or seeds, or vegetables and fruit such as roasted corn, chiles, bell peppers, mushrooms, tomatoes, beans, olives, or dried fruit. Always be prepared to compensate for certain ingredients; for example, if using a sun-dried tomato paste, which is invariably salty, reduce the amount of salt used. Always use unsalted butter.

FLAVORED FILLINGS

We all use fillings in most of our tamales, and there are almost as many options as there are tamales. The trick is to carefully enclose the filling inside the masa dough so that it does not leak out or cook too quickly and dry out.

WRAPPINGS

By far the most common form of tamale wrapper is the cream to pale yellow–colored dried corn husks, available at Mexican stores and Latin markets. They need to be soaked in warm water for 30 minutes until they become pliable, and then they can be rolled up to enclose the dough. To keep the husks submerged in the water, weigh them down with a small plate or other heavy object. Corn husks are not edible, although guests at our restaurants have been known to attempt it. Do not try this at home! If the husks seem too small to contain the masa dough called for in the recipe, use two husks per tamale. Just place the square ends together, overlapping, with the narrow, pointed ends of the husk at each end. Add the filling and roll up carefully (see "Assembly"). You may wish to secure the husk by tying an additional strip around the middle where the two husks join, although this is not usually necessary.

Wrapping tamales in banana leaves, a style favored in tropical regions, gives a dramatic presentation and imparts a pleasant, unique flavor to the dough. Whole fresh banana leaves (measuring, on average, 36 inches long and 12 inches wide) can be bought at Latin markets, as can the precut squares, which are usually found in the frozen section. However, whole leaves do vary in size, and since the ends are tapered, you will need to cut them into squares for the tamale wrappings. Be aware that the measurements for whole leaves called for in the recipes are usually larger than what you will need for the trimmed-up squares. You are likely to have parts of the leaf left over, or at least some scraps, but nature has yet to invent consistently sized, rectangular banana leaves! Like dried corn husks, banana leaves are not edible. Other wrappings can be used; the only limit is your imagination.

Like Stephan and Mark, John also wraps some of his tamales in corn husks, but usually he prefers to wrap the dough in plastic wrap, steam the tamales, and then unwrap the tamales for presentation in a soaked corn husk. (Be sure to have plastic wrap on hand when preparing one of John's recipes.) This makes for a little easier handling at the table, since it is unnecessary to slice the corn husk open or untie the ends, but sometimes that's part of the fun of eating tamales. Most of Stephan and Mark's recipes can be prepared like John's, if you wish, and vice versa.

Sometimes, for a visually striking presentation, nothing beats red corn husks. However, the carmine-colored husks from Burgundy corn and other red corn are hard to come by, and an alternative is to soak regular yellow husks in hibiscus tea. To prepare the tea, soak 1 part dried hibiscus flowers (also sold in Latin stores and such specialty markets as Flor de Jamaica) in 4 parts warm water and let steep for 1 to 2 hours.

ASSEMBLY

If you are using corn husks, the masa dough should be divided evenly and spread or flattened gently with a tortilla press, a heavy pan, or with your fingers to cover all but the edges of the wrapper. In general, about 1 1/2 inches of corn husk should be left uncovered by masa at each end and about 3/4 inch at each side. After adding any filling, bring the sides of the corn husks together, folding the dough so that it encloses the filling. Then tuck one side of the husk under the other and roll up the tamale tightly so that the dough is completely enclosed inside the husk. Avoid rolling up jelly-roll style with one side of the husk inside the dough and filling. Fold the ends of the husk under the tamale in a neat envelope style, or twist the ends of the tamale wrapper and secure with strips of corn husk torn from extra husks. If you like, or if the occasion suggests it, you can use different materials for tying the tamales, such as strips of banana leaf or festively colored ribbons.

STEAMING

Tamales are almost always steamed, and you can buy Mexican tamale steamers for the purpose. Alternatively, use a Chinese bamboo steamer, a couscous pot, or a saucepan fitted with a strainer or vegetable basket. Fill the bottom of the pan with 2 to 3 inches of water, bring to a boil, and place the tamales in the steamer, seam-side down (or they can be steamed in an upright position). Space the tamales as much as possible and make sure they are not close to touching the water. If the tamales are in more than one layer, allow a little more time for them to cook. Cover the steamer or pan tightly with a lid or foil (it is important that little or no steam escapes while cooking). Steam the tamales for the suggested time over lightly boiling water, adding more boiling water as needed. The tamales are done when they feel firm to the touch but are not hard and the dough comes away easily from the husk when it is peeled back. If you can fend off your guests, let the tamales sit for 5 minutes or so after they have cooked to let the texture and flavors set up. The steaming process leaches saltiness from the tamales, so bear this in mind when seasoning the dough.

Do not try cooking or rewarming tamales in a microwave oven—this makes the dough tough.

PRESENTATION

Placing the tamales seam-side down on a work surface or serving plates, slice open the top of the tamales with a knife (or you can let your guests do this at the table). Draw the sides of the corn husk back to reveal the masa and filling or, as Stephan prefers, gently push the ends of the tamale together as you would for a baked potato. When using plastic wrap to cook the tamales, John transfers the unwrapped tamale to pristine open-face "serving husks and then unwraps the tamales." And voilà!—or, as we should more properly say, ¡mira!

Tamale Masa Dough and Tamale Base Recipes

Masa Seca Tamale Dough

(S T E P H A N   P Y L E S)

MY BASIC TAMALE DOUGH RECIPE USES MASA HARINA, A TYPE OF CORN FLOUR THAT IS WIDELY AVAILABLE IN SUPERMARKETS.

PLAIN CORN TAMALES, MADE WITH THIS RECIPE ALONE, MAKE GREAT ACCOMPANIMENTS TO ANY MAIN COURSE.

1³/₄ cups masa harina
1¹/₄ cups hot water
10 tablespoons chilled vegetable shortening
1¹/₂ teaspoons salt
1 teaspoon baking powder
¹/₄ cup chilled Chicken Stock (page 160)

Place the masa harina in the bowl of an electric mixer fitted with a paddle attachment. With the machine on low speed, add the water in a slow, steady stream until the dough forms a ball. Continue mixing on medium speed for 5 minutes, then transfer the dough to a clean bowl. Refrigerate for 1 hour.

Return the masa to the bowl of the electric mixer and beat for 5 minutes on high speed. With the machine running, slowly add the shortening 2 tablespoons at a time. Continue mixing for about 5 minutes, until the dough is smooth and light. Stop the mixer to scrape the sides of the bowl as necessary. Reduce the speed to low and continue to beat.

While the dough is mixing, combine the salt, baking powder, and chicken stock in a small mixing bowl. Slowly add the stock mixture to the masa in a steady stream and continue mixing until thoroughly combined. Increase the speed to high and mix for 5 minutes longer.

Sweet Corn Tamale Mixture

(J O H N   S E D L A R)

THIS TAMALE DOUGH, MADE WITH FRESH CORN, HAS A DISTINCTIVELY INTENSE FLAVOR.

THE FRESHER AND YOUNGER THE CORN, AND THE LESS STARCHY IT IS, THE BETTER.

Heat the corn oil in a saucepan. Add the corn and bell peppers and sauté over medium heat for 10 to 15 minutes, stirring frequently, until tender. Remove from the heat and let cool to room temperature. Transfer three-quarters of this mixture to a blender and blend for 1 minute; do not overmix. Add the remaining mixture and other ingredients and pulse until thoroughly combined.

1 tablespoon corn oil
3 cups fresh corn kernels
¹/₂ red bell pepper, seeded and diced
¹/₂ green bell pepper, seeded and diced
1 tablespoon semolina flour
1 teaspoon salt
¹/₂ teaspoon freshly ground white pepper
¹/₄ cup heavy cream
1 large egg

Fresh and Dried Corn Tamale Masa Dough

(M A R K   M I L L E R)

THIS IS THE BASE RECIPE I USE FOR MY PLAIN TAMALES, AND IT IS ALSO THE JUMPING-OFF POINT FOR THE FLAVORED MASA DOUGHS I LIKE TO USE. IT'S MADE WITH BOTH DRIED MASA HARINA AND FRESH CORN—A HYBRID OF MY COLLEAGUES' TWO PREVIOUS RECIPES, WHICH PROVES THAT THERE'S MORE THAN ONE WAY TO SWING SOME MASA DOUGH! FOR THIS RECIPE, YOU'LL NEED TWO EARS OF CORN. WHEN CUTTING THE CORN KERNELS FROM THE COB, SCRAPE THE COBS WITH THE BACK OF A KNIFE TO SQUEEZE OUT AS MUCH OF THE CORN GERM AND CORN "MILK" AS POSSIBLE.

$1^1/_2$ cups masa harina
$^3/_4$ teaspoon salt
1 teaspoon sugar
$^1/_2$ teaspoon baking powder
$^1/_4$ cup unsalted butter, softened
$^1/_4$ cup vegetable shortening, at room temperature
1 cup warm water
1 cup fresh corn kernels, including corn germ
   and milk

Place the masa harina, salt, sugar, and baking powder in the bowl of an electric mixer fitted with a paddle attachment. Add the butter and shortening and beat together for 3 minutes, until thoroughly incorporated. Add the water and beat for 2 minutes longer, stopping the mixer to scrape down the sides of the bowl with a spatula as necessary. Add the fresh corn and beat for about 1 minute longer, until incorporated. Take the masa dough out of the bowl, wrap in plastic wrap, and let rest for 30 minutes at room temperature so the dough can thoroughly absorb the moist ingredients.

Roasted Corn Tamale Masa Dough

(M A R K   M I L L E R)

THIS VARIATION ON THE PREVIOUS RECIPE USES ROASTED CORN INSTEAD OF FRESH, GIVING THE DOUGH A SMOKY AND MORE COMPLEX FLAVOR. ADD ANOTHER SERRANO CHILE FOR A HOTTER DOUGH.

Place the masa harina, salt, and baking powder in the bowl of an electric mixer fitted with a paddle attachment. Add the butter and shortening and beat together for 3 minutes, until thoroughly incorporated. Add the water and beat for 2 minutes longer, stopping the mixer to scrape down the sides of the bowl with a spatula as necessary. Add the roasted corn kernels and serrano and beat for about 1 minute longer, until incorporated. Take the masa dough out of the bowl, wrap in plastic wrap, and let rest for 30 minutes at room temperature so the dough can thoroughly absorb the moist ingredients.

$1^1/_2$ cups masa harina
1 teaspoon salt
1 teaspoon baking powder
$^1/_4$ cup unsalted butter, softened
$^1/_4$ cup vegetable shortening, at room temperature
$^3/_4$ cup warm water
1 cup roasted corn kernels,
   without corn germ or milk (page 164)
1 serrano chile, minced, with seeds (optional)

Potato Tamale Masa Dough

(J O H N   S E D L A R)

KEEPING THE POTATOES UNPEELED THROUGH THE COOKING PROCESS RETAINS MOST OF THEIR STARCH CONTENT.

THIS HELPS TO BIND THE TAMALES AND GIVES THEM A GOOD CONSISTENCY.

3 large russet potatoes (about 12 ounces each)
1 cup Masa Seca Tamale Dough (page 2)
1/2 cup (8 tablespoons) unsalted butter
1/2 cup heavy cream
1 teaspoon salt
1 teaspoon freshly ground white pepper
2 large eggs

Place the potatoes in a small saucepan, cover with cold water, and bring to a boil. Reduce the heat to medium and cook the potatoes for about 40 minutes, until tender. Drain and let cool. Peel the potatoes and place in a food processor. Add the prepared tamale masa, butter, cream, salt, and pepper and pulse until the mixture is smooth, scraping down the sides of the bowl as necessary. Add the eggs and pulse just to incorporate, being careful not to overprocess. Cover and refrigerate for 2 hours.

Spinach Tamale Mixture

(J O H N   S E D L A R)

THIS MASA CONTAINS NO CORN—NOT THE ONLY MASA RECIPE OF MINE THAT ESCHEWS THE TRADITIONAL BASE FOR TAMALE FILLINGS.

IT MAKES FOR A STRIKING AS WELL AS FLAVORFUL AND INNOVATIVE TAMALE BASE.

Bring the water to a boil. Add the kosher salt and the spinach and blanch for 1 minute. Drain in a strainer or colander and let cool while it continues to drain.

Melt the butter in a small sauté pan or skillet over medium heat. Add the red bell pepper and 1/2 teaspoon of the white pepper and sauté for 2 minutes, until the bell pepper is just tender but still crisp. Set aside.

Using your hands, squeeze out the excess moisture from the spinach. Place the spinach in a food processor and process until pureed. Add the eggs, cream, salt, and remaining pepper and pulse until well blended. Transfer the mixture to a mixing bowl and fold in the sautéed bell pepper. Set aside.

2 quarts water
2 tablespoons kosher salt
4 bunches fresh spinach leaves (about 2 pounds),
  thoroughly washed
1 tablespoon unsalted butter
1/2 red bell pepper, seeded and diced
1/2 teaspoon freshly ground white pepper
2 large eggs
1/2 cup heavy cream
1/2 teaspoon salt

Red Bell Pepper Tamale Masa Dough

(M A R K   M I L L E R)

THIS FILLING IS DISTINGUISHED BY THE SWEET RED BELL PEPPER PUREE. THE FLAVORS AND SWEETNESS OF THE BELL PEPPER
ARE INTENSIFIED BY THE ROASTING PROCESS.

1¹/₂ cups masa harina
1 teaspoon salt
¹/₂ cup olive oil
1 cup warm water
¹/₂ large roasted red bell pepper, seeded, skin left
    on, and pureed (about ¹/₂ cup) (page 164)

Place the masa harina and salt in the bowl of an electric mixer fitted with a paddle attachment. Add the olive oil and beat together for 3 minutes, until thoroughly incorporated. Add the water and bell pepper puree and beat for 2 minutes longer, stopping the mixer to scrape down the sides of the bowl with a spatula as necessary. Take the masa dough out of the bowl, wrap in plastic wrap, and let rest for 30 minutes at room temperature so the dough can thoroughly absorb the moist ingredients.

Wild Mushroom–Chipotle Tamale Masa Dough

(M A R K   M I L L E R)

THE MUSHROOM POWDER, HOT AND SMOKY CHIPOTLES, AND ROASTED GARLIC COMBINE TO GIVE THIS MASA DOUGH A DELIGHTFULLY COMPLEX FLAVOR.
SUBSTITUTE A DIFFERENT TYPE OF WILD MUSHROOM POWDER IF YOU PREFER.

Place the masa harina, salt, sugar, baking powder, and mushroom powder in the bowl of an electric mixer fitted with a paddle attachment. Add the butter and shortening and beat together for 3 minutes, until thoroughly incorporated. Add the water, chipotle puree, garlic, and corn and beat for 2 minutes longer, stopping the mixer to scrape down the sides of the bowl with a spatula as necessary. Take the masa dough out of the bowl, wrap in plastic wrap, and let rest for 30 minutes at room temperature so the dough can thoroughly absorb the moist ingredients.

1¹/₂ cups masa harina
1 teaspoon salt
¹/₂ teaspoon sugar
1 teaspoon baking powder
2 tablespoons porcini mushroom powder or
    ground dried porcini
6 tablespoons unsalted butter, softened
2 tablespoons vegetable shortening,
    at room temperature
³/₄ cup warm water
2 teaspoons chipotle chile puree (page 165)
1 clove roasted garlic (page 165)
³/₄ cup roasted corn kernels (page 164)

Saffron Tamale Masa Dough

(M A R K   M I L L E R)

SAFFRON IS THE MOST EXPENSIVE SPICE IN THE WORLD; IT TAKES A QUARTER OF A MILLION CROCUS STIGMAS TO YIELD A POUND OF SAFFRON. WE ARE ONLY USING HALF A TEASPOON OF SAFFRON IN THIS RECIPE, BUT IT IS ENOUGH TO TURN THE MASA DOUGH A SPECTACULAR YELLOW COLOR.

1/2 teaspoon saffron threads
1 cup hot water
1 1/2 cups masa harina
1 teaspoon salt
1 teaspoon baking powder
1/2 cup olive oil
2 cloves roasted garlic (page 165)

Stir the saffron threads with the water in a stainless steel bowl. Let stand for 10 minutes. Place the masa harina, salt, and baking powder in the bowl of an electric mixer fitted with a paddle attachment. Add the olive oil and garlic and beat together for 3 minutes. Add the saffron-water mixture and beat for 2 minutes longer, until thoroughly mixed, stopping the mixer to scrape down the sides of the bowl with a spatula as necessary. Take the masa dough out of the bowl, wrap in plastic wrap, and let rest for 30 minutes at room temperature.

Chipotle Tamale Masa Dough

(M A R K   M I L L E R)

CHIPOTLE CHILES ARE DRIED SMOKED JALAPEÑOS AND ONE OF MY FAVORITE CULINARY ALLIES. THEY ARE AVAILABLE CANNED, PACKED IN A SPICY, TOMATO-BASED, VINEGARY ADOBO SAUCE, OR DRIED.

Place the masa harina, salt, and baking powder in the bowl of an electric mixer fitted with a paddle attachment. Add the butter and shortening and beat together for 3 minutes. Add the water and chipotle puree and beat for 2 minutes longer, until thoroughly mixed, stopping the mixer to scrape down the sides of the bowl with a spatula as necessary. Take the masa dough out of the bowl, wrap in plastic wrap, and let rest for 30 minutes at room temperature.

1 1/2 cups masa harina
1 teaspoon salt
1/2 teaspoon baking powder
1/4 cup unsalted butter, softened
1/4 cup vegetable shortening, at room temperature
1 1/2 cups warm water
2 tablespoons chipotle chile puree (page 165),
or more to taste

Red Thai Curry Tamale Masa Dough

(S T E P H A N   P Y L E S)

THE SOUTHWEST MEETS SOUTHEAST ASIA IN THIS RECIPE, DEMONSTRATING JUST HOW VERSATILE AND ADAPTABLE TAMALES CAN BE

AS A MEDIUM FOR FLAVORS. THAI CURRY PASTE IS WIDELY AVAILABLE, AND THERE ARE SEVERAL BRANDS TO CHOOSE FROM.

3 stalks lemongrass, outer leaves peeled
   and discarded
1¼ cups water
1¾ cups masa harina
10 tablespoons chilled vegetable shortening
1½ teaspoons salt
1 teaspoon baking powder
¼ cup chilled Chicken Stock (page 160)
2 tablespoons Thai red curry paste

Bruise the lemongrass stalks with the back of a knife, mince, and combine with the water in a small saucepan. Bring to a boil over high heat, then turn off the heat. Cover the pan and allow the lemongrass to infuse for 15 minutes. Strain the water into a clean saucepan, making sure you have 1¼ cups of liquid, adding more water if necessary. Bring to a boil, then remove from the heat and set aside.

Place the masa harina in the bowl of an electric mixer fitted with a paddle attachment. With the machine on low speed, add the infused water in a slow, steady stream until the dough forms a ball. Continue mixing on medium speed for 5 minutes, then transfer the dough to a clean bowl. Refrigerate for 1 hour.

Return the masa to the bowl of the electric mixer and beat for 5 minutes on high speed. With the machine running, slowly add the shortening 2 tablespoons at a time. Continue mixing for about 5 minutes, until the dough is smooth and light. Stop the mixer to scrape the sides of the bowl. Reduce the speed to low and continue to beat.

While the dough is mixing, combine the salt, baking powder, and chicken stock in a small mixing bowl. Slowly add the stock mixture to the masa in a steady stream. Add the red curry paste and continue mixing until thoroughly combined. Increase the speed to high and mix for 5 minutes longer.

Rice Tamale Mixture

(J O H N   S E D L A R)

I PREFER CALROSE RICE FOR THIS RECIPE. WHEN HANDLING RICE, LEAVE THE SERVING SPOON IN A CUP OF WATER

SO THE RICE DOES NOT STICK TO THE SPOON.

3 cups Japanese (long-grain) rice
6 cups water
1 tablespoon salt

Place the rice in a colander and rinse under cold running water until the water runs clear. Place the rice in a saucepan or rice cooker; add the water and salt; stir; and cover. Bring to a boil (alternatively, if using, follow the instructions for the rice cooker). Reduce the heat to a very slow simmer and cook the rice for about 12 minutes, until tender.

Black Olive Tamale Masa Dough

(M A R K  M I L L E R)

TAPENADE, THE INTENSELY FLAVORED PASTE MADE FROM PITTED BLACK OLIVES, GARLIC, AND OLIVE OIL, IS A TRADITIONAL CONDIMENT FROM THE

PROVENCE REGION OF SOUTHERN FRANCE. IT MAKES A WONDERFUL FLAVORING AGENT FOR TAMALE DOUGH, AS THIS RECIPE PROVES.

1¹/₂ cups masa harina
1 teaspoon salt
¹/₄ cup olive oil
¹/₄ cup black olive paste (tapenade) or
  additional olive oil
1 cup warm water

To prepare the masa dough, place the masa harina and salt in the bowl of an electric mixer fitted with a paddle attachment. Add the oil and olive paste and beat together for 3 minutes, until thoroughly mixed. Add the water and beat for 2 minutes longer, stopping the mixer to scrape down the sides of the bowl with a spatula as necessary. Take the masa dough out of the bowl, wrap in plastic wrap, and let rest for 30 minutes at room temperature.

Blue Corn Masa Seca Tamale Dough

(S T E P H A N  P Y L E S)

BLUE CORN HAS A SLIGHTLY SWEETER FLAVOR THAN YELLOW CORN, AND IT MAKES FOR A MOST ATTRACTIVE TAMALE. BLUE CORN ALSO HAS

HIGHER LEVELS OF CERTAIN NUTRIENTS, SUCH AS THE AMINO ACID LYSINE, WHEN COMPARED WITH OTHER CORN.

1 cup masa harina
⁷/₈ cup blue cornmeal
1¹/₄ cups very hot water
6 tablespoons chilled vegetable shortening
1¹/₂ teaspoons salt
1 teaspoon baking powder
¹/₄ cup chilled Chicken Stock (page 160)

Place the masa harina and blue cornmeal in the bowl of an electric mixer fitted with a paddle attachment. With the mixer on low speed, add the water in a slow, steady stream until the dough forms a ball. Change the speed to high and continue mixing for 5 minutes. Transfer the dough to a clean bowl and refrigerate for 1 hour.

Return the dough to the bowl of the electric mixer and beat for 5 minutes on high speed. With the machine running, slowly add the shortening 2 tablespoons at a time. Continue mixing for about 5 minutes, until the dough is smooth and light. Stop the mixer to scrape the sides of the bowl. Reduce the speed to low and continue to beat.

While the dough is mixing, combine the salt, baking powder, and chicken stock in a small bowl. Add the stock mixture to the masa in a slow, steady stream and continue mixing until thoroughly combined. Increase the speed to high and mix for 5 minutes longer.

Jalapeño-Cilantro Tamale Masa Dough

(M A R K   M I L L E R)

CHILES, TOMATOES, AND CILANTRO ARE A CLASSIC COMBINATION IN SOUTHWESTERN CUISINE. ROASTING THE CHILES AND BLACKENING THE TOMATOES
BRINGS OUT THEIR SWEETNESS AND INTENSIFIES THEIR FLAVORS. IT ALSO INCREASES THE "HOTNESS" OF THE CHILES.

1 1/2 cups masa harina
1 teaspoon salt
1/2 cup olive oil
1 1/4 cups warm water
1/4 cup minced cilantro
1/4 cup minced, roasted, and seeded jalapeño
 chiles (page 164)
1 blackened Roma tomato (page 164),
 with skin, diced

Place the masa harina and salt in the bowl of an electric mixer fitted with a paddle attachment. Add the olive oil and beat together for 3 minutes, until thoroughly mixed. Add the water and beat for 2 minutes longer, stopping the mixer to scrape down the sides of the bowl with a spatula as necessary. Add the cilantro, jalapeños, and tomato and beat for 1 to 2 minutes longer, until incorporated. Take the masa dough out of the bowl, wrap in plastic wrap, and let rest for 30 minutes at room temperature.

Guajillo Tamale Masa Dough

(M A R K   M I L L E R)

GUAJILLOS ARE THE DRIED CHILES OF PREFERENCE FOR SALSAS AND SAUCES IN MEXICO, AND THEIR FRUITY, CITRUSY FLAVOR AND MEDIUM HEAT
MAKE THEM AN IDEAL MATCH FOR SEAFOOD. SOMETIMES THE VOLUME OF CHILE PUREE FROM A GIVEN WEIGHT OF DRIED CHILES IS NOT CONSISTENT;
FOR ONE THING, IT DEPENDS ON THE AMOUNT OF WATER YOU USE TO PUREE THE CHILES. IN THIS CASE, YOU WILL NEED ABOUT 1/2 CUP OF
GUAJILLO CHILE PUREE TO GET A GOOD SATURATED COLOR.

Place the masa harina and salt in the bowl of an electric mixer fitted with a paddle attachment. Add the olive oil and beat together for 3 minutes, until thoroughly mixed. Add the water and guajillo puree and beat for 2 minutes longer, stopping the mixer to scrape down the sides of the bowl with a spatula as necessary. Add the orange zest and beat for 1 minute longer, until incorporated. Take the masa dough out of the bowl, wrap in plastic wrap, and let rest for 30 minutes at room temperature.

1 1/2 cups masa harina
3/4 teaspoon salt
1/4 cup olive oil
3/4 cup warm water
1/2 cup guajillo chile puree (page 165)
1 teaspoon finely minced orange zest

Clam and Fennel Tamale Masa Dough

(M A R K   M I L L E R)

MOST CLAM JUICE CONTAINS PLENTY OF SODIUM, SO BY ALL MEANS REDUCE THE AMOUNT OF SALT IN THE TAMALE DOUGH IF YOU LIKE, OR OMIT IT ENTIRELY.

1$^1/_2$ cups masa harina
$^1/_2$ teaspoon salt
$^1/_2$ cup olive oil
1 cup bottled clam juice
$^1/_2$ cup warm water
6 tablespoons chopped fennel tops
   (feathery leaves only)

Place the masa harina and salt in the bowl of an electric mixer fitted with a paddle attachment. Add the olive oil and beat together for 3 minutes, until thoroughly mixed. Add the clam juice and water and beat for 2 minutes longer, stopping the mixer to scrape down the sides of the bowl with a spatula as necessary. Add the fennel and beat for about 1 minute longer, until incorporated. Take the masa dough out of the bowl, wrap in plastic wrap, and let rest for 30 minutes at room temperature.

Mushroom-Truffle Tamale Masa Dough

(M A R K   M I L L E R)

TRUFFLES AND WILD MUSHROOMS ARE TWO NATURAL FLAVOR PARTNERS THAT PERFECTLY COMPLEMENT THE EARTHY MASA.

THE TRUFFLE OIL GIVES THE DOUGH A WONDERFULLY AROMATIC PERFUME.

Place the masa harina, mushroom powder, salt, baking powder, and sugar in the bowl of an electric mixer fitted with a paddle attachment. Add the butter, truffle oil, and shortening and beat together for 3 minutes, until thoroughly mixed. Add the water and beat for 2 minutes longer, stopping the mixer to scrape down the sides of the bowl with a spatula as necessary. Add the corn kernels and beat for about 1 minute longer, until incorporated. Take the masa dough out of the bowl, wrap in plastic wrap, and let rest for 30 minutes at room temperature.

1$^1/_2$ cups masa harina
2 teaspoons mushroom powder or ground dried
   mushrooms (preferably chanterelles or porcini)
1 teaspoon salt
$^1/_2$ teaspoon baking powder
1 teaspoon sugar
2 tablespoons unsalted butter
2 tablespoons truffle oil,
   or 2 additional tablespoons unsalted butter
$^1/_4$ cup vegetable shortening, at room temperature
1 cup warm water
1 cup fresh corn kernels

BBQ Tamale Masa Dough

(M A R K M I L L E R)

TAMALES MADE WITH THIS DOUGH AND A CHEESE OR SHREDDED MEAT FILLING MAKE A WONDERFUL ACCOMPANIMENT FOR ANY COOKOUT OR BARBECUE.

1¹/₂ cups masa harina
1 teaspoon salt
1 teaspoon baking powder
¹/₂ cup vegetable shortening, at room temperature
¹/₂ cup barbecue sauce (see Barbecued Brisket
    Tamales with Jicama Coleslaw, page 108)
1 cup warm water

Place the masa harina, salt, and baking powder in the bowl of an electric mixer fitted with a paddle attachment. Add the shortening and beat together for 3 minutes, until thoroughly incorporated. Add the barbecue sauce and water and beat for 2 minutes longer, stopping the mixer to scrape down the sides of the bowl with a spatula as necessary. Take the masa dough out of the bowl, wrap in plastic wrap, and let rest for 30 minutes at room temperature so the dough can thoroughly absorb the moist ingredients.

Achiote–Black Bean Tamale Masa Dough

(M A R K M I L L E R)

ACHIOTE IS THE SEED OF THE ANNATTO TREE, AND THE TWO NAMES ARE USED INTERCHANGEABLY. FOR NOTES ON ACHIOTE AND ANNATTO, SEE THE

HEADNOTE ON PAGE 60. THE BEANS SHOULD BE COOKED ONLY UNTIL JUST TENDER OR THEY WILL BECOME MUSHY DURING THE STEAMING PROCESS.

Place the achiote in a bowl of hot water and soften for 45 minutes. Drain and set aside. Place the masa harina and salt in the bowl of an electric mixer fitted with a paddle attachment. Add the butter, shortening, and achiote and beat together for 3 minutes, until thoroughly incorporated. Add the chicken stock and beat for 2 minutes longer, stopping the mixer to scrape down the sides of the bowl with a spatula as necessary. Fold in the black beans by hand. Take the masa dough out of the bowl, wrap in plastic wrap, and let rest for 30 minutes at room temperature so the dough can thoroughly absorb the moist ingredients.

2 tablespoons achiote seeds
1¹/₂ cups masa harina
1 teaspoon salt
¹/₄ cup unsalted butter, softened
¹/₄ cup vegetable shortening, at room temperature
1¹/₂ cups warm Chicken Stock (page 160)
³/₄ cup rinsed, cooked black beans

Canela Tamale Masa Dough

(M A R K   M I L L E R)

CANELA IS A SWEETER TYPE OF CINNAMON DERIVED FROM A DIFFERENT TYPE OF TREE BARK THAN REGULAR CINNAMON. IT IS AVAILABLE IN MEXICAN OR LATIN MARKETS. IF YOU ARE SUBSTITUTING REGULAR CINNAMON, USE HALF AS MUCH. IF YOU PREFER, USE APPLE CIDER INSTEAD OF STOCK— IT WILL HELP TO INTENSIFY THE FLAVORS OF THE MASA DOUGH AND FILLING AND GIVE THE MASA A NATURAL SWEETNESS.

1^1/$_2$ cups masa harina
1 teaspoon sugar
1 teaspoon ground canela
^{1}/$_4$ cup unsalted butter, softened
^{1}/$_4$ cup vegetable shortening, at room temperature
1^1/$_2$ cups warm Chicken Stock (page 160),
  apple cider, or water

Place the masa harina, sugar, and canela in the bowl of an electric mixer fitted with a paddle attachment. Add the butter and shortening and beat together for 3 minutes, until thoroughly incorporated. Add the chicken stock and beat for 2 minutes longer, stopping the mixer to scrape down the sides of the bowl with a spatula as necessary. Take the masa dough out of the bowl, wrap in plastic wrap, and let rest for 30 minutes at room temperature so the dough can thoroughly absorb the moist ingredients.

Mushroom Tamale Dough

(J O H N   S E D L A R)

YOU CAN ADAPT THIS RECIPE IF YOU WISH BY USING AN ASSORTMENT OF WILD MUSHROOMS.

Prepare the masa dough.

Sweat the mushrooms in a large dry skillet over medium heat until they have released their liquid. Add the butter and continue cooking, partially covered, until the liquid has almost evaporated. Add the cream and continue cooking until the liquid thickens and become pastelike, 5 to 6 minutes. Remove from the heat, season with the salt and pepper, and mix well.

Combine the mushrooms with the masa dough in a mixing bowl until thoroughly combined.

Masa Seca Tamale Dough (page 2)
1 pound mushrooms, finely chopped
1 tablespoon unsalted butter
^{1}/$_4$ cup heavy cream
^{1}/$_4$ teaspoon salt
^{1}/$_4$ teaspoon freshly ground white pepper

Habanero–Blackened Tomato Tamale Masa Dough

(M A R K   M I L L E R)

THIS IS A SPICY MASA DOUGH WITH COMPLEX FRUITY TONES, NOT ONLY BECAUSE OF THE HOT HABANERO CHILES BUT ALSO

BECAUSE OF THE ORANGE ZEST AND BLACKENED TOMATOES.

2 habanero chiles
3 Roma tomatoes
1 clove garlic
2 teaspoons chopped orange zest
1 1/2 cups masa harina
1/4 teaspoon salt
1/2 cup vegetable shortening, at room temperature
1/3 cup warm water
1/2 cup fresh corn kernels
1 tablespoon chopped cilantro

Heat a dry cast-iron skillet over medium heat. When hot, add the habaneros, tomatoes, and garlic. Blacken over medium heat, turning frequently, for 25 to 30 minutes. Roughly chop and transfer to a blender or food processor. Add the orange zest and puree.

Place the masa harina and salt in the bowl of an electric mixer fitted with a paddle attachment. Add the shortening and beat together for 3 minutes, until thoroughly incorporated.

Add the water and pureed mixture and beat for 2 minutes longer, stopping the mixer to scrape down the sides of the bowl with a spatula as necessary. Add the corn kernels and cilantro and beat for about 1 minute longer, until incorporated. Take the masa dough out of the bowl, wrap in plastic wrap, and let rest for 30 minutes at room temperature so the dough can thoroughly absorb the moist ingredients.

Black Bean–Mint Tamale Masa Dough

(M A R K   M I L L E R)

YOU CAN SUBSTITUTE THE MINT WITH STRONGLY FLAVORED FRESH *EPAZOTE* IF YOU PREFER A MORE DISTINCTIVELY MEXICAN

FLAVOR COMBINATION IN THIS MASA DOUGH, OR USE A COMBINATION OF MINT, CILANTRO, AND *EPAZOTE*.

Place the masa harina, salt, sugar, and baking powder in the bowl of an electric mixer fitted with a paddle attachment. Add the butter and shortening and beat together for 3 minutes, until thoroughly incorporated. Add the water and beat for 2 minutes longer, stopping the mixer to scrape down the sides of the bowl with a spatula as necessary. Add the beans and mint and beat for about 1 minute longer, until incorporated. Take the masa dough out of the bowl, wrap in plastic wrap, and let rest for 30 minutes at room temperature so the dough can thoroughly absorb the moist ingredients.

1 1/2 cups masa harina
3/4 teaspoon salt
3/4 teaspoon sugar
3/4 teaspoon baking powder
1/4 cup unsalted butter, softened
1/4 cup vegetable shortening, at room temperature
3/4 cup warm water
1/4 cup cooked and mashed black beans
3 tablespoons chopped fresh mint

Red Chile–Cilantro Tamale Masa Dough

(S T E P H A N   P Y L E S)

THIS RED- AND GREEN-SPECKLED MASA DOUGH HAS A BITE TO IT BECAUSE OF THE CAYENNE CHILE POWDER. YOU CAN RAISE OR LOWER

THE HEAT TO SUIT YOUR TASTE BY EXPERIMENTING WITH DIFFERENT TYPES OF CHILE POWDER. POWDERED CHIPOTLE CHILE

WILL GIVE THE DOUGH A SMOKY FLAVOR.

1³/₄ cups masa harina
1 teaspoon ground cumin
1 tablespoon pure red chile powder
¹/₂ teaspoon cayenne powder
1¹/₄ cups hot water
¹/₂ cup plus 2 tablespoons chilled
   vegetable shortening
1¹/₂ teaspoons salt
1 teaspoon baking powder
¹/₄ cup chilled Chicken Stock (page 160)
¹/₃ cup chopped cilantro

Place the masa harina, cumin, chile powder, and cayenne in the bowl of an electric mixer fitted with a paddle attachment. With the machine on low speed, add the water in a slow, steady stream until the dough forms a ball. Increase the speed to medium and continue mixing for 5 minutes, then transfer the dough to a clean bowl. Refrigerate for 1 hour.

Return the masa to the bowl of the electric mixer and beat for 5 minutes on high speed. With the machine running, slowly add the shortening 2 tablespoons at a time. Continue mixing for about 5 minutes, until the dough is smooth and light. Stop the mixer to scrape the sides of the bowl. Reduce the speed to low and continue to beat.

While the dough is mixing, combine the salt, baking powder, and chicken stock in a small mixing bowl. Slowly add the stock mixture to the masa in a steady stream and continue mixing until thoroughly combined. Increase the speed to high and mix for 5 minutes longer. Add the cilantro and mix for 1 more minute to incorporate.

Vegetarian Tamales

Chipotle Tamales with Sweet Browned Onions

Candied Sweet Potato Tamales with
Crystallized Ginger

Smashed Potato Tamales with Carrot-Ginger Broth

Roasted Potato, Garlic,
and Sun-Dried Tomato Tamales

Wild Mushroom and White Truffle Tamales
with Tomatillo-Chipotle Sauce

The *Self* Tamale with Vegetables and Carrot Sauce

Ratatouille Tamales with
Rosemary–Queso Fresco Pesto

Blue Corn–Gorgonzola Huevos Rancheros
Tamales with Red Chile Sauce

Black Bean–Roasted Banana Tamales with Coconut-
Lemongrass Broth and Tortilla-Jicama Salad

Artichoke and Sun-Dried Tomato Tamales
with Olive Oil and Saffron

Fresh Corn Tamales with Black Truffles
and Black Truffle Butter

Gazpacho Tamales

Caramelized Onion Tamales with
Tomato-Basil Salad

Vegetarian Cobb Tamale Salad with
Dijon Vinaigrette

Roasted Corn and *Huitlacoche* Tamales

Asparagus and Hollandaise Tamales

Vegetable *Escabeche* Tamales with
Salsa Cruda Roja

Goat Cheese Tamales with Black Olive Masa
and Lemon-Fig Salsa

Chipotle Tamales with Sweet Browned Onions

(M A R K   M I L L E R)

THESE ARE THE PERFECT TAMALES FOR A BARBECUE OR STEAK DINNER, OR WITH GRILLED VEGETABLES FOR BRUNCH. CHIPOTLE CHILES ARE SMOKED JALAPEÑOS, AND THEIR SMOKINESS AND HEAT MAKE THEM THE PERFECT MATCH FOR THE SWEET CARAMELIZED ONIONS WITH THEIR DEEP, RICH FLAVOR AND AROMA. FOR A VARIATION, YOU CAN ADD A LITTLE ROASTED GARLIC AND SOME MINCED THYME TO THE MASA DOUGH. ASADERO IS A TANGY MEXICAN COW CHEESE FROM THE SOUTHERN STATE OF OAXACA THAT'S ALSO WONDERFUL FOR MELTING IN QUESADILLAS OR NACHOS.

Chipotle Tamale Masa Dough (page 6)
1 tablespoon unsalted butter
3 cups finely sliced white onion
   (1-inch lengths or less)
3 tablespoons chipotle chile puree (page 165)
10 large dried corn husks, soaked in
   warm water for 30 minutes
4 tablespoons shredded asadero or
   picante provolone cheese

Prepare the masa dough.

To prepare the filling, melt the butter in a sauté pan, add the onion, and sauté over medium heat, stirring occasionally, until dark brown, 25 to 30 minutes. Add the chipotle puree, mix thoroughly, and remove from the heat.

Drain the corn husks and shake dry. Tear 16 thin strips (about $^1/_8$ inch wide) from 2 of the husks and set aside for tying the tamales. Lay out the remaining 8 corn husks on a flat work surface. Take a 2-ounce ($^1/_4$-cup) portion of masa dough and, using a tortilla press or heavy pan, flatten to a thickness of about $^1/_4$ inch. Place the masa dough inside each husk, leaving about $1^1/_2$ inches of exposed corn husk at each end and $^3/_4$ inch at each side. Spread about 2 heaping tablespoons of the filling on top of the masa. Bring the sides of the corn husk together, folding the dough; tuck one side of the husk under the other and roll up the tamale so the dough is completely enclosed inside the husk. Twist each end and tie with the reserved strips of corn husk. Repeat for the remaining tamales.

Fill the bottom of a steamer or saucepan fitted with a strainer or vegetable basket with 2 to 3 inches of water. Bring the water to a boil and place the tamales in the steamer. Cover tightly with a lid or foil (it is important that little or no steam escapes while cooking). Steam the tamales for 35 to 40 minutes over lightly boiling water, adding more boiling water as needed. The tamales are done when they feel firm to the touch but are not hard and the dough comes away easily from the husk. Let rest for at least 5 minutes before serving.

Transfer the tamales to serving plates and, with a knife, slice open the top of the wrappers from end to end. Sprinkle the cheese over the tamales.

SERVES 8

Candied Sweet Potato Tamales with Crystallized Ginger

(S T E P H A N   P Y L E S)

HERE'S A RECIPE THAT'S PERFECT FOR THE HOLIDAY SEASON BECAUSE THE BUTTERY DOUGH AND SWEET POTATO–AND–MAPLE SYRUP FILLING MAKE THESE TAMALES AN IDEAL ACCOMPANIMENT TO TURKEY OR GOOSE. THESE TAMALES ALSO LIVEN UP LEFTOVER TURKEY OR MAKE A GREAT SIDE WITH A GREEN SALAD MADE WITH NUTS. SWEET POTATOES ARE TROPICAL TUBERS NATIVE TO CENTRAL AMERICA, AND THE CRYSTALLIZED GINGER, WHICH IS AVAILABLE IN ASIAN MARKETS AND SPECIALTY FOOD STORES, GIVES AN UNEXPECTED AND INTERESTING DIMENSION TO THEIR EARTHY, RICH FLAVOR.

Masa Seca Tamale Dough (page 2)

FOR THE SWEET POTATO FILLING

2 sweet potatoes, about 12 ounces each
1 tablespoon maple syrup
1 teaspoon cayenne powder
1 teaspoon pure red chile powder
1 teaspoon salt

FOR THE TAMALES

10 large dried corn husks, soaked in warm water
* for 30 minutes*
5 tablespoons minced crystallized ginger

Prepare the masa dough.

Preheat the oven to 350°F. Place the sweet potatoes in a roasting pan or on a baking sheet and place in the oven. After 20 minutes, remove 1 potato. When cool enough, peel, finely dice, and place in a bowl. Roast the remaining potato for an additional 40 minutes, until completely soft. When cool enough, peel the soft potato and combine it with the maple syrup, cayenne, chile powder, and salt in a food processor. Process the mixture until smooth and pureed, about 3 minutes.

Combine half the pureed sweet potato mixture with the tamale dough in a bowl, stir to combine thoroughly, and set aside. Add the remaining sweet potato puree to the bowl with the diced sweet potato and stir to mix well.

Drain the corn husks and shake dry. Tear 16 thin strips (about 1/8 inch wide) from 2 of the husks and set aside for tying the tamales. Lay out the remaining 8 corn husks on a flat work surface. Divide the dough into 8 even portions and place 1 portion on each husk. Evenly spread out the masa mixture, leaving about 1 1/2 inches of exposed corn husk at each end and 3/4 inch at each side. Top each portion of the masa with the sweet potato mixture and the crystallized ginger and spread out evenly. Bring the sides of the corn husk together, folding the dough; tuck one side of the husk under the other and roll up the tamale so that the dough is completely enclosed inside the husk. Twist each end and tie with the reserved strips of corn husk. Repeat for the remaining tamales.

Fill the bottom of a steamer or saucepan fitted with a strainer or vegetable basket with 2 to 3 inches of water. Bring the water to a boil and place the tamales in the steamer. Cover tightly with a lid or foil (it is important that little or no steam escapes while cooking). Steam the tamales for 30 to 35 minutes over lightly boiling water, adding more boiling water as needed. The tamales are done when they feel firm to the touch but are not hard and the dough comes away easily from the husk. Let rest for at least 5 minutes before serving.

Transfer the tamales to serving plates and, with a knife, slice open the top of the tamale wrappers from end to end. Gently push the ends together, as for a baked potato.

SERVES 8

Smashed Potato Tamales with Carrot-Ginger Broth

(J O H N   S E D L A R)

THIS STYLE OF TAMALE, MADE WITHOUT CORN MASA DOUGH, IS IN THE SOUTH AMERICAN TRADITION OF *HUMITAS*. IN FACT, THE CHILEAN *HUMITAS*

MADE WITH SWEET CORN ARE A NATIONAL DISH, AND *HUMITAS* ARE ALSO COMMON IN BOLIVIA AND PERU. THIS IS A SOUPY KIND OF DISH THAT

I RECOMMEND SERVING IN PASTA BOWLS. THE SPICY GINGER AND CARROT BROTH COMBINES PERFECTLY WITH THE INTENSE GARLIC,

THE JUST-OVERCOOKED NEW POTATOES, AND THE BASIL OIL.

Potato Tamale Masa Dough (page 4)

FOR THE CARROT-GINGER BROTH
6 small new potatoes (2 to 3 ounces each)
6 cups fresh carrot juice
2 tablespoons peeled and sliced fresh ginger
2 tablespoons olive oil
Salt and freshly ground white pepper

FOR THE TAMALES
Olive oil, for brushing
6 large dried corn husks, soaked in warm water
  for 30 minutes

Prepare the potato masa dough.

To prepare the broth, place the new potatoes in a saucepan, cover with lightly salted water, and bring to a boil. Reduce the heat to medium and cook the potatoes for about 20 minutes, until tender. Drain and let cool. Finely dice the potatoes, being careful not to tear the skins. Set aside.

Combine the carrot juice and ginger in a nonreactive saucepan and let sit for 1 hour to let the flavors combine. Just before you are ready to serve, bring to a boil, then stir in the olive oil. Add the diced potatoes and season with salt and white pepper to taste. Remove the ginger with a slotted spoon or tongs.

To prepare the tamales, cut 6 square pieces of plastic wrap measuring about 6 inches by 6 inches each. Lay out each piece of plastic on a flat work surface and brush lightly with the olive oil. Divide the potato masa dough evenly among them and mold into a rectangular shape. Fold two of the sides of the plastic wrap over, and then fold over the other two sides to form a tight envelope package. Repeat for the remaining tamales.

Fill the bottom of a steamer or saucepan fitted with a strainer or vegetable basket with 2 to 3 inches of water. Bring the water to a boil and place the tamales in the steamer. Cover tightly with a lid or foil (it is important that little or no steam escapes while cooking). Steam the tamales for about 15 minutes over lightly boiling water until firm, adding more boiling water as needed. Let rest for at least 5 minutes before serving.

Drain the corn husks and shake dry. Lay out each husk in the center of a large shallow pasta bowl. Unwrap the tamales from the plastic wrap and place one in the center of each corn husk. Carefully spoon the broth around each tamale.

SERVES 6

Roasted Potato, Garlic, and Sun-Dried Tomato Tamales

(STEPHAN PYLES)

I THINK OF THE COMBINATION OF POTATOES AND GARLIC AS A REAL COMFORT FOOD, AND THEIR RUSTIC FLAVORS ARE ENLIVENED IN THIS DISH BY
THE PLEASANTLY FRUITY ACIDITY AND INTENSITY OF THE SUN-DRIED TOMATOES. IF YOU WANT TO GIVE THESE TAMALES A MEDITERRANEAN TWIST,
ADD SOME CHOPPED BLACK OLIVES, CRUMBLED FETA CHEESE, AND A LITTLE MINCED LEMON ZEST. ALTHOUGH THESE TAMALES STAND VERY WELL
ON THEIR OWN, THEY MAKE A WONDERFUL MATCH WITH A GOAT CHEESE SALAD.

Masa Seca Tamale Dough (page 2)
1 large baking potato (about 12 ounces), peeled
*   and cut into ¼-inch dice (about 2 cups)*
20 cloves garlic (about ½ cup)
2 teaspoons salt
2 tablespoons olive oil
1 tomato, blanched, peeled, seeded, and chopped
10 large dried corn husks, soaked in warm water
*   for 30 minutes*

FOR THE SUN-DRIED TOMATO SAUCE

1 cup sun-dried or oven-dried cherry tomatoes,
*   julienned*
3 cups Vegetable Stock (page 162) or
*   Chicken Stock (page 160)*
2 teaspoons olive oil
1 cup finely diced onion
1 tablespoon chopped fresh basil
1 teaspoon chopped cilantro
1 teaspoon chopped fresh oregano
Salt

Prepare the masa dough. Preheat the oven to 350°F.

To prepare the filling, toss the potato, garlic, and salt with the olive oil in a roasting pan. Roast in the oven for 25 to 30 minutes, until cooked through and golden. Combine half the potato, all the garlic, and half the tomato in the bowl of an electric mixer fitted with a paddle attachment. Add the tamale dough and beat on high speed to thoroughly mash the potato and garlic, about 2 minutes.

Drain the corn husks and shake dry. Tear 16 thin strips (about ⅛ inch wide) from 2 of the husks and set aside for tying the tamales. Lay out the remaining husks. Divide the dough into 8 even portions and place 1 portion on each husk. Evenly spread out the masa mixture, leaving about 1½ inches of exposed corn husk at each end and ¾ inch at each side. Bring the sides of the corn husk together, folding the dough; tuck one side of the husk under the other and roll up the tamale so that the dough is completely enclosed inside the husk. Twist each end and tie with the reserved strips of corn husk. Repeat for the remaining tamales.

Fill the bottom of a steamer or saucepan fitted with a strainer or vegetable basket with 2 to 3 inches of water. Bring the water to a boil

and place the tamales in the steamer. Cover tightly with a lid or foil. Steam the tamales for 30 to 35 minutes over lightly boiling water, adding more boiling water as needed. The tamales are done when they feel firm to the touch but are not hard and the dough comes away easily from the husk. Let rest for at least 5 minutes before serving.

Meanwhile, to prepare the sauce, combine ½ cup of the sun-dried tomatoes and the vegetable stock in a small saucepan and bring to a boil. Transfer the mixture to a blender and puree for 1 minute. Transfer to a clean saucepan and keep warm.

In another saucepan, heat the olive oil until lightly smoking. Add the onion and sauté over high heat for 3 to 4 minutes, stirring occasionally, until it begins to brown. Add the remaining chopped tomato and sauté for 1 minute. Add the sun-dried tomato puree and the remaining potato and sun-dried tomatoes. Bring the mixture to a boil, add the herbs, and season with salt to taste.

Transfer the tamales to serving plates and, with a knife, slice open the top of the tamale wrappers from end to end. Gently push the ends together, as for a baked potato. Spoon the sauce over the tamales and serve.

SERVES 8

Wild Mushroom and White Truffle Tamales with Tomatillo-Chipotle Sauce

(M A R K   M I L L E R)

THE INTENSE TRUFFLE PASTE AND THE FULL-FLAVORED WILD MUSHROOMS IN THIS RECIPE GIVE THESE TAMALES A NATURALLY EARTHY AND WOODSY QUALITY. YOU CAN USE PORCINI, SHIITAKES, MORELS, OR CHANTERELLES OR ANY COMBINATION; THE MORE TYPES OF MUSHROOM YOU USE, THE MORE COMPLEX THE FLAVORS WILL BE. TRUFFLES, WHICH LIKE MUSHROOMS ARE A FUNGUS, HAVE LONG BEEN A DELICACY, DATING BACK AT LEAST TO BABYLONIAN TIMES; WHITE TRUFFLES ARE A SPECIALTY OF THE PIEDMONT REGION OF NORTHERN ITALY. THEY ARE USUALLY ADDED TO DISHES, OR GRATED AND SPRINKLED OVER THEM, AT THE LAST MINUTE, AND BUYING TRUFFLES IN PASTE FORM IS THE MOST CONVENIENT AS WELL AS THE MOST AFFORDABLE WAY TO GO.

Mushroom-Truffle Tamale Masa Dough
  (page 10)
2 tablespoons unsalted butter
1 tablespoon minced garlic
1 pound mixed wild mushrooms, sliced
1/2 teaspoon salt
1/2 teaspoon freshly ground black pepper
2 tablespoons chopped fresh Italian parsley
1 teaspoon white truffle paste,
  or 2 tablespoons white truffle oil
10 large dried corn husks, soaked in warm water
  for 30 minutes

FOR THE TOMATILLO-CHIPOTLE SAUCE

20 tomatillos (about 1 1/4 pounds), husked,
  rinsed, blackened, and chopped (page 164)
2 cloves roasted garlic (page 165)
3/4 teaspoon sugar
3/4 teaspoon salt
6 canned chipotle chiles in adobo sauce
  plus 3 tablespoons adobo sauce
1/2 cup minced cilantro

Prepare the masa dough.

To prepare the filling, heat the butter in a saucepan and sauté the garlic over medium-low heat for 3 to 4 minutes. Add the mushrooms, salt, and pepper and sauté for 6 to 8 minutes longer, stirring occasionally. Add the parsley and remove the pan from the heat. Stir in the truffle paste and add a little water if necessary to thin.

Drain the corn husks and shake dry. Tear 16 thin strips (about 1/8 inch wide) from 2 of the husks and set aside for tying the tamales. Lay out the remaining 8 corn husks on a flat work surface. Take a 2-ounce (1/4-cup) portion of masa dough and, using a tortilla press or heavy pan, flatten to a thickness of about 1/4 inch. Place the masa dough inside each husk, leaving about 1 1/2 inches of exposed corn husk at each end and 3/4 inch at each side. Spread about 2 heaping tablespoons of the filling on top of the masa. Bring the sides of the corn husk together, folding the dough; tuck one side of the husk under the other and roll up the tamale so the dough is completely enclosed inside the husk. Twist each end and tie with the reserved strips

of corn husk. Repeat for the remaining tamales.

Fill the bottom of a steamer or saucepan fitted with a strainer or vegetable basket with 2 to 3 inches of water. Bring the water to a boil and place the tamales in the steamer. Cover tightly with a lid or foil (it is important that little or no steam escapes while cooking). Steam the tamales for 35 to 40 minutes over lightly boiling water, adding more boiling water as needed. The tamales are done when they feel firm to the touch but are not hard and the dough comes away easily from the husk. Let rest for at least 5 minutes before serving.

While the tamales are steaming, prepare the sauce. Place the tomatillos, garlic, sugar, and salt in a food processor and puree. Add the chipotles, adobo sauce, and cilantro and puree briefly. The sauce should be slightly textured rather than smooth. Transfer to a saucepan and warm through.

With a knife, slice open the top of the tamale wrappers from end to end and place on serving plates. Spoon the sauce next to the tamales.

SERVES 8

The *Self* Tamale with Vegetables and Carrot Sauce

(J O H N   S E D L A R)

MY FRIEND DEBORAH SHARPE, THE WEST COAST EDITOR OF *SELF* MAGAZINE, WAS QUITE SURPRISED BY THE ABSOLUTE FRESHNESS OF THE TAMALES I WAS

SERVING AT MY RESTAURANT, ABIQUIU. HER IMAGE OF TAMALES WAS THAT THEY WERE LUMPY AND DOUGHY. INSPIRED BY WHAT SHE HAD TASTED, SHE

ASKED ME TO CREATE A TAMALE FOR HER READERS THAT WOULD BE LOW IN FAT AND SALT, YET WITH EXPLOSIVE FLAVORS. THIS TAMALE, WHICH MAKES

THE MOST OF DELICATELY FLAVORED SUMMER PRODUCE, WAS CALLED "THE *SELF* TAMALE FOR THE SEXY WOMAN" ON THE MENU FROM THEN ON.

Sweet Corn Tamale Mixture (page 2)
4 cups fresh carrot juice
1 clove garlic, minced
1 tablespoon minced fresh ginger
4 tablespoons chilled unsalted butter, diced
Salt and freshly ground black pepper
1 large banana leaf (about 12 inches by 36 inches),
*   cut into 6 squares of 6 inches by 6 inches*
Olive oil, for brushing

FOR THE VEGETABLES

6 small cauliflower florets
6 baby carrots
6 whole baby eggplants, halved lengthwise
6 baby zucchini
2 yellow pattypan squash, each cut into 3 wedges
2 tablespoons fresh peas
6 teardrop tomatoes, halved
Salt and freshly ground black pepper
1 teaspoon olive oil

Prepare the tamale mixture.

To prepare the sauce, place the carrot juice, garlic, and ginger in a small nonreactive saucepan. Bring to a boil, reduce the heat to a simmer, and reduce the juice by one-half, about 20 minutes. Remove the pan from the heat and whisk in the butter, one piece at a time. Season with salt and pepper to taste and keep warm.

To prepare the tamales, lay out each square of banana leaf on a flat work surface and brush lightly with the olive oil. Divide the sweet corn tamale mixture evenly among the leaves and mold into a rectangular shape. Fold two of the sides of the leaf over, and then fold over the other two sides to form a tight envelope package. Repeat for the remaining tamales.

Fill the bottom of a steamer or saucepan fitted with a strainer or vegetable basket with 2 to 3 inches of water. Bring the water to a boil and place the tamales in the steamer. Cover tightly with a lid or foil (it is important that

little or no steam escapes while cooking). Steam the tamales for about 15 minutes over lightly boiling water until firm, adding more boiling water as needed.

While the tamales are steaming, bring a large saucepan of lightly salted water to a boil. Add the cauliflower and carrots and blanch for 7 to 8 minutes. Remove with a slotted spoon and drain. Add the eggplants, zucchini, squash, peas, and tomatoes and blanch for 3 minutes. Remove immediately and drain. Just before you are ready to serve, season the vegetables with salt and pepper to taste and heat the olive oil in a sauté pan. Sauté the blanched vegetables over medium heat for about 2 minutes, until warm.

Transfer the tamales to large shallow pasta bowls. Unwrap one side of each tamale to expose the filling and sprinkle the sautéed vegetables over and around the tamale, on top of the banana leaf. Generously spoon the sauce over the tamale and vegetables.

SERVES 6

Ratatouille Tamales with Rosemary–Queso Fresco Pesto

(S T E P H A N   P Y L E S)

IN THIS RECIPE, THE SOUTH OF FRANCE (RATATOUILLE AND THE ROSEMARY IN THE PESTO) MEETS MEXICO (QUESO FRESCO, MARIGOLD MINT, AND TAMALES). MARIGOLD MINT IS A ROBUST HERB POPULAR IN MEXICO AND INCREASINGLY AVAILABLE IN THE SOUTHWEST. IT IS MORE ASSERTIVE THAN TARRAGON, WHICH CAN READILY BE SUBSTITUTED FOR IT. SOME CHEFS, LIKE ME, PREFER TO COOK THE VEGETABLES FOR RATATOUILLE SEPARATELY BEFORE STEWING THEM TOGETHER TO ACHIEVE A SMOOTHER CONSISTENCY, WHILE OTHERS SWEAR BY A MORE RUSTIC TEXTURE; IT'S YOUR CALL.

Masa Seca Tamale Dough (page 2)
10 large dried corn husks, soaked in warm water
*   for 30 minutes*

FOR THE ROSEMARY–QUESO FRESCO PESTO

1 tablespoon fresh rosemary needles
1/2 cup fresh basil leaves
1/4 cup pine nuts, toasted and cooled (page 165)
2 cloves garlic, chopped
3/4 cup extra-virgin olive oil
1/4 cup queso fresco cheese or feta, crumbled
Juice of 2 lemons
Salt and freshly ground black pepper

FOR THE RATATOUILLE

5 ripe tomatoes
2 tablespoons olive oil
2 small onions, 1 roughly chopped
*   and 1 finely diced*
1 tablespoon minced garlic
1 teaspoon ground cumin
1 teaspoon cayenne powder
1 tablespoon chopped fresh basil

Prepare the masa dough.

Drain the corn husks and shake dry. Tear 16 thin strips (about 1/8 inch wide) from 2 of the husks and set aside for tying the tamales. Lay out the remaining 8 corn husks on a flat work surface. Divide the dough into 8 even portions and place 1 portion on each husk. Evenly spread out the masa mixture, leaving about 1 1/2 inches of exposed corn husk at each end and 3/4 inch at each side. Bring the sides of the corn husk together, folding the dough; tuck one side of the husk under the other and roll up the tamale so that the dough is completely enclosed inside the husk. Twist each end and tie with the reserved strips of corn husk. Repeat for the remaining tamales.

Fill the bottom of a steamer or saucepan fitted with a strainer or vegetable basket with 2 to 3 inches of water. Bring the water to a boil and place the tamales in the steamer. Cover tightly with a lid or foil (it is important that little or no steam escapes while cooking). Steam the tamales for 30 to 35 minutes over lightly boiling water, adding more boiling water as needed. The tamales are done when they feel firm to the touch but are not hard and the dough comes away easily from the husk. Let rest for at least 5 minutes before serving.

While the tamales are steaming, prepare the pesto and ratatouille. For the pesto, combine the rosemary, basil, pine nuts, and garlic in a food processor and process for about 1 minute, until finely chopped. Slowly add the olive oil, cheese, and lemon juice in turn and process until smooth. Season with salt and pepper to taste and refrigerate until ready to serve.

To prepare the ratatouille, quarter the tomatoes. Cut away the seeds and inner pulp with a paring knife and reserve. Leaving the skin attached to the outer flesh, dice and reserve separately. Heat 1 tablespoon of the olive oil in a saucepan until lightly smoking. Add the roughly chopped onion and the garlic and sauté for 2 to 3 minutes over high heat, until the onion begins to brown slightly. Add the reserved tomato pulp and cook for 3 minutes longer, stirring occasionally. Add the cumin and cayenne and cook for 3 minutes more,

(continues)

1 tablespoon chopped fresh marigold mint
    or tarragon
1 small zucchini, unpeeled and finely diced
1 yellow squash, unpeeled and finely diced
2 Japanese eggplants, or 1 small Italian eggplant,
    unpeeled and finely diced
2 tablespoons balsamic vinegar
1 red bell pepper, roasted, peeled, seeded,
    and diced (page 164)
1 yellow bell pepper, roasted, peeled, seeded,
    and diced (page 164)
1 tablespoon chopped cilantro
Salt

stirring frequently. Add the basil and marigold mint and transfer the mixture to a blender. Puree on high speed until smooth, about 1 minute. Strain the sauce through a medium sieve into a clean saucepan and keep warm.

Heat the remaining 1 tablespoon of olive oil in a sauté pan over high heat until lightly smoking. Sauté the remaining diced onion for about 3 minutes, until it begins to brown, stirring occasionally. Add the zucchini and yellow squash and sauté for about 2 minutes longer, until they begin to soften. Add the eggplants and sauté for 1 minute more. Add the vinegar, deglaze the pan, and stir in the reserved sauce. Bring the mixture to a light boil, stirring occasionally, and turn down the heat to a simmer. Add the roasted peppers, reserved diced tomatoes, and cilantro. Season with salt to taste.

Transfer the steamed tamales to serving plates and, with a knife, slice open the top of the tamale wrappers from end to end. Gently push the ends together, as for a baked potato. Spoon the ratatouille over the top of each tamale and drizzle the pesto around the plate.

SERVES 8

Blue Corn–Gorgonzola Huevos Rancheros Tamales with Red Chile Sauce

(J O H N  S E D L A R)

JUST AS BLUE CORN TASTES LIKE INTENSIFIED CORNMEAL, SO THE BLUE-VEINED ITALIAN GORGONZOLA IS AN INTENSELY FLAVORED CHEESE. THESE TWO BLUE FOODS REALLY ADD SPARK TO A TRADITIONAL SOUTHWESTERN BREAKFAST OR BRUNCH DISH. BEFORE MAKING THE CHILE SAUCE, CLEAN THE DRIED RED CHILES WITH A DRY CLOTH OR TOWEL TO REMOVE ANY SURFACE DUST OR DIRT (THIS IS ALWAYS A GOOD IDEA WHENEVER USING DRIED CHILES).

FOR THE TAMALES

Masa Seca Tamale Dough (page 2)
6 large dried corn husks, soaked in warm water for 30 minutes
Olive oil, for brushing
6 tablespoons crumbled gorgonzola cheese

FOR THE RED CHILE SAUCE

2 quarts water
12 ounces dried New Mexico or Anaheim red chiles, stemmed and seeded
$1/2$ teaspoon minced garlic
$1/4$ teaspoon dried oregano
1 teaspoon salt

FOR THE POTATOES

4 tablespoons clarified unsalted butter
2 russet potatoes (8 to 10 ounces each), peeled and finely diced
Salt and freshly ground black pepper

FOR THE EGGS

2 quarts water
1 tablespoon red wine vinegar
12 large eggs

Prepare the masa dough.

Drain the corn husks and shake dry. Lay out the husks on a flat work surface. Brush the inside of each husk with the olive oil and then divide the tamale masa dough evenly among them. Evenly spread out the masa, leaving about $1^{1}/_{2}$ inches of exposed corn husk at each end and $^{3}/_{4}$ inch at each side. Top each portion of the dough with 1 tablespoon of the gorgonzola cheese and spread out evenly. Bring the sides of the corn husks together, tightly around the dough; tuck one side of the husk under the other and then fold the ends over to form a neat envelope package. Repeat for the remaining tamales.

Fill the bottom of a steamer or saucepan fitted with a strainer or vegetable basket with 2 to 3 inches of water. Bring the water to a boil and place the tamales in the steamer. Cover tightly with a lid or foil (it is important that little or no steam escapes while cooking). Steam the tamales for about 45 minutes over lightly boiling water, adding more boiling water as needed. The tamales are done when they feel firm to the touch but are not hard and the dough comes away easily from the husk. Let rest for at least 5 minutes before serving.

While the tamales are steaming, prepare the sauce. Bring the water to a boil in a saucepan. Add the chiles, turn down the heat to a simmer, and cook until the chiles are soft, about 20 minutes. Remove the chiles with a slotted spoon and place in a blender. Add 2 cups of the poaching water to the chiles and blend until smooth. Add the garlic, oregano, and salt and blend until well mixed. Transfer to a saucepan and warm through before serving.

Preheat the oven to 200°F. To prepare the potatoes, heat the clarified butter in a sauté pan. Add the potatoes, season with salt and pepper to taste, and sauté over medium-high heat for about 10 minutes, until crisp and golden, stirring occasionally. Remove the potatoes with a spatula and drain on paper towels. Transfer to an ovenproof dish and place in the oven to keep warm.

To prepare the eggs, combine the water and vinegar in a saucepan and bring to a boil. Turn down the heat to a simmer, gently break 2 eggs at a time into the water, and cook just until the white is cooked. Remove gently with a slotted spoon and place in a single layer in a large warmed dish.

(continues)

Vegetable oil, for deep-frying
3 blue corn tortillas, finely julienned
Salt
2 tablespoons chopped red onion
6 sprigs cilantro

To prepare the garnish, heat a deep fryer or large saucepan and heat the vegetable oil to 350°F. Add the julienned tortillas and deep-fry for about 45 seconds, until crispy. Remove with a slotted spoon and drain on paper towels. Sprinkle with salt to taste.

Unwrap each tamale and, leaving the dough lying on the husks, place each in the center of a large pasta bowl. Place 2 poached eggs on top of (or next to) each tamale and spoon about $1/3$ cup of the sauce over each serving. Sprinkle the potato cubes and chopped onion over the eggs and top with the fried tortilla strips and a sprig of cilantro.

SERVES 6

Black Bean–Roasted Banana Tamales with Coconut-Lemongrass Broth and Tortilla-Jicama Salad

(S T E P H A N P Y L E S)

THE COMBINATION OF BLACK BEANS AND BANANAS OR PLANTAINS IS DISTINCTIVE OF TROPICAL REGIONS OF MEXICO SUCH AS THE YUCATÁN AND CENTRAL AMERICAN COUNTRIES SUCH AS GUATEMALA, AND IT'S ONE OF MY FAVORITES. THE COCONUT AND LEMONGRASS IN THE BROTH INTRODUCES A THAI INFLUENCE TO THE EQUATORIAL NEW WORLD FLAVORS, TAKING THESE INGREDIENTS TO NEW HEIGHTS. ROASTING BANANAS IN THEIR SKINS CARAMELIZES THEIR SUGARS AND GIVES AN INCREDIBLY DEEP BANANA FLAVOR. THESE TAMALES ALSO MAKE A WONDERFUL ACCOMPANIMENT TO GRILLED OR SAUTÉED SALMON OR SCALLOPS.

Masa Seca Tamale Dough (page 2)

FOR THE COCONUT-LEMONGRASS BROTH

1 tablespoon olive oil
1/2 carrot, peeled and roughly chopped
1 stalk celery, chopped
1/2 onion, peeled and chopped
2 serrano chiles, seeded and chopped
1/2 teaspoon ground cumin
1 stalk lemongrass, chopped
1 kaffir lime leaf
1/2 cup sherry
1 1/2 14-ounce cans coconut milk
1/2 cup chilled Chicken Stock (page 160)
1/2 cup cilantro sprigs
1/4 cup fresh basil sprigs
Salt

FOR THE BLACK BEAN PUREE

1 cup black beans, soaked overnight
6 cups chilled Chicken Stock (page 160)
*   or chilled Vegetable Stock (page 162)*
5 cloves garlic, peeled

Prepare the masa dough.

To prepare the broth, heat the olive oil in a large saucepan. Sauté the carrot, celery, and onion over high heat for 3 minutes, until the onion is translucent. Add the serranos, cumin, lemongrass, and lime leaf and sauté for 1 minute longer.

Add the sherry to deglaze the pan and reduce until syrupy, about 10 minutes. Add the coconut milk and stock and bring to a boil. Turn down the heat and simmer for 5 minutes. Transfer to a blender and puree until smooth. Strain the broth through a fine sieve into a clean saucepan. Tie the cilantro and basil together with kitchen twine and steep in the broth for 15 to 20 minutes. Season with salt to taste, remove the tied herbs, and reheat when ready to serve.

To prepare the black bean puree, drain the beans, reserving the water. Combine the beans, stock, garlic, and thyme in a saucepan and bring to a boil. Turn down the heat to a simmer and cook for 45 minutes, until the beans are cooked through. Drain the beans, reserving the liquid in a clean saucepan, and set aside.

Add the reserved water in which the beans were soaked to the saucepan with the liquid and bring to a boil. Reduce until syrupy and about 1/4 cup remains, about 15 minutes. The mixture will begin to thicken toward the end of the cooking process.

Place the cooked beans into the bowl of a food processor and puree, adding enough of the reduced liquid to make pureeing possible. Add the chile powder and cumin and mix thoroughly. Season with salt to taste. Spoon the puree into a bowl and allow to cool to room temperature.

Preheat the oven to 350°F.

To prepare the banana filling, place the bananas on a baking sheet and bake until the skin is blackened and the flesh begins to seep from the skin, about 15 minutes. Remove from the oven and allow to cool to room temperature. Peel the bananas and puree them in a food processor. Combine half the banana

(continues)

2 sprigs fresh thyme
1 tablespoon pure red chile powder
1 teaspoon ground cumin
Salt

FOR THE BANANA FILLING AND TAMALES

4 ripe bananas, unpeeled
2 large banana leaves, about 12 inches
    by 36 inches each

FOR THE TORTILLA-JICAMA SALAD

3¹/₂ cups vegetable oil
2 corn tortillas, julienned
1 blue corn tortilla, julienned
1 red corn tortilla, julienned
    (or another blue corn tortilla)
1 jicama, peeled and julienned
¹/₂ red onion, julienned
¹/₂ red bell pepper, julienned
¹/₂ yellow bell pepper, julienned
8 ounces mesclun mix
1 tomato, julienned
¹/₄ cup red wine vinegar
¹/₂ tablespoon ground cumin
¹/₂ tablespoon pure red chile powder
Pinch of cayenne powder
Juice of 2 limes
1 teaspoon sugar
Salt

puree with half of the masa dough in a mixing bowl. In a separate mixing bowl, combine half the black bean puree with the remaining masa dough.

Soften the banana leaves over an open flame for 10 seconds on each side, being careful not to burn them. Cut each leaf crosswise into 4 even pieces, about 8 inches by 10 inches, and lay out on a flat work surface. Divide the banana masa dough into 8 even portions and place a portion in the center of each leaf. Spread into a 4-inch square, leaving at least a 1¹/₂-inch border at the ends and ³/₄ inch on the long sides. Repeat this procedure for the banana puree, followed by the black bean puree and black bean dough mixture, respectively, creating layers of each. To fold the tamales, pick up the two long sides of the banana leaf and bring them together (the dough will surround the filling). Tuck one side under the other and fold the flaps on each end underneath the tamale. Repeat for the remaining tamales.

Fill the bottom of a steamer or saucepan fitted with a strainer or vegetable basket with 2 to 3 inches of water. Bring the water to a boil and place the tamales in the steamer. Cover tightly with a lid or foil (it is important that little or no steam escapes while cooking). Steam the tamales for 30 to 35 minutes over lightly boiling water, adding more boiling water as needed. The tamales are done when they feel firm to the touch but are not hard and the dough comes away easily from the leaves. Let rest for at least 5 minutes before serving.

While the tamales are steaming, prepare the salad. Heat 3 cups of the oil in a saucepan until lightly smoking and deep-fry the tortillas until crisp. Remove with a slotted spoon and drain on paper towels. In a mixing bowl, mix together the jicama, onion, bell peppers, mesclun mix, and tomato. Pour the vinegar into a separate bowl and using a whisk to incorporate, slowly add the remaining ¹/₂ cup oil until emulsified. Add the remaining ingredients and whisk until incorporated. Toss the salad with the vinaigrette just before serving.

Unwrap the tamales and, leaving the filling lying on the leaves, place each in the center of a large serving bowl. Pour about ¹/₄ cup of the broth over each. Serve with the tossed salad.

SERVES 8

Artichoke and Sun-Dried Tomato Tamales with Olive Oil and Saffron

(M A R K   M I L L E R)

ON OUR CONTINUING TOUR OF THE GLOBE IN TAMALE WRAPPERS, THIS RECIPE GIVES US ANOTHER TASTE OF THE MEDITERRANEAN, THIS TIME BEAUTIFULLY COLORED AND WITH A SPANISH ACCENT. SAFFRON WAS BROUGHT OVER TO SPAIN BY THE MOORS. THE MOORS ALSO BROUGHT OVER ARTICHOKES FROM THEIR NATIVE SICILY; THEY USED TO GROW THEM EXTENSIVELY AROUND THEIR CAPITAL OF GRENADA. SPAIN ALSO PRODUCES SOME OF THE BEST OLIVE OIL AND TOMATOES IN THE WORLD. IN THIS RECIPE, YOU CAN ADD DICED ROASTED RED BELL PEPPERS OR PITTED BLACK OLIVES TO THE MASA DOUGH TO GIVE MORE COLOR AND FLAVOR, IF YOU WISH, AND 2 TEASPOONS OF CRUMBLED GOAT CHEESE TO THE FILLING.

Saffron Tamale Masa Dough (page 6)

FOR THE SALSA ROMANA

8 Roma tomatoes (about 1 pound), diced
$1/4$ cup finely diced red onion
$1/2$ tablespoon minced garlic
1 cup finely sliced basil leaves
$1/4$ cup extra-virgin olive oil
$1/2$ tablespoon salt

FOR THE FILLING

8 baby artichokes, or 2 large or 3 medium artichokes
2 teaspoons sun-dried tomato paste
1 clove roasted garlic (page 165)

FOR THE TAMALES

10 large dried corn husks, soaked in warm water for 30 minutes

Prepare the masa dough.

To prepare the salsa, place all the ingredients in a mixing bowl and thoroughly combine. Let the mixture sit at room temperature for 1 hour before serving to allow the flavors to mingle.

To prepare the filling, trim the tops and bottoms of the artichokes and peel away the tough, darker outer leaves. Cook in boiling salted water for about 10 minutes, until the tip of a knife easily pierces the artichoke heart. Cut the artichokes into eighths and set aside.

In a bowl, mix together the sun-dried tomato paste and garlic. Add the artichokes and combine thoroughly.

Drain the corn husks and shake dry. Tear 16 thin strips (about $1/8$ inch wide) from 2 of the husks and set aside for tying the tamales. Lay out the remaining 8 corn husks on a flat work surface. Take a 2-ounce ($1/4$-cup) portion of masa dough and, using a tortilla press or heavy pan, flatten to a thickness of about $1/4$ inch. Place the masa dough inside each husk, leaving about $1^1/2$ inches of exposed corn husk at each end and $3/4$ inch at each side. Spread

about 2 heaping tablespoons of the filling on top of the masa. Bring the sides of the corn husk together, folding the dough; tuck one side of the husk under the other and roll up the tamale so the dough is completely enclosed inside the husk. Twist each end and tie with the reserved strips of corn husk. Repeat for the remaining tamales.

Fill the bottom of a steamer or saucepan fitted with a strainer or vegetable basket with 2 to 3 inches of water. Bring the water to a boil and place the tamales in the steamer. Cover tightly with a lid or foil (it is important that little or no steam escapes while cooking). Steam the tamales for 35 to 40 minutes over lightly boiling water, adding more boiling water as needed. The tamales are done when they feel firm to the touch but are not hard and the dough comes away easily from the husk. Let rest for at least 5 minutes before serving.

Transfer the steamed tamales to serving plates and, with a knife, slice open the top of the tamale wrappers from end to end. Serve with the salsa.

SERVES 8

Fresh Corn Tamales with Black Truffles and Black Truffle Butter

(M A R K   M I L L E R)

THESE WONDERFULLY AROMATIC AND LIGHT MINI-TAMALES ARE NOTHING IF NOT VERSATILE. THEY ARE THE PERFECT FINGER-FOOD SIZE FOR PARTIES OR HORS D'OEUVRES, AND SERVED WARM THEY MAKE IDEAL AND ELEGANT ACCOMPANIMENTS FOR STEAMED LOBSTER, GRILLED HALIBUT, OR ANY VEGETARIAN ENTRÉE. YOU CAN ALSO SERVE THESE TAMALES COLD FOR BRUNCH OR WITH SOUP OR EGGS. IF TRUFFLES ARE UNAVAILABLE OR IF THE WALLET DOES NOT STRETCH THAT FAR, SUBSTITUTE SAUTÉED WILD MUSHROOMS SUCH AS MORELS OR PORCINI. FOR NOTES ON TRUFFLES, SEE THE HEADNOTE ON PAGE 21.

FOR THE TAMALES

8 ears fresh sweet corn
$1/2$ cup yellow cornmeal, preferably stone-ground
1 tablespoon sugar
1 large egg plus 1 egg white
$1/2$ teaspoon salt
$1/2$ teaspoon baking powder
$1/4$ cup unsalted butter, melted
3 tablespoons shaved and minced fresh black truffle

FOR THE BLACK TRUFFLE BUTTER

$1/4$ cup unsalted butter
1 tablespoon fresh black truffle, shaved
    and finely julienned

To prepare the tamales, cut the kernels from the corn cobs and place in a blender. Puree until smooth (there should be about $2^{1}/_{2}$ cups). Using the back of a knife, scrape down the sides of the cut cobs to release the corn germ and "milk" and add to the puree. Transfer to a mixing bowl and mix in the cornmeal, sugar, egg and egg white, salt, and baking powder. Add the butter in small increments while whisking and whisk until smooth. Fold in the minced truffle.

Cut kitchen foil into 24 squares measuring 4 inches by 5 inches and spray with nonstick vegetable spray. Place 4 teaspoons of the batter in the center of each piece of foil and form into a rectangular loaf shape. Fold up the long side of each piece of foil like a letter, into thirds. Then fold up the sides, forming a neat package measuring about 2 inches by 3 inches. Repeat for the remaining tamales.

Fill the bottom of a steamer or saucepan fitted with a strainer or vegetable basket with 2 to 3 inches of water. Bring the water to a boil and place the tamales in the steamer. Cover tightly with a lid or foil (it is important that little or no steam escapes while cooking). Steam the tamales for 30 to 35 minutes over lightly boiling water, adding more boiling water as needed. The tamales are done when they feel firm to the touch but are not hard and the dough comes away easily from the foil. Let rest for at least 5 minutes before serving.

To prepare the truffle butter, place the butter in a small saucepan and melt over low heat. Add the julienned truffle and stir into the melted butter.

Unwrap the tamales and place 3 on each serving plate. Pour the truffle butter around the tamales.

SERVES 8

Gazpacho Tamales

(J O H N   S E D L A R)

THE SECRET OF A GREAT GAZPACHO IS LEARNING THE FINE LINE BETWEEN TOO HOT AND SPICY, AND JUST RIGHT. THE KEY IS TO COUNTERPOINT THE COOLNESS OF THE CUCUMBERS WITH THE INCENDIARY STIMULATION OF THE CHILES. THIS RECIPE CONTAINS MORE CUCUMBER AND FAR LESS TOMATO THAN TRADITIONAL GAZPACHO, AND IT REMINDS ME OF THE FIRST GAZPACHO I FELL IN LOVE WITH. THAT VERSION WAS MADE BY MY GRANDMOTHER, ELOISA, WHO WORKED AS A CHEF AT THE LANDMARK LA FONDA HOTEL, LOCATED ON THE DOWNTOWN PLAZA IN SANTA FE, NEW MEXICO. THIS TAMALE CAN BE SERVED WARM, AT ROOM TEMPERATURE, OR CHILLED DEPENDING ON THE SEASON AND YOUR PREFERENCE.

FOR THE TAMALES
Spinach Tamale Mixture (page 4)
1 teaspoon olive oil
1/2 cup diced celery
1/2 cup peeled, seeded, and diced tomato
Olive oil, for brushing

FOR THE GAZPACHO
2 cups chilled Vegetable Stock (page 162)
2 cucumbers, peeled, seeded, and chopped
1 teaspoon minced garlic
1/2 cup olive oil
1/4 cup red wine vinegar
1 jalapeño chile, seeded, deveined, and minced
1/2 green bell pepper, seeded and quartered
Salt and freshly ground white pepper

FOR THE TAMALES AND GARNISH
1/2 cup peeled, seeded, and diced tomato
1/2 cucumber, unpeeled, seeded, and finely diced
1/2 cup seeded and finely diced green bell pepper
3 tablespoons finely diced red onion
6 sprigs cilantro
Salt and freshly ground white pepper
*6 large dried corn husks, soaked in warm water
    for 30 minutes*

Prepare the spinach mixture.

Heat the olive oil in a small nonstick sauté pan. Add the diced celery and sauté for 5 minutes, until tender. Let cool. Thoroughly mix together the spinach mixture, sautéed celery, and the diced tomato in a mixing bowl.

Cut 6 square pieces of plastic wrap measuring about 6 inches by 6 inches each. Lay out each piece of plastic on a flat work surface and brush lightly with the olive oil. Divide the spinach mixture evenly among them and mold into a rectangular shape. Fold two sides of the plastic wrap over, and then fold over the other two sides to form a tight envelope package. Repeat for the remaining tamales.

Fill the bottom of a steamer or saucepan fitted with a strainer or vegetable basket with 2 to 3 inches of water. Bring the water to a boil and place the tamales in the steamer. Cover tightly with a lid or foil (it is important that little or no steam escapes while cooking).

Steam the tamales for about 15 minutes over lightly boiling water until firm, adding more boiling water as needed.

Meanwhile, to prepare the gazpacho, combine the stock, cucumbers, garlic, olive oil, vinegar, jalapeño, bell pepper, and salt and white pepper to taste in a blender or food processor. Blend the mixture on high speed until liquefied. Let sit over a bowl in a sieve for 30 minutes. Discard the solids or use for soup, place the gazpacho liquids in a bowl, and refrigerate until chilled.

Thoroughly mix together all the ingredients for the garnish except the corn husks in a mixing bowl.

Drain the corn husks and shake dry. Lay out each husk in the center of a shallow pasta bowl. Unwrap the tamales from the plastic wrap and place in the center of each corn husk. Spoon the chilled gazpacho around the tamales. Sprinkle the garnish over the tamales and gazpacho.

SERVES 6

Caramelized Onion Tamales with Tomato-Basil Salad

(S T E P H A N  P Y L E S)

THINK OF THIS TAMALE AS ITALIAN BREAD SALAD BY WAY OF MEXICO! IT TASTES LIKE THE ESSENCE OF SUMMER, WHEN TOMATOES ARE AT THEIR

RIPEST AND BASIL IS IN PEAK SEASON. THE INTENSELY SWEET CARAMELIZED ONIONS ARE THE PERFECT FOIL FOR THE PLEASANT ACIDITY

OF THE TOMATILLOS AND VINAIGRETTE IN THIS VIBRANTLY FLAVORED DISH. THE TEXTURAL CONTRAST BETWEEN THE CRUNCHY CROUTONS

AND THE SOFT, CREAMY TAMALE DOUGH ROUNDS OUT AN INTRIGUING COMBINATION OF ELEMENTS IN THIS RECIPE.

Masa Seca Tamale Dough (page 2)

FOR THE ROASTED CHILE–GARLIC CROUTONS

3 tablespoons olive oil
Salt
1 tablespoon roasted garlic (page 165)
*4 slices French or sourdough bread,
    crust removed, cut into 1-inch cubes*
2 teaspoons pure red chile powder

FOR THE FILLING AND TAMALES

1 tablespoon olive oil
3 onions, thinly sliced
1 cup white wine vinegar
1 cup sugar
1 teaspoon salt
*10 large dried corn husks, soaked in warm water
    for 30 minutes*

FOR THE BASIL-PESTO VINAIGRETTE

1 small clove garlic
1/2 cup fresh basil leaves
1/4 cup grated Parmesan cheese
2 tablespoons toasted pine nuts (page 165)
1/4 cup extra-virgin olive oil
3 tablespoons balsamic vinegar
6 tablespoons olive oil

Prepare the masa dough.

To prepare the croutons, preheat the oven to 350°F. Combine the olive oil, salt to taste, and roasted garlic in a bowl. Add the bread cubes. Mix thoroughly so the cubes are well seasoned. Place on a baking sheet and roast in the oven until the cubes are golden brown, 5 to 7 minutes, turning after about 3 minutes. Transfer the croutons to a bowl, sprinkle with the chile powder, and toss until they are thoroughly covered. Set aside.

To prepare the filling, heat the olive oil in a large sauté pan over high heat, until lightly smoking. Sauté the onions, stirring occasionally, until they are dark brown, 10 to 12 minutes. Add the vinegar; deglaze the pan; add the sugar and salt; and stir. Bring the mixture to a boil and reduce to a syrupy consistency, 5 to 7 minutes. Strain the liquid and discard. Transfer the onions to a baking sheet and let cool to room temperature. When cool, combine the onions with the tamale dough in a mixing bowl. Set aside.

Drain the corn husks and shake dry. Tear 16 thin strips (about 1/8 inch wide) from 2 of the husks and set aside for tying the tamales. Lay out the remaining 8 corn husks on a flat work surface. Divide the dough into 8 even portions and place 1 portion on each husk. Evenly spread out the masa mixture, leaving about 1 1/2 inches of exposed corn husk at each end and 3/4 inch at each side. Bring the sides of the corn husk together, folding the dough; tuck one side of the husk under the other and roll up the tamale so that the dough is completely enclosed inside the husk. Twist each end and tie with the reserved strips of corn husk. Repeat for the remaining tamales.

Fill the bottom of a steamer or saucepan fitted with a strainer or vegetable basket with 2 to 3 inches of water. Bring the water to a boil and place the tamales in the steamer. Cover tightly with a lid or foil (it is important that little or no steam escapes while cooking). Steam the tamales for 30 to 35 minutes over lightly boiling water, adding more boiling water as needed. The tamales are done when they feel firm to the touch but are not hard and the dough comes away easily from the husk. Let rest for at least 5 minutes before serving.

While the tamales are cooking, prepare the vinaigrette. Place the garlic, basil, cheese, and pine nuts in a food processor and puree until smooth. With the machine running, slowly drizzle in the extra-virgin olive oil. When the

(continues)

FOR THE TOMATO-BASIL SALAD

1 yellow tomato, cored and cut into 1-inch cubes

1 red tomato, cored and cut into 1-inch cubes

4 tomatillos (about 5 ounces), husks removed,
*   rinsed, cored, and cut into 1-inch cubes*

¹/₃ cup minced fresh basil leaves

Salt

mixture is smooth, drizzle in the balsamic vinegar and olive oil.

To prepare the salad, combine the tomatoes, tomatillos, and vinaigrette in a mixing bowl. Add the basil and croutons. Mix the salad to coat all the ingredients and season with salt to taste.

Place the tamales on serving plates and, with a knife, slice open the top of the wrappers from end to end. Gently push the ends together, as for a baked potato, and spoon the salad over the top and around the sides of the tamales.

SERVES 8

Vegetarian Cobb Tamale Salad with Dijon Vinaigrette

(J O H N   S E D L A R)

IN LOS ANGELES, SALAD IS KING. IN HIS FAMOUS NOVEL *THE BONFIRE OF THE VANITIES*, TOM WOLFE CALLED ULTRATHIN SOCIALITE WOMEN

"SOCIAL X-RAYS"; WELL, THE "RAYS" ARE ALWAYS OUT IN FORCE AT LUNCHTIME IN THE CITY'S RESTAURANTS. SALADS ARE ALL THAT PEOPLE SEEM TO EAT

IN THE CITY OF ANGELS, SO IT IS FITTING THAT THE KING OF SALADS, THE COBB, WAS INVENTED AT THE BROWN DERBY RESTAURANT IN HOLLYWOOD.

I DECIDED TO GIVE THIS CLASSIC A TWIST, AND, SINCE IT IS ALREADY HEAVY ON THE VEGGIES, IT MAKES A WONDERFUL VEGETARIAN TAMALE.

FOR THE TAMALES

Masa Seca Tamale Dough (page 2)
6 large dried corn husks, soaked in warm water for 30 minutes
Olive oil, for brushing

FOR THE DIJON VINAIGRETTE

²/₃ cup extra-virgin olive oil
¹/₂ cup red wine vinegar
2 tablespoons safflower oil
2 tablespoons Dijon mustard
2 tablespoons minced fresh chives
2 teaspoons dried mixed herbs, such as oregano, tarragon, and chervil
1 teaspoon honey
¹/₂ teaspoon freshly ground black pepper
Pinch of salt

FOR THE SALAD

2 heads romaine lettuce (outer leaves discarded), thinly sliced crosswise
2 large ripe avocados, halved, pitted, peeled, and diced
6 Roma tomatoes, seeded and finely diced
1 cup crumbled blue cheese
2 cups cooked pinto beans, fresh or canned
¹/₂ cup diced celery
¹/₂ cup diced carrot
¹/₂ cup seeded and diced red bell pepper
Freshly ground black pepper

Prepare the masa dough.

Drain the corn husks and shake dry. Lay out the husks on a flat work surface. Brush the inside of each husk with the olive oil and then divide the masa evenly among them. Evenly spread out the masa, leaving about 1¹/₂ inches of exposed corn husk at each end and ³/₄ inch at each side. Bring the sides of the corn husks together, tightly around the dough; tuck one side of the husk under the other and then fold the ends over to form a neat envelope package. Repeat for the remaining tamales.

Fill the bottom of a steamer or saucepan fitted with a strainer or vegetable basket with 2 to 3 inches of water. Bring the water to a boil and place the tamales in the steamer. Cover tightly with a lid or foil (it is important that little or no steam escapes while cooking). Steam the tamales for about 45 minutes over lightly boiling water, adding more boiling water as needed. The tamales are done when they feel firm to the touch but are not hard and the dough comes away easily from the husk.

Combine all the ingredients for the vinaigrette in a glass jar with a tight-fitting lid and shake well. Toss together all the ingredients for the salad except the pepper in a large mixing bowl. Pour the vinaigrette over the salad and toss again.

Unwrap each tamale and, leaving the dough lying on the husks, place one in the center of each serving plate. Arrange the salad around each tamale, on top of the husks. Season with the pepper and serve immediately.

SERVES 6

Roasted Corn and *Huitlacoche* Tamales

(M A R K   M I L L E R)

HUITLACOCHE, CONSIDERED A DELICACY IN MEXICO, IS A GRAYISH BLACK FUNGUS THAT GROWS ON CORN AND TASTES LIKE WILD MOREL MUSHROOMS. IT MAKES A WONDERFUL FLAVOR PARTNER WITH CORN, AND IT'S AVAILABLE BY MAIL ORDER (SEE "SOURCES," PAGE 167). IF YOU PREFER, YOU CAN SUBSTITUTE 1$^{1}/_{2}$ CUPS OF SAUTÉED BLACK CHANTERELLE, MOREL, OR TRUMPET MUSHROOMS (OR A MIXTURE) FOR THE *HUITLACOCHE*. GIVEN THE RELATIONSHIP BETWEEN *HUITLACOCHE* AND FRESH CORN, IT IS FITTING THAT THESE TAMALES ARE SERVED IN FRESH CORN HUSKS. THE SAUCE CONTAINS *EPAZOTE*, A COMMON MEXICAN HERB WITH A UNIQUE, ASSERTIVE FLAVOR, WHICH CAN BE EASILY GROWN ON A WINDOWSILL OR IN AN HERB GARDEN. IT'S INCREASINGLY AVAILABLE IN GOOD PRODUCE STORES, BUT IF NECESSARY, SUBSTITUTE CILANTRO.

Roasted Corn Tamale Masa Dough (page 3)
8 ears fresh sweet corn

FOR THE FILLING

1 cup shredded Monterey Jack or mozzarella cheese
2 tablespoons minced cilantro

FOR THE *HUITLACOCHE* SAUCE

2 tablespoons vegetable or peanut oil
2 cloves roasted garlic, minced (page 165)
$^{1}/_{3}$ cup finely diced white onion
3 Roma tomatoes, blackened and chopped
  (page 164)
1 canned chipotle chile in adobo sauce, minced,
  plus 1 tablespoon adobo sauce
2 serrano chiles with seeds, blackened
  and minced (page 164)
12 ounces fresh or frozen huitlacoche
$^{1}/_{2}$ teaspoon salt
1 cup roasted corn kernels (page 164)
2 tablespoons epazote leaves (no stems),
  roughly chopped

Prepare the masa dough.

Carefully fold back the leaves of the corn husks, exposing the cobs, and break off the cobs at the base, leaving the leaves and husks intact. Remove the silks and set aside. Reserve the husks and use the corn for another purpose (1 cup of kernels can be roasted for the sauce).

To prepare the tamales, cut 8 square pieces of plastic wrap measuring about 6 inches by 6 inches each. Lay out each piece of plastic on a flat work surface and spray with nonstick vegetable spray. Take a 2-ounce ($^{1}/_{4}$-cup) portion of masa dough and, using a tortilla press or heavy pan, flatten to a thickness of about $^{1}/_{4}$ inch. Place the masa dough on top of the plastic wrap. Mix the cheese and cilantro for the filling in a bowl and sprinkle about 2 heaping tablespoons on top of the masa. Fold the dough over to enclose the filling and mold into a rectangular shape. Fold over two sides of the plastic wrap, and then fold over the other two sides to form a tight envelope package. Repeat for the remaining tamales.

Fill the bottom of a steamer or saucepan fitted with a strainer or vegetable basket with 2 to 3 inches of water. Bring the water to a boil and place the tamales in the steamer. Cover tightly with a lid or foil (it is important that little or no steam escapes while cooking). Steam the tamales for 35 to 40 minutes over lightly boiling water, adding more boiling water as needed. The tamales are done when they feel firm to the touch but are not hard and the dough comes away easily from the plastic wrap. Let rest for at least 5 minutes before serving.

While the tamales are steaming, prepare the sauce. Heat the oil in a sauté pan, add the garlic and onion, and sauté over medium heat for 10 minutes. Add the tomatoes, chiles, and *huitlacoche* and cook for 10 minutes, stirring occasionally. Add the salt and roasted corn and cook for 5 to 7 minutes longer, until thick in consistency. Turn the heat down to low, add the *epazote*, and cook for a further 10 minutes.

Spoon about $^{1}/_{2}$ cup of the sauce onto each serving plate. Unwrap the tamales from the plastic wrap and place inside the reserved corn husks. Garnish the husks with the reserved corn silks, if desired.

SERVES 8

Asparagus and Hollandaise Tamales

(J O H N   S E D L A R)

YOU MAY LOOK AT THIS RECIPE AND THINK THAT I AM OVERCOOKING THE ASPARAGUS, BUT I LIKE IT TO BE SOFT AND MUSHY TO COMPLEMENT THE LIGHT AND AIRY MASA DOUGH. I LEARNED THIS MATCHING OF TEXTURES FROM ROGER JALOUX, PAUL BOCUSE'S CHEF DE CUISINE. I WORKED WITH ROGER AT L'ERMITAGE IN LOS ANGELES MANY YEARS AGO WHEN HE WAS THE GUEST CHEF THERE; ONE OF HIS TRADEMARK DISHES WAS AN ASPARAGUS AND HOLLANDAISE *FEUILLETÉE*. TO THIS DAY, I CAN RECALL HIM EXPLAINING THAT THE MELTING, DELICATE TEXTURE OF THE ASPARAGUS SHOULD BE COMPATIBLE WITH THAT OF THE *FEUILLETÉE*, NOT CONTRASTING WITH IT. PEAK SEASON FOR ASPARAGUS IS LATE WINTER AND SPRING, WHEN TENDER, THIN YOUNG SPEARS ARE AT THEIR BEST.

FOR THE TAMALES

Spinach Tamale Mixture (page 4)
2 pounds thin asparagus spears, stem ends trimmed
1 small white onion, coarsely chopped
Olive oil, for brushing

FOR THE HOLLANDAISE SAUCE

5 egg yolks
1 tablespoon Dijon mustard
1 teaspoon lukewarm water
2 cups warm clarified unsalted butter
1/2 cup freshly squeezed lemon juice
Salt and freshly ground white pepper

FOR THE GARNISH

2 tablespoons unsalted butter, softened
Salt and freshly ground white pepper
6 large dried corn husks, soaked in warm water for 30 minutes

Prepare the spinach mixture.

To prepare the asparagus, cut off the top half-inch from each spear and set aside. Bring a large saucepan of salted water to a boil. Cut the asparagus spears into 1/2-inch lengths and blanch in the boiling water for about 5 minutes, until almost tender. Remove from the water with a slotted spoon and place in an ice bath to cool. Drain, then blot the asparagus dry with paper towels or a kitchen towel. Set aside.

Thoroughly combine the spinach mixture and asparagus spears (not the tips) in a mixing bowl. Mix in the onion until incorporated.

Cut 6 square pieces of plastic wrap measuring about 6 inches by 6 inches each. Lay out each piece of plastic on a flat work surface and brush lightly with the olive oil. Divide the spinach mixture evenly among them and mold into a rectangular shape. Fold two of the sides of the plastic wrap over, then fold over the other two sides to form a tight envelope package. Repeat for the remaining tamales.

Fill the bottom of a steamer or saucepan fitted with a strainer or vegetable basket with 2 to 3 inches of water. Bring the water to a boil and place the tamales in the steamer. Cover tightly with a lid or foil (it is important that little or no steam escapes while cooking). Steam the tamales for about 15 minutes over lightly boiling water until firm, adding more boiling water as needed. Keep warm.

Meanwhile, to prepare the hollandaise sauce, combine the egg yolks, mustard, and water in the top of a double boiler over medium heat.

Whisk continuously until the mixture turns lemon yellow and a ribbon forms, about 5 minutes. Slowly drizzle in the clarified butter and continue whisking. As the sauce thickens, whisk in the lemon juice and season with salt and white pepper to taste. Keep warm.

For the garnish, heat the butter in a sauté pan. Add the reserved asparagus tips, season with salt and white pepper to taste, and sauté over medium heat for about 2 minutes to heat through.

Drain the corn husks and shake dry. Lay out each husk in the center of a serving plate. Spoon the hollandaise sauce onto each husk. Unwrap the tamales from the plastic wrap and place in the center of each corn husk on top of the sauce. Sprinkle the asparagus tips over the top of the tamales.

SERVES 6

Vegetable *Escabeche* Tamales with *Salsa Cruda Roja*

(S T E P H A N   P Y L E S)

PICKLING VEGETABLES—*ESCABECHE* IN SPANISH—IS THE PERFECT METHOD FOR PRESERVING THEIR FLAVOR, OR EVEN PERKING IT UP WITH A ZESTY

MARINADE. THE TRADITION OF *ESCABECHE* WAS BROUGHT TO MEXICO FROM SPAIN, WHERE IT WAS LONG USED TO "COOK" AND PRESERVE MEATS AND FISH

AS WELL AS VEGETABLES WITH AN ACIDIC MARINADE, USUALLY VINEGAR. THE SAME TECHNIQUE WAS USED IN EARLIER CENTURIES BY THE INCAS AND

OTHER CIVILIZATIONS OF SOUTH AMERICA, WHO USED CITRUS JUICE TO "COOK" SEAFOOD FOR CEVICHES. THESE TAMALES ARE DELICIOUS ON THEIR OWN

OR AS A SIDE WITH ALMOST ANY MAIN DISH.

FOR THE VEGETABLE MARINADE

2 oranges, zested, halved, and juiced

$^1/_4$ cup olive oil

1 cup white wine vinegar

1 cup dry white wine

3 allspice seeds

1 stick cinnamon

2 tablespoons lightly toasted cumin seeds
    (page 165)

1 teaspoon black peppercorns

1 bay leaf

1 tablespoon dried thyme

4 dried pequín chiles, or $^1/_4$ teaspoon cayenne
    powder

1 tablespoon kosher salt

1 tablespoon sugar

FOR THE GRILLED VEGETABLES

1 small white baking potato, about 10 ounces

1 small sweet potato, about 8 ounces

1 large blue or yellow potato, about 6 ounces

1 red bell pepper, roasted, peeled, and seeded
    (page 164)

1 small onion, cut into $^1/_2$-inch slices

1 small zucchini, cut into $^1/_2$-inch diagonal slices

$^1/_4$ cup olive oil

Masa Seca Tamale Dough (page 2)

To prepare the marinade, place the orange zest and juice in a saucepan. Add the olive oil and combine with the remaining marinade ingredients. Bring to a boil and simmer for 5 minutes. Remove from the heat, cover, and let stand for at least 6 hours and preferably overnight.

To prepare the vegetables, place the baking potato and sweet potato in a saucepan of salted water and bring to a boil. Cook until tender but firm, 25 to 30 minutes. In another saucepan, boil the blue potato likewise, about 15 minutes. Drain the potatoes and when cool enough, peel and cut into $^1/_4$-inch slices. Transfer to a large bowl. Cut the roasted pepper in half lengthwise and then crosswise, and reserve with the potatoes, onion, and zucchini.

Prepare the grill. (As an alternative to grilling, the vegetables and the boiled potatoes can be roasted or sautéed.) Brush the vegetables with the olive oil and grill until tender, about 3 minutes. Set aside in a large bowl. Meanwhile, bring the reserved marinade to a boil and pour over the grilled vegetables. Let stand for 2 to 3 hours.

Prepare the masa dough.

Drain the corn husks and shake dry. Tear 16 thin strips (about $^1/_8$ inch wide) from 2 of the husks and set aside for tying the tamales. Lay out the remaining 8 corn husks on a flat work surface. Divide the dough into 16 even portions and place 1 portion on each husk. Evenly spread out the masa mixture, leaving about $1^1/_2$ inches of exposed corn husk at each end and $^1/_4$ inch at each side. Bring the sides of the corn husk together, folding the dough; tuck one side of the husk under the other and roll up the tamale so that the dough is completely enclosed inside the husk. Twist each end and tie with the reserved strips of corn husk. Repeat for the remaining tamales.

Fill the bottom of a steamer or saucepan fitted with a strainer or vegetable basket with 2 to 3 inches of water. Bring the water to a boil and place the tamales in the steamer. Cover tightly with a lid or foil (it is important that little or no steam escapes while cooking). Steam the tamales for 30 to 35 minutes over lightly boiling water, adding more boiling

(continues)

10 large dried corn husks, soaked in warm water
for 30 minutes

FOR THE *SALSA CRUDA ROJA*
3 ripe tomatoes, halved
1 tablespoon olive oil
¹/₂ cup sliced onion
3 jalapeño chiles, seeded and sliced
2 cloves garlic, chopped
1 tablespoon chipotle chile puree (page 165)
¹/₄ cup chopped cilantro
¹/₄ cup freshly squeezed lime juice
1 teaspoon salt

water as needed. The tamales are done when they feel firm to the touch but are not hard and the dough comes away easily from the husk. Let rest for at least 5 minutes before serving.

To prepare the salsa, place a large cast-iron skillet over high heat for about 3 minutes, until smoking. Place the tomatoes in the skillet and char on all sides until black and somewhat soft. Remove from the skillet and turn down the heat to medium. After 2 minutes, pour the olive oil into the skillet and immediately add the onion, jalapeños, and garlic. Cook for about 3 minutes, stirring occasionally, until the vegetables are soft.

Remove the onion, jalapeños, and garlic from the skillet and place in a food processor with the griddled tomatoes and chipotle puree. Process until all the ingredients are blended. Transfer to a bowl and add the cilantro, lime juice, and salt. Set aside.

Place the tamales on serving plates and, with a knife, slice open the top of the wrappers from end to end. Gently push the ends together, as for a baked potato. Remove the vegetables from the marinade with a slotted spoon and place around the tamales. Serve the *salsa cruda roja* on top of the tamales.

SERVES 8

Goat Cheese Tamales with Black Olive Masa and Lemon-Fig Salsa

(M A R K M I L L E R)

FLAVORING MASA DOUGH CAN TURN A TAMALE INTO A MEDIUM FOR DISTINCTIVE TASTES—IN THIS CASE, THE FLAVORS OF THE MEDITERRANEAN. BLACK OLIVE PASTE (TAPENADE) IS AVAILABLE IN JARS FROM SUPERMARKETS (USUALLY NEXT TO THE OLIVE OIL SECTION), OR AT GOURMET STORES. YOU CAN MAKE YOUR OWN BY BLENDING PITTED OLIVES—PREFERABLY THE LESS SALTY VARIETIES SUCH AS NIÇOISE OR GAETA—WITH A LITTLE OLIVE OIL AND GARLIC. THIS TAMALE IS A TAKEOFF ON THE CLASSIC OLIVE BREAD, WITH THE GOAT CHEESE ALREADY ADDED! USE A FULL-FLAVORED, FIRM GOAT CHEESE SUCH AS MONTRACHET, WHICH WILL NOT BECOME TOO RUNNY WHEN STEAMED, UNLIKE A FRESH GOAT CHEESE. SUN-DRIED TOMATOES ADDED TO THE MASA DOUGH INSTEAD OF BLACK OLIVES MAKES ANOTHER GREAT PARTNERSHIP WITH THE GOAT CHEESE.

10 large dried corn husks, soaked in warm water for 30 minutes

Black Olive Tamale Masa Dough (page 8)

8 ounces semihard ripened goat cheese, sliced or crumbled

FOR THE LEMON-FIG SALSA

3 cups dried figs (about 30)

Zest of 2 lemons, finely minced

3 tablespoons minced fresh Italian parsley

1 tablespoon minced fresh thyme

3/4 teaspoon cayenne powder

1 tablespoon pure lemon extract

1 cup extra-virgin olive oil

Drain the corn husks and shake dry. Tear 16 thin strips (about 1/8 inch wide) from 2 of the husks and set aside for tying the tamales. Lay out the remaining 8 corn husks on a flat work surface. Take a 2-ounce (1/4-cup) portion of masa dough and, using a tortilla press or heavy pan, flatten to a thickness of about 1/4 inch. Place the masa dough inside each husk, leaving about 1 1/2 inches of exposed corn husk at each end and 3/4 inch at each side. Place about 2 tablespoons of the goat cheese on top of each portion of masa. Bring the sides of the corn husk together, folding the dough; tuck one side of the husk under the other and roll up the tamale so the dough is completely enclosed inside the husk. Make sure the cheese is completely enclosed by the masa dough or it will run out during the steaming process. Twist each end and tie with the reserved strips of corn husk. Repeat for the remaining tamales.

Fill the bottom of a steamer or saucepan fitted with a strainer or vegetable basket with 2 to 3 inches of water. Bring the water to a boil and place the tamales in the steamer. Cover tightly with a lid or foil (it is important that little or no steam escapes while cooking). Steam the tamales for about 45 minutes over lightly boiling water, adding more boiling water as needed. The tamales are done when they feel firm to the touch but are not hard and the dough comes away easily from the husk. Let the tamales sit for 5 minutes before serving to allow the cheese filling to firm up a little.

While the tamales are steaming, prepare the salsa. Place all the salsa ingredients in a food processor or blender and puree until smooth.

Place the tamales on serving plates and, with a knife, slice open the top of the wrappers from end to end. Serve with the salsa.

SERVES 8

Seafood Tamales

SALMON AND *HOJA SANTA* TAMALES WITH
ANCHO-ORANGE SAUCE

SALMON TAMALES WITH RED PEPPER MASA
AND MOLE AMARILLO

SMOKED SALMON TAMALES WITH
HORSERADISH *CREMA*

TAMALES TOKYO

TUNA TAMALES WITH OLIVES AND SMOKED
TOMATO–JALAPEÑO SAUCE

RED SNAPPER TAMALES WITH RED CURRY MASA

CARIBBEAN JERK SHRIMP TAMALES

ANNATTO SHRIMP–BLUE CORN TAMALES

SHRIMP TAMALES WITH RANCHO SAUCE

BACKYARD BARBECUE SHRIMP TAMALES

LOBSTER AND ROASTED POBLANO TAMALES
WITH GUAJILLO SAUCE

LOBSTER NEWBURG TAMALES

MOULES MARINIÈRE TAMALES WITH PIPÉRADE

SAFFRON RISOTTO TAMALES WITH SEARED SCALLOPS
AND MANGO–RED PEPPER RELISH

CLAM TAMALES WITH FENNEL AND
CHAYOTE-MELON SALSA

Salmon and *Hoja Santa* Tamales with Ancho-Orange Sauce

(STEPHAN PYLES)

HOJA SANTA IS AN AROMATIC MEXICAN HERB WITH LARGE HEART-SHAPED, VELVETY LEAVES THAT TASTE LIKE SASSAFRAS WITH OVERTONES OF FENNEL. IT'S USED EXTENSIVELY IN MEXICAN COOKING AND IT IS BECOMING MORE READILY AVAILABLE IN THE UNITED STATES. IT IS BEING GROWN COMMERCIALLY IN TEXAS, FLORIDA, AND CALIFORNIA (FOR SOURCES, SEE PAGE 167); I HAVE ALSO SEEN IT GROWING WILD ALONG THE RIVER WALK IN SAN ANTONIO, TEXAS! A DECADE AGO, I DISCOVERED THAT *HOJA SANTA* HAD A NATURAL AFFINITY WITH SALMON, A PAIRING THAT I AM HAPPY TO SAY MANY OTHERS HAVE EMULATED SINCE. THIS TAMALE, IN SOME FORM OR OTHER, HAS BEEN ON THE MENU AT MY RESTAURANT, STAR CANYON, EVER SINCE WE OPENED IN 1994.

Masa Seca Tamale Dough (page 2)

FOR THE ANCHO-ORANGE SAUCE

1 tablespoon olive oil
1 small yellow onion, diced
2 cloves garlic, minced
Juice of 5 oranges
Juice of 1/2 lemon
2 tablespoons ancho chile puree (page 165)

FOR THE TAMALES

2 large hoja santa leaves, stemmed and julienned
* (about 1/2 cup)*
12 ounces salmon fillet, skin and
* pin bones removed*
Salt
10 large dried corn husks, soaked in warm water
* for 30 minutes*

Prepare the masa dough.

To prepare the sauce, heat the olive oil in a saucepan until hot and lightly smoking. Sauté the onion and garlic over medium heat for 2 to 3 minutes, stirring until the onion is translucent. Add both citrus juices and cook until reduced by three-quarters. Whisk in the ancho puree and strain through a fine mesh strainer. Set aside.

To prepare the filling, combine the tamale dough and the *hoja santa* in a mixing bowl. Cut the salmon into 8 thin rectangular slices and season them lightly with the salt.

Drain the corn husks and shake dry. Tear 16 thin strips (about 1/8 inch wide) from 2 of the husks and set aside for tying the tamales. Lay out the remaining 8 corn husks on a flat work surface. Divide the dough into 16 even portions and place 1 portion on each husk. Evenly spread out the masa mixture, leaving about 1 1/2 inches of exposed corn husk at each end and 3/4 inch at each side. Place a slice of the salmon on top of each portion of masa. Top the salmon with the remaining portions of masa, spreading it out evenly. Bring the sides of the corn husk together, folding the dough; tuck one side of the husk under the other and roll up the tamale so that the dough is completely enclosed inside the husk. Twist each end and tie with the reserved strips of corn husk. Repeat for the remaining tamales.

Fill the bottom of a steamer or saucepan fitted with a strainer or vegetable basket with 2 to 3 inches of water. Bring the water to a boil and place the tamales in the steamer. Cover tightly with a lid or foil (it is important that little or no steam escapes while cooking). Steam the tamales for 30 to 35 minutes over lightly boiling water, adding more boiling water as needed. The tamales are done when they feel firm to the touch but are not hard and the dough comes away easily from the husk. Let rest for at least 5 minutes before serving.

Ladle the ancho-orange sauce onto serving plates. With a knife, slice open the top of the tamale wrappers from end to end. Gently push the ends together, as for a baked potato, and serve.

SERVES 8

Salmon Tamales with Red Pepper Masa and Mole Amarillo

(M A R K   M I L L E R)

THE SWEETNESS OF THE RED BELL PEPPER IN THE MASA DOUGH AND THE SUBTLE SWEET HEAT OF THE YELLOW MOLE SAUCE MAKE TASTY MUSIC TOGETHER! DON'T OVERCOOK THESE FAUX TAMALES OR THE SALMON WILL DRY OUT AND LOSE ITS SILKY TEXTURE. YOU CAN USE ANOTHER FIRM-FLESHED FISH, SUCH AS TUNA, INSTEAD OF THE SALMON AND A RED CHILE SAUCE INSTEAD OF THE YELLOW MOLE IF YOU PREFER. THE YELLOW MOLE IS AN ELEGANT SAUCE FROM THE OAXACA REGION OF MEXICO THAT ALSO SHOULD NOT BE OVERCOOKED, OR IT WILL LOSE ITS EDGE.

FOR THE MOLE AMARILLO

1/2 cup vegetable oil
2 large yellow bell peppers
1 tablespoon unsalted butter
1 onion, diced
8 ounces guero or yellow banana wax chiles,
* seeded and chopped*
10 tomatillos, husked and rinsed
3 cloves roasted garlic (page 164)
3/4 teaspoon ground canela, or 1/2 teaspoon
* ground cinnamon*
3/4 teaspoon sugar
1/8 teaspoon ground allspice
Salt
2 tablespoons peanut oil

FOR THE RED PEPPER MASA AND SALMON

3 1/2 cups masa harina
3 red bell peppers, roasted, peeled, seeded,
* and pureed (page 164)*
1 cup olive oil
3 tablespoons sweet paprika
1/2 tablespoon salt
1/2 cup water
8 boneless salmon fillets, about 4 ounces each

To prepare the mole sauce, heat the vegetable oil in a saucepan until almost smoking. Add the bell peppers and turn for 45 seconds to 1 minute to blister the skins. Transfer to a bowl, cover with plastic wrap, and let steam for 10 minutes, then peel, seed, and chop. Meanwhile, melt the butter in a heavy skillet and sauté the onion over medium heat for 5 minutes. Add the chiles and bell peppers and cook over low heat until soft, about 30 minutes.

Blanch the tomatillos in boiling water for 20 seconds and roughly chop. Transfer to a food processor and add the chile mixture. Add the garlic, canela, sugar, allspice, and salt to taste, and puree until smooth; add a little water if necessary. Heat the peanut oil in a high-sided skillet until almost smoking. Add the sauce and fry at a sizzle over medium heat for 5 to 6 minutes, stirring constantly; add water if necessary to prevent it from becoming too thick. Strain through a fine mesh strainer into a saucepan and warm just before serving.

To prepare the masa, place the masa harina in the bowl of an electric mixer fitted with a paddle attachment. Add the red pepper puree and olive oil and beat together until combined.

With the machine running, add the paprika and salt, and the water last. When a dough forms, remove from the bowl and cover with plastic wrap. Let sit for 30 to 60 minutes.

Trim the salmon fillets into squares about 1 inch thick. Divide the dough into 8 equal portions and roll into squares measuring about 6 inches by 5 inches and 3/4 inch thick. Place the salmon in the middle of each square, fold up the edges of the masa, and cut off any excess dough. Wrap the salmon pieces in squares of foil, securing tightly.

Fill the bottom of a steamer or saucepan fitted with a strainer or vegetable basket with 2 to 3 inches of water. Bring the water to a boil and place the tamales in the steamer. Cover tightly with a lid or foil (it is important that little or no steam escapes while cooking). Steam the tamales for about 25 minutes over lightly boiling water, adding more boiling water as needed.

Unwrap the foil and cut each salmon in half on a diagonal. Stand the salmon triangles upright on serving plates and serve with the mole sauce.

SERVES 8

Smoked Salmon Tamales with Horseradish *Crema*

(S T E P H A N   P Y L E S)

SMOKED SALMON WITH HORSERADISH IS A CLASSIC COMBINATION, AND THESE TAMALES MAKE GREAT HORS D'OEUVRES OR APPETIZERS. HORSERADISH, A MEMBER OF THE MUSTARD FAMILY, IS NATIVE TO EASTERN EUROPE, AND ITS CLEANSING, PUNGENT BITE REVEALS AN UNDERLYING SWEETNESS. IF YOU FEEL SO INCLINED, BY ALL MEANS BRINE AND SMOKE YOUR OWN SALMON, BUT BUYING IT ALREADY SMOKED IS OBVIOUSLY THE EASIEST WAY TO GO. MY PREFERENCE IS FOR NORWEGIAN OR SWEDISH SMOKED SALMON.

Masa Seca Tamale Dough (page 2)

FOR THE HORSERADISH *CREMA*

1 cup sour cream or crème fraîche
3 tablespoons prepared horseradish
1 teaspoon minced lemon zest
1 tablespoon minced shallot
Cream or milk, for thinning
Salt

FOR THE TAMALES

1 tablespoon minced lemon zest
1 tablespoon drained and minced capers
2 tablespoons chopped chives
*10 large dried corn husks, soaked in warm water
   for 30 minutes*
8 ounces smoked salmon, thinly cut into 16 slices

Prepare the masa dough.

To prepare the horseradish *crema*, whisk together the sour cream, horseradish, lemon zest, and shallot in a small mixing bowl. Thin with the cream to the consistency of thin sour cream and season with salt to taste. Refrigerate until ready to serve.

To prepare the filling, combine the masa dough, lemon zest, capers, and chives in the bowl of an electric mixer and blend thoroughly.

Drain the corn husks and shake dry. Tear 16 thin strips (about $1/8$ inch wide) from 2 of the husks and set aside for tying the tamales. Lay out the remaining 8 corn husks on a flat work surface. Divide the dough into 8 even portions and place 1 portion on each husk. Evenly spread out the masa mixture, leaving about $1 1/2$ inches of exposed corn husk at each end and $3/4$ inch at each side. Bring the sides of the corn husks together, folding the dough; tuck one side of the husk under the other and roll up the tamale so that the dough is com-pletely enclosed inside the husk. Twist each end and tie with the reserved strips of corn husk. Repeat for the remaining tamales.

Fill the bottom of a steamer or saucepan fitted with a strainer or vegetable basket with 2 to 3 inches of water. Bring the water to a boil and place the tamales in the steamer. Cover tightly with a lid or foil (it is important that little or no steam escapes while cooking). Steam the tamales for 30 to 35 minutes over lightly boiling water, adding more boiling water as needed. The tamales are done when they feel firm to the touch but are not hard and the dough comes away easily from the husk. Let rest for at least 5 minutes before serving.

Place the tamales on serving plates. Remove the tie at one end and pull back the husk to expose the dough. Place 2 slices of the smoked salmon on top of each tamale, criss-crossed to form an X. Spoon a dollop of the horseradish *crema* on top of each tamale.

SERVES 8

Tamales Tokyo

(J O H N S E D L A R)

I LOVE JAPAN AND JAPANESE CUISINE. THE LAST TIME I WAS IN TOKYO, MY FRIEND MURAMASA KUDO, ONE OF THE COUNTRY'S PREMIER PAINTERS,

TOOK ME ON A SERIES OF TRIPS TO THE CITY'S BEST RESTAURANTS. THE FIRST NIGHT, HE TOOK ME TO A WONDERFUL FRENCH RESTAURANT; THE NEXT,

WE WENT TO AN ITALIAN RESTAURANT; ONLY ONCE DID WE GO FOR A FINE JAPANESE MEAL. AS SOON AS I RETURNED TO LOS ANGELES, I WENT STRAIGHT

FROM THE AIRPORT TO MATSUHISA, ONE OF THE BEST JAPANESE RESTAURANTS IN THE WORLD. WITH RICE, SASHIMI-QUALITY TUNA, WASABI, AND PONZU

SAUCE, THESE TAMALES CAPTURE THE ESSENCE OF ONE OF MY FAVORITE CUISINES. FOR A SHORTCUT, BUY READY-MADE BOTTLED PONZU SAUCE.

Rice Tamale Mixture (page 7)

FOR THE PONZU SAUCE

1 cup freshly squeezed orange juice
1/2 cup freshly squeezed lemon juice
1/4 cup unsweetened pineapple juice
3/4 cup soy sauce
1/4 cup unseasoned rice vinegar
1 tablespoon bonito flakes
1 teaspoon arrowroot
1 teaspoon water

FOR THE TAMALES

Olive oil, for brushing
6 large dried corn husks, soaked in warm water
* for 30 minutes*
1 1/2 pounds sashimi-quality ahi tuna, cut into
* 1/4-inch-thick slices*
1/2 cup pickled ginger
3 tablespoons prepared wasabi
1 tablespoon toasted sesame seeds (page 165)
6 tablespoons daikon sprouts

Prepare the rice tamale mixture.

To prepare the ponzu sauce, combine the citrus juices, pineapple juice, soy sauce, vinegar, and bonito flakes in a saucepan. Bring to a boil, turn down the heat, and simmer for 3 minutes, stirring occasionally. Combine the arrowroot and water in a bowl. Remove the pan from the heat and stir in the arrowroot mixture. Set aside; the sauce will thicken slightly as it cools.

To prepare the tamales, cut 6 square pieces of plastic wrap measuring about 6 inches by 6 inches each. Lay out each piece of plastic on a flat work surface and brush lightly with the olive oil. Divide the rice mixture evenly among them and mold into a rectangular shape. Fold two of the sides of the plastic wrap over, and then fold over the other two sides to form a tight envelope package. Repeat for the remaining tamales.

Fill the bottom of a steamer or saucepan fitted with a strainer or vegetable basket with 2 to 3 inches of water. Bring the water to a boil and place the tamales in the steamer. Cover tightly with a lid or foil (it is important that little or no steam escapes while cooking). Steam the tamales for about 8 minutes over lightly boiling water until firm, adding more boiling water as needed.

Drain the corn husks and shake dry. Lay out each husk in the center of a large shallow pasta bowl. Unwrap the tamales from the plastic wrap and place in the center of each corn husk. Fan out the tuna slices on top of the tamales. Mound the pickled ginger next to the tamales and place a dollop of the wasabi next to the ginger. Place the ponzu sauce in small dishes or ramekins and place in the bowl (or to one side). Sprinkle the sesame seeds and sprouts over the tamales.

SERVES 6

Tuna Tamales with Olives and
Smoked Tomato–Jalapeño Sauce

(M A R K M I L L E R)

IF YOU USE FRESH TUNA IN THESE TAMALES, IT WILL DRY OUT TOO MUCH DURING THE STEAMING PROCESS SO MAKE SURE THAT YOU USED CANNED.

THE EGG YOLKS BIND THE FILLING WELL AND MAKE IT THAT MUCH RICHER IN FLAVOR AND TEXTURE. THE SMOKY-FLAVORED SAUCE IS VERY VERSATILE—

IT GOES WONDERFULLY WITH GRILLED PORK AND CHICKEN, SCALLOPS, AND MOST EGG DISHES.

FOR THE SMOKED
TOMATO–JALAPEÑO SAUCE

$1^{1}/_{4}$ pounds Roma tomatoes (about 10),
    halved lengthwise

4 jalapeño chiles, halved lengthwise and seeded

1 tablespoon olive oil

$^{3}/_{4}$ cup finely sliced white onion

3 cloves garlic, roasted and peeled (page 165)

1 tablespoon dark brown sugar

$^{1}/_{2}$ teaspoon salt

6 tablespoons softened unsalted butter

$^{1}/_{2}$ tablespoon balsamic vinegar

FOR THE TAMALES

Red Bell Pepper Tamale Masa Dough (page 5)

1 can (6 ounces) white albacore tuna packed in
    water or pure olive oil

2 tablespoons finely diced black olives
    (preferably Niçoise or Gaeta)

2 tablespoons finely diced green olives
    (preferably French or Italian)

2 tablespoons finely diced sun-dried tomatoes
    packed in oil

2 egg yolks

$^{1}/_{2}$ teaspoon crushed red pepper (optional)

10 large dried corn husks, soaked in warm water
    for 30 minutes

To prepare the sauce, arrange the tomatoes and jalapeños, cut-side up, in a home smoker or on a very low covered grill. Smoke lightly over a sweet fruit wood such as apple (or use fruit wood chips) for about 1 hour. Heat the olive oil in a sauté pan, add the onion, and sauté over medium-low heat until brown, about 25 minutes. Transfer the onion to a blender or food processor, add the tomatoes, 2 of the jalapeños, the garlic, brown sugar, and salt. Puree until smooth and strain through a medium sieve into a saucepan. Just before you are ready to serve, warm the sauce gently and stir in the butter and vinegar. Julienne the remaining 2 jalapeños and use to garnish the sauce on each plate.

Prepare the masa dough.

Combine all the ingredients except the corn husks in a mixing bowl for the filling.

Drain the corn husks and pat dry. Tear 16 thin strips (about $^{1}/_{8}$ inch wide) from 2 of the husks and set aside for tying the tamales. Lay out the remaining 8 corn husks on a flat work surface. Take a 2-ounce ($^{1}/_{4}$-cup) portion of masa dough and, using a tortilla press or heavy pan, flatten to a thickness of about $^{1}/_{4}$ inch. Place the masa dough inside each husk, leav-ing about $1^{1}/_{2}$ inches of exposed corn husk at each end and $^{3}/_{4}$ inch at each side. Spread about 2 heaping tablespoons of the filling on top of the masa. Bring the sides of the corn husk together, folding the dough; tuck one side of the husk under the other and roll up the tamale so the dough is completely enclosed inside the husk. Twist each end and tie with the reserved strips of corn husk. Repeat for the remaining tamales.

Fill the bottom of a steamer or saucepan fitted with a strainer or vegetable basket with 2 to 3 inches of water. Bring the water to a boil and place the tamales in the steamer. Cover tightly with a lid or foil (it is important that little or no steam escapes while cooking). Steam the tamales for 15 to 20 minutes over lightly boiling water, adding more boiling water as needed. The tamales are done when they feel firm to the touch but are not hard and the dough comes away easily from the husk. Let rest for at least 5 minutes before serving.

Ladle the sauce onto serving plates and arrange the tamales on the sauce. With a knife, slice open the top of the tamale wrappers from end to end. Gently push the ends together, as for a baked potato, and serve.

SERVES 8

Red Snapper Tamales with Red Curry Masa

(STEPHAN PYLES)

ALL TOO OFTEN, WHAT IS LABELED AS "RED SNAPPER FILLET" IS IN FACT A DIFFERENT TYPE OF SNAPPER, OR SOMETIMES ROCKFISH. IT'S HARD

TO TELL UNLESS THE SKIN IS ATTACHED OR YOU CAN SEE THE WHOLE DISTINCTIVELY COLORED FISH, SO BUY FROM A SOURCE YOU CAN TRUST.

RED SNAPPER IS ONE OF THE GULF'S MOST PRIZED FISH, AND ITS FIRM FLESH IS MEATY AND DELICIOUS. SUBSTITUTE ANOTHER FIRMLY TEXTURED

WHITE-FLESHED FISH SUCH AS HALIBUT OR GROUPER IF RED SNAPPER IS UNAVAILABLE. THE THAI RED CURRY PASTE IN THE MASA DOUGH IS

AVAILABLE IN MANY SUPERMARKETS AND ASIAN GROCERIES; IT'S A SPICY, STRONGLY FLAVORED CONDIMENT MADE WITH CHILES, GARLIC,

CORIANDER, LEMONGRASS, SHRIMP PASTE, CLOVES, NUTMEG, AND PEPPER.

Red Thai Curry Tamale Masa Dough
(page 7)
1¹/₂ pounds red snapper fillet, skinned, boned,
and cut into 8 portions, about 3 ounces each
Salt
2 tablespoons chopped fresh mint
2 large banana leaves, about 12 inches
by 36 inches each

Prepare the masa dough.

Place the fillets on a flat work surface and season on both sides with salt. Roll both sides of the fillets in the chopped mint, pressing gently so it adheres.

Soften the banana leaves over an open flame for 10 seconds on each side, being careful not to burn them. Cut each leaf crosswise into 4 even pieces, about 8 inches by 10 inches, and lay out on a flat work surface. Divide the masa mixture into 16 even portions and roll them each into a ball. Flatten each ball between 2 layers of plastic wrap with your hand to a thickness of ¹/₈ inch. (Alternatively, use a tortilla press.) Place 1 masa portion in the center of each banana leaf leaving 8 left over. Spread into a 4-inch square, leaving at least a 1¹/₂-inch border at the ends and ³/₄ inch on the long sides. Place 1 piece of snapper in the center of each portion of masa and spread another flattened masa portion over the snapper to make a sandwich. Repeat

for the remaining tamales. To fold the tamales, pick up the two long sides of the banana leaf and bring them together (the dough will surround the filling). Tuck one side under the other and roll up. Fold the flaps on each end underneath the tamale.

Fill the bottom of a steamer or saucepan fitted with a strainer or vegetable basket with 2 to 3 inches of water. Bring the water to a boil and place the tamales in the steamer. Cover tightly with a lid or foil (it is important that little or no steam escapes while cooking). Steam the tamales for 25 to 30 minutes over lightly boiling water, adding more boiling water as needed. The tamales are done when they feel firm to the touch but are not hard and the dough comes away easily from the leaves. Let rest for at least 5 minutes before serving.

Unwrap the tamales and, leaving the filling lying on the leaves, place each in the center of a large serving bowl.

SERVES 8

Caribbean Jerk Shrimp Tamales

(J O H N  S E D L A R)

THE SCOTCH BONNET CHILE SOUNDS LIKE A SWEET LITTLE THING. IN REALITY, HOWEVER, THIS CLOSE RELATIVE OF THE HABANERO IS THE MOST

INCENDIARY, SCORCHING, FIERY CHILE ON THE FACE OF THE EARTH—WHICH IS WHY ONLY ONE IS CALLED FOR IN THIS RECIPE! "JERK SHRIMP"

DOES NOT REFER TO ANNOYING CRUSTACEANS BUT TO THE TRADITIONAL SEASONING MIXTURE THAT IS A HALLMARK OF JAMAICAN COOKING

IN PARTICULAR. JERK SEASONING IS A DRY RUB USUALLY MADE WITH CHILES, GARLIC, SPICES, AND HERBS THAT IS MASSAGED INTO MEAT

(TYPICALLY CHICKEN OR PORK) OR COMBINED WITH A LIQUID TO MAKE A MARINADE.

FOR THE JERK SHRIMP

8 scallions, all of the white part and
*   a little of the green, coarsely chopped*
1 Scotch Bonnet chile, seeded and minced
2 cloves garlic, coarsely chopped
2 tablespoons allspice berries, toasted and ground
*   (page 165)*
1 teaspoon ground cinnamon
¼ teaspoon ground cloves
1½ pounds rock shrimp or small shrimp
*   (45 to 50)*

FOR THE TAMALES

Sweet Corn Tamale Mixture (page 2)
Olive oil, for brushing
6 large dried corn husks, soaked in warm water
*   for 30 minutes*

FOR THE SAUCE

6 cups Chicken Stock (page 160)
1 onion, finely diced
2 stalks celery, finely diced
4 carrots, finely diced
¼ cup rum
1 vanilla bean, halved lengthwise, seeds scraped out
Salt

Combine all the ingredients for the jerk shrimp except the shrimp in a blender and puree to a paste. If the mixture is too thick, add a little water. Place the shrimp in a mixing bowl, add the jerk mixture, and toss to coat well. Cover the bowl with plastic wrap and marinate in the refrigerator for 1 hour.

Prepare the tamale mixture.

To prepare the tamales, cut 6 square pieces of plastic wrap measuring about 6 inches by 6 inches each. Lay out each piece of plastic on a flat work surface and brush lightly with the olive oil. Divide the tamale mixture evenly among them and mold into a rectangular shape. Fold two of the sides of the plastic wrap over, and then fold over the other two sides to form a tight envelope package. Repeat for the remaining tamales.

Fill the bottom of a steamer or saucepan fitted with a strainer or vegetable basket with 2 to 3 inches of water. Bring the water to a boil and place the tamales in the steamer. Cover tightly with a lid or foil (it is important that little or no steam escapes while cooking). Steam the tamales for about 15 minutes over lightly boiling water, adding more boiling water as needed. Transfer to a plate, cover, and keep warm.

Prepare the grill (alternatively, the shrimp can be broiled).

Remove the shrimp from the jerk marinade; reserve the jerk mixture. Thread the shrimp onto 6 thin wooden skewers (or cook the shrimp without the skewers). After you have made the sauce, grill (or broil) the shrimp until firm but still juicy, about 3 minutes, turning once; do not overcook.

To prepare the sauce, combine the reserved jerk mixture, the chicken stock, onion, celery, and carrots in a saucepan. Cook over medium heat for 30 minutes, until reduced by half. Stir in the rum and vanilla bean and seeds, and reduce by half again. Strain through a fine mesh sieve into a clean saucepan, season with salt to taste, and keep warm.

To serve the tamales, drain the corn husks and shake dry. Place the husks in the center of each serving plate. Unwrap the tamales from the plastic wrap and place in the center of each corn husk. Place the skewers with the shrimp next to the tamales (or, if not using skewers, scatter the shrimp around the tamales). Spoon the sauce over the tamales and shrimp.

SERVES 6

Annatto Shrimp–Blue Corn Tamales

(S T E P H A N   P Y L E S)

ANNATTO IS MADE FROM THE SMALL ORANGE OR RUST-COLORED SEEDS OF THE TROPICAL ACHIOTE TREE. ANNATTO, IN PASTE OR POWDERED FORM,

IS USED COMMERCIALLY AS A NATURAL FOOD DYE, ESPECIALLY IN BUTTER AND CHEESE. IN THESE TAMALES, IT NOT ONLY TURNS THE SHRIMP BRIGHT

ORANGE BUT ALSO IMPARTS A SUBTLE, EARTHY FLAVOR. THE SHRIMP CONTRAST STRIKINGLY WITH THE BLUE-GRAY CORN OF THE MASA DOUGH.

BLUE CORN IS PARTICULARLY NUTRITIOUS AND HOLDS A SPECIAL SIGNIFICANCE IN NATIVE AMERICAN CULTURE.

$^1/_4$ cup annatto seeds
$^1/_2$ cup olive oil
1 sprig fresh rosemary
2 cloves garlic, crushed
8 large shrimp, peeled and deveined
Blue Corn Masa Seca Tamale Dough
   (page 8)
10 large dried corn husks, soaked in warm water
   for 30 minutes
Salt
One recipe Salsa cruda roja (see Vegetable
   Escabeche Tamales with Salsa Cruda Roja,
   page 45), optional
$^1/_2$ cup sour cream or crème fraîche (optional)

To prepare the marinade, heat the annatto seeds in a saucepan with the olive oil, rosemary, and garlic until the oil becomes very hot. Remove from the heat, cover the pan, and let infuse for 3 hours. Carefully skim off the colored oil, leaving the bottom layer and solids undisturbed, and transfer to a bowl. Add the shrimp to the marinade and let sit for at least 30 minutes (and up to 2 days in the refrigerator).

Prepare the masa dough.

Drain the corn husks and shake dry. Tear 16 thin strips (about $^1/_8$ inch wide) from 2 of the husks and set aside for tying the tamales. Lay out the remaining 8 corn husks on a flat work surface. Divide the dough into 8 even portions and place 1 portion on each husk. Evenly spread out the masa mixture, leaving about $1^1/_2$ inches of exposed corn husk at each end and $^3/_4$ inch at each side. Bring the sides of the corn husk together, folding the dough; tuck one side of the husk under the other and roll up the tamale so that the dough is completely enclosed inside the husk. Twist each end and tie with the reserved strips of corn husk. Repeat for the remaining tamales.

Fill the bottom of a steamer or saucepan fitted with a strainer or vegetable basket with 2 to 3 inches of water. Bring the water to a boil and place the tamales in the steamer. Cover tightly with a lid or foil (it is important that little or no steam escapes while cooking). Steam the tamales for 30 to 35 minutes over lightly boiling water, adding more boiling water as needed. The tamales are done when they feel firm to the touch but are not hard and the dough comes away easily from the husk. Let rest for at least 5 minutes before serving.

While the tamales are steaming, remove the shrimp from the marinade with a slotted spoon, let drain, and season with salt to taste. In a hot, dry sauté pan, sauté the shrimp for $1^1/_2$ minutes on each side.

Prepare the salsa, if desired.

Transfer the tamales to serving plates and, with a knife, slice open the top of the wrappers from end to end. Gently push the ends together, as for a baked potato. Serve the shrimp next to the tamales and garnish with the sour cream, if desired. Serve with salsa, if desired.

SERVES 8

Shrimp Tamales with Rancho Sauce

(M A R K   M I L L E R)

WHEN YOU MAKE THESE TAMALES WITH THE FRESHEST SHRIMP, THEY ARE HARD TO BEAT, ESPECIALLY FOR BREAKFAST OR BRUNCH. THEY ALSO MAKE A GREAT LUNCH WITH A SALAD, OR DINNERTIME APPETIZERS. A DELICIOUS SPECIALTY OF SOUTHERN MEXICO, ESPECIALLY IN THE OAXACA REGION, IS TAMALES MADE WITH SUN-DRIED SALTED SHRIMP; IN OTHER COASTAL REGIONS, FRESH SHRIMP ARE USED—THE INSPIRATION FOR THIS RECIPE. YOU CAN USE SAUTÉED BAY OR SEA SCALLOPS INSTEAD OF THE SHRIMP, IF YOU PREFER, AND YOU CAN ADD A TEASPOON OF GROUND DRIED ANCHO OR GUAJILLO CHILE TO THE MASA DOUGH FOR SPICIER TAMALES.

*Jalapeño-Cilantro Tamale Masa Dough
    (page 9)*
*16 large shrimp (about 1 pound),
    unpeeled and heads removed*
Juice of $1/2$ lime
Salt and freshly ground black pepper
*8 large dried corn husks, soaked in warm water
    for 30 minutes*

FOR THE RANCHO SAUCE
*4 pounds Roma tomatoes, lightly blackened
    (page 164)*
5 serrano chiles, lightly blackened (page 164)
2 tablespoons peanut oil
$1^1/_2$ cups diced white onion
$1^1/_2$ tablespoons minced garlic
*5 poblano chiles, roasted, peeled, seeded,
    and diced (page 164)*
1 bunch cilantro, tied
$1/_2$ tablespoon salt

Prepare the masa dough. Preheat the oven to 350°F.

To prepare the filling, place the shrimp on a glass ovenproof plate, sprinkle with the lime juice, and season with salt and pepper to taste. Cover with foil and bake for 10 minutes. Peel the shrimp when cool enough and set aside.

Drain the corn husks, shake dry, and lay out on a flat work surface. Take a 2-ounce ($1/_4$-cup) portion of masa dough and form into a rectangular block. Place 2 of the seasoned shrimp on a work surface and gently press the masa dough over the shrimp, imprinting them into the dough while keeping its shape intact. Place the dough inside the corn husk and bring the sides of the husk together, folding the dough; tuck one side of the husk under the other and roll up the tamale so the dough is completely enclosed inside the husk. Fold each end neatly and securely under the tamale (there is no need to tie these tamales).

Fill the bottom of a steamer or saucepan fitted with a strainer or vegetable basket with 2 to 3 inches of water. Bring the water to a boil and place the tamales in the steamer. Cover tightly with a lid or foil (it is important that little or no steam escapes while cooking). Steam the tamales for 15 to 20 minutes over lightly boiling water, adding more boiling water as needed. The tamales are done when they feel firm to the touch but are not hard and the dough comes away easily from the husk.

While the tamales are steaming, prepare the sauce. Chop the blackened tomatoes and serranos and set them aside. Heat the peanut oil in a sauté pan or skillet and sauté the onion and garlic over low heat until soft but not brown, about 10 minutes. Transfer to a saucepan, add the tomatoes, serranos, and remaining ingredients and simmer over low heat for 20 to 30 minutes, adding a little water if necessary. Remove the cilantro.

Ladle the warm sauce onto serving plates. Remove the husks from the tamales and discard. Serve the masa shrimp-side up on the sauce.

SERVES 8

Backyard Barbecue Shrimp Tamales

(J O H N  S E D L A R)

ONE OF THE HALLMARKS OF WESTERN COOKING IS THE BARBECUE. RIBS, CHOPS, STEAKS, BURGERS—MEATS OF ALL KINDS. SEAFOOD IS NOT USUALLY THOUGHT OF WHEN PREPARING THE GRILL, BUT THE SMOKY, COMPLEX FLAVORS THAT WOOD AND CHARCOAL NATURALLY IMPART ENLIVEN MANY TYPES OF FISH AND SEAFOOD, AND SHRIMP ARE PARTICULARLY WELL SUITED TO GRILLING. FOR THOSE WITH BOLD PALATES, FEEL FREE TO ADD MORE SPICE AND LEMON JUICE TO THE MARINADE.

FOR THE SHRIMP MARINADE

2/3 cup freshly squeezed lemon juice
1 1/2 tablespoons extra-virgin olive oil
1 tablespoon water
1 teaspoon Tabasco sauce
2/3 teaspoon cayenne powder
2 teaspoons coarsely ground black pepper
2 tablespoons minced fresh oregano
2 tablespoons minced rosemary needles
24 jumbo shrimp (about 2 pounds),
*   peeled and deveined*

FOR THE TAMALES

Rice Tamale Mixture (page 7)
1 large banana leaf (about 12 inches by 36 inches)
*   cut into 6 squares, 6 inches by 6 inches*
Olive oil, for brushing

Whisk together all the ingredients for the marinade except the shrimp in a mixing bowl. Add the shrimp and toss to coat well. Cover the bowl with plastic wrap and marinate in the refrigerator for 2 hours.

Prepare the rice mixture. Prepare the grill.

To prepare the tamales, lay out each square of banana leaf on a flat work surface and brush lightly with the olive oil. Divide the rice evenly among the leaves and mold into a rectangle shape. Fold two of the sides of the leaf over, and then fold over the other two sides to form a tight envelope package. Repeat for the remaining tamales.

Fill the bottom of a steamer or saucepan fitted with a strainer or vegetable basket with 2 to 3 inches of water. Bring the water to a boil and place the tamales in the steamer. Cover tightly with a lid or foil (it is important that little or no steam escapes while cooking). Steam the tamales for about 6 minutes over lightly boiling water, adding more boiling water as needed. Remove the tamales from the pan and set aside; do not unwrap.

Remove the shrimp from the marinade and place on the hot grill. Cook for about 3 minutes, until firm yet still juicy; do not overcook.

Transfer the tamales to serving plates. Unwrap one side of each tamale to expose the rice and place the shrimp over the rice.

SERVES 6

Lobster and Roasted Poblano Tamales
with Guajillo Sauce

(M A R K M I L L E R)

LOBSTER MEAT AND CORN IS A CLASSIC COMBINATION, AND A RICHLY FLAVORED ONE. EARLY EUROPEAN SETTLERS TO THE NEW WORLD DISCOVERED THAT NATIVE AMERICANS ON THE EASTERN SEABOARD HAD LONG COOKED LOBSTER AND CORN TOGETHER ON THE SHORE OVER SEAWEED ON HOT ROCKS AND COALS—THE ORIGINAL CLAMBAKE! YOU CAN SUBSTITUTE SHRIMP OR CRAWFISH FOR THE LOBSTER IN THIS RECIPE. FOR A RICHER MASA DOUGH, SUBSTITUTE 2 TABLESPOONS OF REDUCED LOBSTER OR SHRIMP STOCK FOR THE OTHER LIQUID. NOTE THAT FOR THE MASA DOUGH AND THE SAUCE YOU WILL NEED A TOTAL OF ABOUT 10 OUNCES OF CHILES.

Guajillo Tamale Masa Dough (page 9)

FOR THE GUAJILLO SAUCE

2 teaspoons toasted pumpkin seeds (page 165)
8 ounces dried guajillo chiles, stemmed, seeded,
    toasted, and rehydrated (page 165)
3 cups water
5 large cloves roasted garlic (page 165)
1 teaspoon ground cumin
1 teaspoon salt
8 ounces Roma tomatoes, chopped (1 cup)
1 1/2 tablespoons cider vinegar
1/2 teaspoon dried oregano
2 tablespoons peanut oil

FOR THE FILLING AND TAMALES

1 tablespoon plus 1/2 cup softened unsalted butter
1/2 cup fresh corn kernels
6 ounces cooked lobster meat, chopped
1 small poblano chile, roasted, peeled,
    and diced (page 164)
2 tablespoons minced cilantro
Salt and freshly ground black pepper
10 large dried corn husks, soaked in warm water
    for 30 minutes

Prepare the masa dough.

Place all the sauce ingredients except the peanut oil in a food processor or blender and puree. Heat the peanut oil in a large high-sided skillet and, when hot, fry the puree at a sizzle for 4 to 5 minutes, stirring constantly. Add a little water to thin if necessary. Set aside and rewarm just before serving.

To prepare the filling, heat 1 tablespoon of the butter in a small sauté pan. Sauté the corn for 3 to 4 minutes over medium heat, until tender. Transfer to a mixing bowl and thoroughly combine with the remaining filling ingredients except the corn husks.

Drain the corn husks and pat dry. Tear 16 thin strips (about 1/8 inch wide) from 2 of the husks and set aside for tying the tamales. Lay out the remaining 8 corn husks on a flat work surface. Take a 2-ounce (1/4-cup) portion of masa dough and, using a tortilla press or heavy pan, flatten to a thickness of about 1/4 inch. Place the masa dough inside each husk, leaving about 1 1/2 inches of exposed corn husk at each end and 3/4 inch at each side. Spread about

2 heaping tablespoons of the filling on top of the masa. Bring the sides of the corn husk together, folding the dough; tuck one side of the husk under the other and roll up the tamale so the dough is completely enclosed inside the husk. Twist each end and tie with the reserved strips of corn husk. Repeat for the remaining tamales.

Fill the bottom of a steamer or saucepan fitted with a strainer or vegetable basket with 2 to 3 inches of water. Bring the water to a boil and place the tamales in the steamer. Cover tightly with a lid or foil (it is important that little or no steam escapes while cooking). Steam the tamales for about 30 minutes over lightly boiling water, adding more boiling water as needed. The tamales are done when they feel firm to the touch but are not hard and the dough comes away easily from the husk. Let rest for at least 5 minutes before serving.

Ladle the sauce onto serving plates. With a knife, slice open the top of the tamale wrappers from end to end. Arrange the tamales on the sauce.

SERVES 8

Lobster Newburg Tamales

(J O H N   S E D L A R)

THE STORY GOES THAT LOBSTER NEWBURG WAS INVENTED BY THE CHEF OF NEW YORK'S DELMONICO RESTAURANT IN 1876, BASED ON A RECIPE GIVEN HIM BY A NAVAL CAPTAIN AND GOOD CUSTOMER NAMED WENBERG. "LOBSTER WENBERG" PROVED IMMENSELY POPULAR, BUT AFTER THE CHEF AND WENBERG HAD A FALLING OUT, THE CHEF CHOSE TO CHANGE THE DISH'S NAME. SUCH IS THE STUFF OF CULINARY LORE! THE DIET SQUAD WOULD HEARTILY DISAPPROVE OF THIS DISH, BUT IT'S SO OUTRAGEOUSLY DELICIOUS AND LUXURIOUS, WHO CARES? THE PRESENTATION OF THE TAMALE IN THE LOBSTER SHELL NOT ONLY LOOKS ORIGINAL, BUT IT ALSO SERVES A PRACTICAL PURPOSE: THE TAMALE TAKES ON SOME OF THE SHELL'S BRINY FLAVOR.

Masa Seca Tamale Dough (page 2)
1 cup fresh corn kernels
3 tablespoons chopped fresh sage
Olive oil, for brushing

FOR THE LOBSTER NEWBURG
6 small live Maine lobsters
(about 1¼ pounds each)
3 tablespoons unsalted butter
1 cup cognac
3 cups heavy cream
1 teaspoon sweet paprika
4 sprigs cilantro, for garnish

Prepare the masa dough. Blanch the corn for 3 minutes in lightly boiling salted water and drain. Mix the corn and sage into the masa dough and set aside.

To prepare the tamales, cut six 6-inch squares of plastic wrap. Brush lightly with the olive oil. Divide the masa dough evenly among them and mold into a rectangular shape. Fold two of the sides of the plastic wrap over, and then fold over the other two sides to form a tight envelope package. Repeat for the remaining tamales.

Steam the tamales (see page 65 for method) for about 15 minutes over lightly boiling water, adding more boiling water as needed. Transfer to a plate, cover, and keep warm. Let rest for at least 5 minutes before serving.

To prepare the Lobster Newburg, place the lobsters right side up on a cutting board and sever the spinal cord by cutting the lobster at the neck where the tail meets the body shell; this will kill the lobsters immediately. Break off the head and reserve for garnish. Slice the lobsters in half lengthwise. Crack the claws and remove the meat in one piece. Dice the tail meat and reserve separately.

Bring a saucepan of water to a boil. Clean the lobster heads and tail shells, removing all interior matter and cartilage. Add the heads and tail shells to the pan and boil for 10 minutes. Remove with a slotted spoon and let cool.

Melt the butter in a sauté pan. Add the lobster meat and sauté for about 3 minutes over medium heat. Turn up the heat to high, carefully add the cognac, and flambé the lobster until the alcohol has burned off. Add the cream and paprika and remove the lobster meat with a slotted spoon so it will not overcook; place the lobster on a plate and reserve. Turn down the heat to medium and reduce the cream mixture for about 10 minutes, until thickened to a saucelike consistency. Place the lobster back in the sauce and heat through.

Unwrap the tamales from the plastic wrap and carefully arrange inside the reserved lobster tail shells. Place the shells in the center of each serving plate and spoon the Lobster Newburg around each tamale (do not spoon over the tamale). Garnish each plate with a cooked lobster head, standing upright to the side of each tamale, and a cilantro sprig.

SERVES 6

Moules Marinière Tamales with Pipérade

(J O H N   S E D L A R)

THE FRENCH STYLE OF PREPARING SEAFOOD—USUALLY MUSSELS—"À LA MARINIÈRE" ("MARINER STYLE") INVOLVES COOKING WITH WHITE WINE

AND HERBS. WHILE THE LARGE GREEN-LIPPED MUSSELS, USUALLY IMPORTED FROM NEW ZEALAND, HAVE BECOME VERY POPULAR OVER THE LAST FEW

YEARS, THE SMALLER COMMON OR BLUE MUSSELS (WHICH ARE USUALLY BLACK IN COLOR) REMAIN, FOR ME, AN EPIPHANY. THEY ARE IMBUED WITH

THE ESSENCE OF OCEAN, ELEVATED TO CELESTIAL HEIGHTS—SAUTÉED IN A LITTLE OLIVE OIL AND SPRINKLED WITH SOME COARSE SALT AND FRESHLY

CRACKED BLACK PEPPER, I BELIEVE I COULD EAT THEM FOR DAYS OR EVEN WEEKS ON END. PIPÉRADE IS A TRADITIONAL SIDE DISH ON MENUS

IN THE FRENCH BASQUE COUNTRY, CONTAINING SWEET PIMIENTOS OR BELL PEPPERS AND TOMATOES.

FOR THE TAMALES
Sweet Corn Tamale Mixture (page 2)
1 can (18 ounces) pimientos,
*   drained and coarsely chopped*
Olive oil, for brushing
6 large dried corn husks, soaked in warm water
*   for 30 minutes*

FOR THE MUSSELS AND PIPÉRADE
6 dozen fresh blue mussels,
*   scrubbed and debearded*
3 cups dry white wine
3 cups bottled clam juice
3 tablespoons extra-virgin olive oil
1 teaspoon chopped fresh oregano
1 teaspoon chopped fresh tarragon
8 saffron threads, chopped
1 lemon, cut in half
2 tablespoons chopped garlic
3 Roma tomatoes, peeled, seeded,
*   and coarsely chopped*
2 tablespoons minced fresh parsley

Prepare the tamale mixture. Add half of the pimientos and mix well.

To prepare the tamales, cut 6 square pieces of plastic wrap measuring about 6 inches by 6 inches each. Lay out each piece of plastic on a flat work surface and brush lightly with the olive oil. Divide the masa dough evenly among them and mold into a rectangular shape. Fold two of the sides of the plastic wrap over, and then fold over the other two sides to form a tight envelope package. Repeat for the remaining tamales.

Fill the bottom of a steamer or saucepan fitted with a strainer or vegetable basket with 2 to 3 inches of water. Bring the water to a boil and place the tamales in the steamer. Cover tightly with a lid or foil (it is important that little or no steam escapes while cooking). Steam the tamales for about 15 minutes over lightly boiling water, adding more boiling water as needed. Transfer to a plate, cover, and keep warm.

Meanwhile, place all the ingredients for the mussels and pipérade except the parsley in a large saucepan and add the remaining pimientos. Cover tightly, bring to a boil, and cook, stirring occasionally, until all of the mussels open, about 10 minutes; discard any mussels that do not open. Stir in the parsley.

To serve the tamales, drain the corn husks and shake dry. Place the husks in the center of large pasta bowls. Unwrap the tamales from the plastic wrap and place in the center of each corn husk. Using a slotted spoon, remove the mussels and place in the bowls around the husks. Spoon the pipérade over the tamales and mussels.

SERVES 6

Saffron Risotto Tamales with Seared Scallops and Mango–Red Pepper Relish

(S T E P H A N  P Y L E S)

HERE IS ANOTHER TAMALE THAT DISPENSES WITH THE TRADITIONAL CORN MASA AND INSTEAD USES RISOTTO AS THE BASE FOR THE FILLING. RISOTTO IS AS POPULAR IN THE NORTH OF ITALY AS PASTA IS IN THE SOUTH, AND WHILE BOTH STARCHES ARE HIGH IN CARBOHYDRATES, RICE IS MORE DIGESTIBLE AS IT LACKS CELLULOSE. I HAVE ALWAYS ENJOYED THE COMBINATION OF RISOTTO AND SCALLOPS, AND I OFTEN SERVE IT AS A MAIN COURSE SPECIAL AT STAR CANYON. THE YELLOW SAFFRON IN THE RISOTTO AND THE COLORFUL RELISH MAKE A STRIKING COMBINATION ON THE PLATE. MAKE THE RELISH AS CLOSE TO SERVING TIME AS POSSIBLE TO MAXIMIZE ITS VIBRANT, FRESH FLAVORS.

FOR THE SCALLOPS

32 fresh sea scallops, washed and dried
3 tablespoons olive oil
4 cloves garlic, minced
2 tablespoons minced fresh ginger
Salt

FOR THE RISOTTO FILLING

6 cups chilled Chicken Stock (page 160)
1 teaspoon saffron powder
5 tablespoons unsalted butter
2/3 cup finely minced onion
4 cloves garlic, minced
2 cups Arborio rice
2/3 cup grated Parmesan cheese
Salt

FOR THE TAMALES

10 large dried corn husks, soaked in warm water for 30 minutes

Combine all the scallop ingredients except the salt in a mixing bowl and marinate in the refrigerator for 1 hour.

To prepare the filling, combine the chicken stock and saffron powder in a saucepan and bring to a boil. Turn down the heat and simmer gently for about 5 minutes, until you are ready to add it to the rice.

Meanwhile, heat 3 tablespoons of the butter in a heavy saucepan over medium-high heat. Add the onion and garlic and sauté for 1 to 2 minutes, until they begin to soften; do not brown.

Add the rice and stir for about 1 minute, making sure all the grains are well coated. Turn down the heat to medium and add the simmering chicken stock and saffron mixture, 1/2 cup at a time, stirring frequently. Wait until each addition is almost completely absorbed before adding the next 1/2 cup. Reserve about 1/2 cup to add at the end. Stir the rice frequently to prevent it from sticking.

After 20 to 25 minutes, when the rice is tender but still firm, add the reserved 1/2 cup stock. Turn off the heat and immediately add the remaining 2 tablespoons butter and the Parmesan cheese. Stir vigorously to combine with the rice and season with salt to taste. Spread the rice onto an 11-inch by 17-inch baking sheet and refrigerate until the rice is cold and has thickened, about 45 minutes.

Drain the corn husks and shake dry. Tear 16 thin strips (about 1/8 inch wide) from 2 of the husks and set aside for tying the tamales. Lay out the remaining 8 corn husks on a flat work surface. Divide the rice mixture into 8 even portions and place 1 portion on each corn husk. Evenly spread out the rice mixture, leaving about 1 1/2 inches of exposed corn husk at each end and 3/4 inch at each side. Bring the sides of the corn husks together, folding the filling; tuck one side of the husk under the other and roll up the tamale so that the filling is completely enclosed inside the husk. Twist each end and tie with the reserved strips of corn husk. Repeat for the remaining tamales.

(continues)

1 red bell pepper, seeded and diced

2 serrano chiles, seeded and diced

1 small cucumber, peeled, seeded, and finely diced

1 mango, peeled, pitted, and finely diced

1 tablespoon dark sweet soy sauce

1 tablespoon chopped cilantro

2 teaspoons chopped fresh basil

1¹/₂ tablespoons freshly squeezed lime juice

Fill the bottom of a steamer or saucepan fitted with a strainer or vegetable basket with 2 to 3 inches of water. Bring the water to a boil and place the tamales in the steamer. Cover tightly with a lid or foil (it is important that little or no steam escapes while cooking). Steam the tamales for 12 to 15 minutes over lightly boiling water, adding more boiling water as needed. The tamales are done when the rice is just tender but still firm.

While the tamales are steaming, combine all the ingredients for the relish in a mixing bowl and refrigerate until ready to serve.

Remove the scallops from the marinade with a slotted spoon. Preheat a large sauté pan over medium-high heat.

Season the scallops with salt and add them to the pan. Allow the scallops to sauté undisturbed for about 2 minutes, until browned. Turn the scallops over in the pan and allow them to brown for about 2 minutes longer.

Place the cooked tamales on serving plates and, with a knife, slice the wrappers from end to end. Gently push the ends together, as for a baked potato. Arrange 4 scallops on each plate, 2 on either side of the tamale, and serve with the relish.

SERVES 8

Clam Tamales with Fennel and Chayote-Melon Salsa

(M A R K   M I L L E R)

THESE ARE THE ONLY CLAM TAMALES I'VE EVER SEEN! THE SUBTLE, LICORICE-ANISE FLAVOR OF FENNEL, A HERB USED EXTENSIVELY IN MEDITERRANEAN COUNTRIES, SUITS CLAMS VERY WELL, AND IT LIGHTENS THE DOUGH IN A PLEASINGLY AROMATIC WAY. YOU CAN SUBSTITUTE BASIL, DILL, OR ITALIAN PARSLEY FOR THE FENNEL, ANY ONE OF WHICH WILL CONTRIBUTE BRIGHT, GREEN FLAVORS TO THE TAMALE. ALTERNATIVELY, IF YOU ENJOY THE CLASSIC COMBINATION OF CLAMS AND SAUSAGE, SUBSTITUTE SOME CHOPPED HOT ITALIAN SAUSAGE FOR HALF THE CLAMS. CHAYOTE, ALSO CALLED MIRLITON AND CHRISTOPHENE, IS A CRISP, MILD-FLAVORED, AVOCADO-SIZED SQUASH THAT WAS CONSIDERED A DELICACY BY THE AZTECS. IT IS NATIVE TO MEXICO AND THE SOUTHWEST BUT WIDELY AVAILABLE DURING THE WINTER MONTHS, ESPECIALLY IN THE NEW ORLEANS AREA.

Clam and Fennel Tamale Masa Dough
  (page 10)
1 tablespoon olive oil
3 cloves garlic, minced
1¼ cups freshly cooked clam meat
  or bottled baby clams
1 Roma tomato, seeded and diced
2 tablespoons minced fresh basil (optional)
10 large dried corn husks, soaked in warm water
  for 30 minutes

FOR THE CHAYOTE-MELON SALSA

1 large chayote, peeled and diced
¾ cup diced honeydew melon
½ cup diced fennel bulb
1 tablespoon chopped fennel tops
1 tablespoon unseasoned rice wine vinegar
1 teaspoon green habanero sauce
1 tablespoon freshly squeezed lime juice
⅛ teaspoon sugar
⅛ teaspoon salt

Prepare the masa dough.

To prepare the filling, heat the olive oil in a sauté pan or skillet and cook the garlic over low heat for 10 minutes. Add the clams, tomato, and basil and cook for 3 to 4 minutes over medium heat.

Drain the corn husks and shake dry. Tear 16 thin strips (about ⅛ inch wide) from 2 of the husks and set aside for tying the tamales. Lay out the remaining 8 corn husks on a flat work surface. Take a 2-ounce (¼-cup) portion of masa dough and, using a tortilla press or heavy pan, flatten to a thickness of about ¼ inch. Place the masa dough inside each husk, leaving about 1½ inches of exposed corn husk at each end and ¾ inch at each side. Spread about 2 heaping tablespoons of the filling on top of the masa. Bring the sides of the corn husk together, folding the dough; tuck one side of the husk under the other and roll up the tamale so the dough is completely enclosed inside the husk. Twist each end and

tie with the reserved strips of corn husk. Repeat for the remaining tamales.

Fill the bottom of a steamer or saucepan fitted with a strainer or vegetable basket with 2 to 3 inches of water. Bring the water to a boil and place the tamales in the steamer. Cover tightly with a lid or foil (it is important that little or no steam escapes while cooking). Steam the tamales for about 30 minutes over lightly boiling water, adding more boiling water as needed. The tamales are done when they feel firm to the touch but are not hard and the dough comes away easily from the husk. Let rest for at least 5 minutes before serving.

While the tamales are steaming, prepare the salsa. Place all the salsa ingredients in a mixing bowl and combine thoroughly. Keep chilled.

Transfer the tamales to serving plates and, with a knife, slice open the top of the wrappers from end to end. Serve with the salsa.

SERVES 8

Poultry and Fowl Tamales

Bombay Taj Tamales with Curry Chicken

Chicken Tamales with BBQ Masa
and Red Chile *Crema*

Chicken Tamales with Mole Poblano

Arroz con Pollo Tamales

Turkey Tamales Yucatán Style with
Black Beans, Chipotle, and Pumpkin Seeds

Seared Foie Gras and Corn Pudding Tamales with
Pineapple Mole and Canela Dust

Caesar Salad with Turkey Tamales

Smoked Duck and Wild Cherry Tamales
with Ancho Sauce

Duck Tamales with Pineapple and Chipotle

Duck Confit–Black Olive *Humitas*

Shanghai Duck Tamales with
Bok Choy and Sake Sauce

Roasted Pheasant–Polenta Tamales with
Gorgonzola and Dried Fruit Compote

Port-Poached Pear Tamales with
Molasses Grilled Quail

Smoked Quail Tamales with Canela, Apple,
and Apple–Green Chile Salsa

Squab Tamales with Château d'Yquem
and Rosemary

Squab-Chestnut Tamales with
Red Cabbage Chow Chow

Bombay Taj Tamales with Curry Chicken

(J O H N   S E D L A R)

"CURRY" COMES FROM THE HINDI WORD *KARI*, MEANING "SAUCE," AND A GOOD CURRY IS HARD TO BEAT. IT'S FUN TO MIX YOUR OWN CURRY POWDER BLEND FROM SPICES SUCH AS CORIANDER, CUMIN, TUMERIC, AND GINGER, BUT BUYING A GOOD-QUALITY CURRY POWDER SAVES TIME. IN EITHER CASE, ONE OF THE SECRETS OF GREAT INDIAN COOKING IS TO ALWAYS "BLOOM" OR TOAST THE SPICES OR CURRY POWDER BEFORE USING. TO DO THIS, PLACE THE DRIED GROUND SPICES IN A VERY HOT DRY SAUTÉ PAN TO UNLOCK THEIR PUNGENT AROMAS. THE EXTREMELY HOT AND FIERY THAI CHILES USED FOR GARNISH MUST BE HANDLED CAREFULLY; USE RUBBER GLOVES IF YOU HAVE SENSITIVE SKIN, AND NEVER TOUCH YOUR FACE OR EYES BEFORE WASHING YOUR HANDS THOROUGHLY.

Rice Tamale Mixture (page 7)

FOR THE CURRY SAUCE

1/2 cup good-quality curry powder
2 cups Chicken Stock (page 160)
1 cup dry white wine
1 shallot, minced
1 1/2 cups heavy cream
Salt and freshly ground white pepper

FOR THE FILLING AND TAMALES

4 cups Chicken Stock (page 160)
1 pound boneless, skinless chicken breast
Salt and freshly ground black pepper
Olive oil, for brushing

FOR THE CUCUMBER RAITA

1/2 Japanese cucumber or hothouse cucumber,
*   peeled, seeded, and very finely sliced*
6 tablespoons plain yogurt
2 teaspoons fresh mint leaves, cut into thin strips
Juice of 1/2 lemon
Salt and freshly ground white pepper

Prepare the rice tamale mixture.

To prepare the sauce, heat a dry heavy skillet or sauté pan over medium heat. When the skillet is hot, add the curry powder and toast, stirring constantly, until very fragrant, about 3 minutes. Transfer to a plate to cool. Combine the chicken stock, wine, and shallot in a saucepan and bring to a boil over medium heat. Turn down the heat to a simmer and reduce by half, about 15 minutes. Add the curry powder and cream and reduce by half again. Pour through a fine mesh strainer into a blender, season with salt and pepper to taste, and blend until smooth. Set aside and rewarm just before you are ready to serve.

To prepare the filling, pour the chicken stock into a saucepan, bring to a boil, and turn down the heat to a simmer. Season the chicken with salt and pepper and poach in the stock for about 20 minutes, until tender. Remove from the heat and let the chicken cool in the stock (this will make it more tender). When cool enough, shred the chicken breast into strips and place in a clean saucepan. Add 1/4 cup of the curry sauce and cook over high heat for about 5 minutes; the chicken will soak up the curry sauce and take on a yellow color. Remove the pan from the heat and let cool.

To prepare the tamales, cut 6 square pieces of plastic wrap measuring about 6 inches by 6 inches each. Lay out each piece of plastic on a flat work surface and brush lightly with the olive oil. Divide the rice mixture evenly among them and mold into a rectangular shape. Top each portion of the rice with the chicken filling mixture and spread out evenly. Fold two of the sides of the plastic wrap over, and then fold over the other two sides to form a tight envelope package. Repeat for the remaining tamales.

Fill the bottom of a steamer or saucepan fitted with a strainer or vegetable basket with 2 to 3 inches of water. Bring the water to a boil and place the tamales in the steamer. Cover tightly with a lid or foil (it is important that little or no steam escapes while cooking). Steam the tamales for about 15 minutes over lightly boiling water until firm, adding more boiling water as needed.

(continues)

FOR THE GARNISH

Peanut oil for deep-frying
1 tablespoon julienned blue corn tortilla
12 strands rice noodle sticks (cellophane noodles)
Salt
6 large dried corn husks, soaked in warm water
*   for 30 minutes*
6 sprigs fresh mint
6 green Thai chiles or serranos, seeded and sliced
6 red Thai chiles or serranos, seeded and sliced

Meanwhile, to prepare the raita, place the cucumber in a bowl and combine with the yogurt, mint, and lemon juice. Season with salt and white pepper to taste. Stir to mix well and chill until ready to serve.

To prepare the garnish, heat the peanut oil in a deep fryer to 350°F. Add the tortilla strips and fry until crisp, about 3 minutes. Remove with a slotted spoon and drain on paper towels. Add the rice noodle sticks to the hot oil until they expand and turn crisp. Remove with a slotted spoon, drain on paper towels, and season lightly with salt to taste.

Drain the corn husks and shake dry. Lay out each husk in the center of a serving plate. Unwrap the tamales from the plastic wrap and place in the center of each corn husk. Spoon about 2 tablespoons of the remaining warm curry sauce at the bottom of each tamale. Place 1 heaping tablespoon of the cucumber raita on top. Garnish with the blue corn tortillas, rice noodle sticks, mint, and Thai chiles spread over the top.

SERVES 6

Chicken Tamales with BBQ Masa and Red Chile *Crema*

(M A R K   M I L L E R)

THIS RECIPE OFFERS THE PERFECT SOLUTION FOR LEFTOVER CHICKEN OR COOKED ROTISSERIE CHICKEN, WHICH CAN BE SUBSTITUTED FOR THE POACHED CHICKEN IN THIS RECIPE. IF YOU DON'T MAKE YOUR OWN, BUY A GOOD-QUALITY (AND NOT A MASS-MARKET) BARBECUE SAUCE—ONE OF MY FAVORITES IS BUCKAROO, A TEXAS BRAND. ALTERNATIVELY, YOU CAN ADAPT A STORE-BOUGHT BARBECUE SAUCE BY ADDING PUREED CHIPOTLE CHILES AND ROASTED GARLIC, A LITTLE CIDER VINEGAR, AND SPICES OF YOUR CHOICE. THE CHIPOTLES WILL GIVE THE SAUCE PLENTY OF HEAT AND A SMOKY FLAVOR, SO USE THEM JUDICIOUSLY. IF YOU LIKE, YOU CAN SERVE THESE TAMALES WITH MORE BARBECUE SAUCE ON THE SIDE.

BBQ Tamale Masa Dough (page 11)

FOR THE RED CHILE *CREMA*

1 cup heavy cream
1 clove roasted garlic (page 165)
1 tablespoon canned chipotle chiles

FOR THE FILLING AND TAMALES

4 cups Chicken Stock (page 160)
1 pound boneless skinless chicken breast
Salt and freshly ground black pepper
2 tablespoons barbecue sauce (see Barbecued
   Brisket Tamales with Jicama Coleslaw,
   page 108)
10 large dried corn husks, soaked in warm water
   for 30 minutes

Prepare the masa dough.

To prepare the red chile *crema*, puree the cream, garlic, and chiles in a blender. Pour the mixture into a plastic ketchup-style squeeze bottle with a nozzle that allows for drizzling.

To prepare the filling, pour the chicken stock into a saucepan, bring to a boil, and turn down the heat to a simmer. Season the chicken with salt and pepper to taste and poach in the stock for about 20 minutes, until tender. Remove from the heat and let the chicken cool in the stock (this will make it more tender). When cool enough, shred the chicken breast into strips and place in a mixing bowl. Add the barbecue sauce to the chicken, and mix well to moisten thoroughly.

Drain the corn husks and shake dry. Tear 16 thin strips (about 1/8 inch wide) from 2 of the husks and set aside for tying the tamales. Lay out the remaining 8 corn husks on a flat work surface. Take a 2-ounce (1/4-cup) portion of masa dough and, using a tortilla press or heavy pan, flatten to a thickness of about 1/4 inch. Place the masa dough inside each husk, leaving about 1 1/2 inches of exposed corn husk

at each end and 3/4 inch at each side. Spread about 2 heaping tablespoons of the filling on top of the masa. Bring the sides of the corn husk together, folding the dough; tuck one side of the husk under the other and roll up the tamale so the dough is completely enclosed inside the husk. Twist each end and tie with the reserved strips of corn husk. Repeat for the remaining tamales.

Fill the bottom of a steamer or saucepan fitted with a strainer or vegetable basket with 2 to 3 inches of water. Bring the water to a boil and place the tamales in the steamer. Cover tightly with a lid or foil (it is important that little or no steam escapes while cooking). Steam the tamales for 30 to 35 minutes over lightly boiling water, adding more boiling water as needed. The tamales are done when they feel firm to the touch but are not hard and the dough comes away easily from the husk. Let rest for at least 5 minutes before serving.

With a knife, slice open the tamales from end to end. Drizzle generously with the red chile *crema*.

SERVES 8

Chicken Tamales with Mole Poblano

(M A R K   M I L L E R)

THERE ARE MANY DIFFERENT TYPES OF MOLE (THE WORD IS DERIVED FROM THE ANCIENT NAHUATL WORD *MOLLI*, MEANING "MIXTURE"), EACH ONE USING DIFFERENT TYPES OF CHILE AND DIFFERENT BLENDS OF SPICES, SEEDS, AND NUTS. MOLE POBLANO IS ONE OF THE CLASSIC SAUCES OF MEXICO AND A TRADITIONAL PARTNER WITH TURKEY AND CHICKEN DISHES. *POBLANO* REFERS TO THIS PARTICULAR SAUCE'S CITY OF ORIGIN—PUEBLA— AND CHOCOLATE IS THIS MOLE'S DISTINGUISHING INGREDIENT. FOR A SHORTCUT, USE A GOOD-QUALITY STORE-BOUGHT BOTTLE OF MOLE POBLANO, SUCH AS DON ALFONSO™, FROM SOUTHWESTERN GOURMET STORES.

FOR THE MOLE POBLANO AND MASA DOUGH

2 ounces Mexican dark chocolate or semisweet chocolate, grated

1/2 cup pumpkin seeds, toasted until they start to pop (page 165)

1/4 cup sesame seeds

4 ounces dried pasilla chile, seeded, toasted, and rehydrated (page 165)

4 ounces dried ancho chile, seeded, toasted, and rehydrated (page 165)

4 ounces dried mulato chile, seeded, toasted, and rehydrated (page 165)

1 canned chipotle chile in adobo sauce

2 cloves roasted garlic (page 165)

2 Roma tomatoes, blackened and chopped (page 164)

1/2 white onion, blackened (page 164)

1 teaspoon ground canela or 1/2 teaspoon ground cinnamon

1/2 teaspoon ground allspice

1/4 teaspoon ground cloves

Juice of 3 limes

Salt

1 1/2 tablespoons peanut oil

3 cups Chicken Stock (page 160)

Roasted Corn Tamale Masa Dough (page 3)

To prepare the mole, melt the chocolate in a stainless steel bowl set over a pan of boiling water. Transfer the chocolate and seeds to a blender. Add the water in which the chiles rehydrated if it does not taste bitter, or use plain water. Add the chiles, garlic, tomatoes, onion, spices, lime juice, and salt to taste, and puree until smooth.

Heat the peanut oil in a large, high-sided sauté pan or skillet until almost smoking. While tilting the pan away from you to prevent spatters, add the sauce and refry at a sizzle, taking care not to scorch it. Add the stock and cook over low heat for 30 to 45 minutes. Strain the sauce through a fine mesh strainer into a clean saucepan; the sauce should be thick. Reheat just before you are ready to serve.

Prepare the masa dough.

To prepare the filling, pour the chicken stock into a saucepan, bring to a boil, and turn down the heat to a simmer. Season the chicken with salt and pepper and poach in the stock for about 20 minutes, until tender. Remove from the heat and let the chicken cool in the stock (this will make it more tender). When cool enough, shred the chicken breast into strips and place in a mixing bowl. Add 1/4 cup of the mole poblano to the chicken and mix well to moisten thoroughly.

Soften the banana leaves over an open flame for 10 seconds on each side, being careful not to burn them. Cut each leaf crosswise into 4 even pieces, about 8 inches by 10 inches, and lay out on a flat work surface. Divide the masa into 8 even portions and place a portion in the center of each leaf. Spread into a 4-inch square, leaving at least a 1 1/2-inch border at the ends and 3/4 inch on the long sides. Spread about 2 heaping tablespoons of the filling mixture on top of the masa and top with 1/2 tablespoon of the mole poblano. To fold the tamales, pick up the two long sides of the banana leaf and bring them together (the dough will surround the filling). Tuck one side under the other and fold the flaps on each end underneath the tamale.

Fill the bottom of a steamer or saucepan fitted with a strainer or vegetable basket with 2 to 3 inches of water. Bring the water to a boil and place the tamales in the steamer. Cover tightly with a lid or foil (it is important that little or no steam escapes while cooking). Steam

(continues)

4 cups *Chicken Stock (page 160)*
1 pound *boneless, skinless chicken breast*
Salt and freshly ground black pepper
2 large *banana leaves, about 12 inches*
  by 36 inches
2 teaspoons *white sesame seeds, for garnish*

the tamales for 30 to 35 minutes over lightly boiling water, adding more boiling water as needed. The tamales are done when they feel firm to the touch but are not hard and the dough comes away easily from the leaves. Let rest for at least 5 minutes before serving.

Unwrap the tamales and, leaving the filling lying on the leaves, place each in the center of serving plates. Serve each tamale with $1/4$ cup of warm mole poblano and garnish the sauce with the sesame seeds.

SERVES 8

Arroz con Pollo Tamales

(J O H N   S E D L A R)

ARROZ CON POLLO WAS A DISH I ENJOYED WHEN I LIVED IN SPAIN AS A CHILD. IT'S A TRADITIONAL CASSOULET-STYLE RECIPE FULL OF

TAPAS INGREDIENTS—ONIONS, CAPERS, GREEN AND BLACK OLIVES, GARLIC CLOVES, SARDINES, PIMIENTOS, SWEET GREEN PEPPERS, AND CHICKEN—

SERVED WITH A GARLIC AND SAFFRON BROTH. WHEN MY FAMILY LIVED IN SEVILLE, OUR HOUSEKEEPER, NIEVES, PREPARED A MEMORABLE

ARROZ CON POLLO THAT SHE SERVED IN THE TRADITIONAL STYLE WITH AN EGG *TORTA*.

Sweet Corn Tamale Mixture (page 2)
2 tablespoons olive oil
1 small yellow onion, diced
3 tablespoons minced garlic
3 scallions, cut into $^1/_2$-inch slices
  (white and green parts separated)
1 red bell pepper, roasted, peeled, and julienned
  (page 164)
1 green bell pepper, roasted, deveined,
  seeded, and julienned (page 164)
Salt and freshly ground white pepper
1 cup short-grain white rice
6 red Japonnaise chiles, or serranos,
  seeded and minced
2 cups Chicken Stock (page 160)
1 teaspoon saffron threads
3 tablespoons capers, drained
$^1/_4$ cup whole green olives, drained
$^1/_4$ cup whole black olives
  (such as kalamatas), drained
6 ounces canned garbanzos (chickpeas), drained
6 boneless chicken breasts, 6 ounces each
Olive oil, for brushing
6 large dried corn husks, soaked in
  warm water for 30 minutes

Prepare the tamale mixture. Preheat the oven to 375°F.

To prepare the *arroz con pollo*, heat the olive oil in a large cast-iron skillet or oven-proof sauté pan. Add the onion and sauté over medium heat for 5 minutes. Add the garlic, white part of the scallions, and bell peppers and sauté until the peppers are tender but firm, about 5 minutes longer. Season with salt and white pepper to taste. Add the rice and cook, stirring constantly, for about 10 minutes. Add the chiles, chicken stock, saffron, capers, olives, and garbanzos and stir to thoroughly combine. Season the chicken with salt and white pepper and add to the skillet, submerging the chicken in the liquid. Cover the skillet with a lid or foil and transfer to the oven. Cook until the rice is tender, 40 to 50 minutes.

Meanwhile, to prepare the tamales, cut 6 square pieces of plastic wrap measuring about 6 inches by 6 inches each. Lay out each piece of plastic on a flat work surface and brush lightly with the olive oil. Divide the tamale mixture evenly among them and mold into a rectangular shape. Fold two of the sides of the plastic wrap over, and then fold over the other two sides to form a tight envelope package. Repeat for the remaining tamales.

Fill the bottom of a steamer or saucepan fitted with a strainer or vegetable basket with 2 to 3 inches of water. Bring the water to a boil and place the tamales in the steamer. Cover tightly with a lid or foil (it is important that little or no steam escapes while cooking). Steam the tamales for about 15 minutes over lightly boiling water until firm, adding more boiling water as needed.

Drain the corn husks and shake dry. Lay out each husk in the center of a large serving plate. Unwrap the tamales from the plastic wrap and place in the center of each corn husk. Place a chicken breast leaning on the side of each tamale and spoon the rice mixture over the chicken. Sprinkle with the green part of the scallions.

SERVES 6

Turkey Tamales Yucatán Style with Black Beans, Chipotle, and Pumpkin Seeds

(M A R K　M I L L E R)

THIS LARGE, FAMILY-STYLE TAMALE IS TYPICAL FARE AT FAMILY FEASTS AND SPECIAL CELEBRATIONS IN MEXICO, ESPECIALLY FOR TRADITIONAL HOLIDAYS SUCH AS THE DAY OF THE DEAD (SEE THE HEADNOTE ON PAGE 139). THESE TAMALES ARE "YUCATÁN" STYLE BECAUSE OF THE ACHIOTE PASTE USED IN THE MASA DOUGH AND THE BANANA LEAVES THAT ARE TYPICAL FOR WRAPPING TAMALES OF THIS TROPICAL REGION. ACHIOTE PASTE IS OFTEN USED IN SIMILAR WAYS AS RECADO PASTES, TRADITIONAL SPICE MIXES THAT ARE A HALLMARK OF THE COOKING OF THE REGIONAL CAPITAL OF MÉRIDA. RECADO PASTES ARE USED AS RUBS FOR MEAT, STUFFINGS, AND ALL-PURPOSE SEASONINGS. THEY ARE TYPICALLY RED, GREEN, OR BLACK, DENSE AND OILY IN CONSISTENCY, AND USUALLY SOLD IN PLASTIC CONTAINERS OR BAGS IN THE MARKETS. IF YOU LIVE NEAR A GOOD MEXICAN MARKET, YOU CAN BUY A RED RECADO PASTE OF ACHIOTE; MY FAVORITE COMMERCIAL BRAND OF ACHIOTE IS PERLA™.

*Achiote—Black Bean Tamale Masa Dough
(page 11)*
4 cups turkey stock or Chicken Stock (page 160)
1 pound boneless, skinless turkey breast
Salt and freshly ground black pepper
*1/2 cup pumpkin seeds, toasted until they
start to pop (page 165)*
2 tablespoons chipotle chile puree (page 164)
2 banana leaves, about 12 inches by 20 inches
1 tablespoon chopped cilantro, for garnish

Prepare the masa dough.

To prepare the filling, pour the stock into a saucepan, bring to a boil, and turn down the heat to a simmer. Season the turkey with salt and pepper and poach in the stock for about 20 minutes, until tender. Remove the pan from the heat and let the turkey cool in the stock (this will make it more tender). When cool enough, shred the turkey breast into strips and place 12 ounces in a mixing bowl; reserve the remaining 4 ounces for garnish. Transfer half of the seeds to a blender and grind coarsely; reserve the remainder for garnish. Add the ground seeds to the mixing bowl with the turkey, then add the chipotle puree, and mix well. Place the filling on top of the masa dough.

Soften the banana leaves over an open flame for 10 seconds on each side, being careful not to burn them. Lay out one of the leaves on a flat work surface and place the masa and filling at the wide end of the leaf. Roll the leaf around and around the masa and filling, creating a package with the masa inside. Place the other leaf on the work surface and roll it around the masa and filling in the opposite direction so that it covers the short side of the first leaf, creating a sealed package.

Fill the bottom of a steamer or saucepan fitted with a strainer or vegetable basket with 2 to 3 inches of water. Bring the water to a boil and place the tamale in the steamer. Cover tightly with a lid or foil (it is important that little or no steam escapes while cooking). Steam the tamale for 50 to 60 minutes over lightly boiling water, adding more boiling water as needed. The tamale is done when it feels firm to the touch but is not hard and the dough comes away easily from the leaf.

Unwrap the tamale and, leaving the masa and filling lying on the leaf, bring to the table on a serving platter. Sprinkle the reserved turkey meat and pumpkin seeds on top of the masa and garnish with the cilantro.

SERVES 8

Seared Foie Gras and Corn Pudding Tamales with Pineapple Mole and Canela Dust

(S T E P H A N   P Y L E S)

THESE STAR CANYON TAMALES WON *GQ* MAGAZINE'S 1996 GOLDEN DISH AWARD, GIVEN TO ACKNOWLEDGE THE 10 BEST DISHES IN THE UNITED STATES THAT YEAR. THIS RECIPE DEMONSTRATES THE INCREDIBLE DIVERSITY THAT TAMALES CAN OFFER, AS IT PAIRS HAUTE CUISINE (FOIE GRAS) WITH RUSTIC CUISINE (MASA, MOLE SAUCE) IN A COMBINATION THAT BLENDS TOGETHER BEAUTIFULLY. TALK ABOUT A CONTRAST BETWEEN DIFFERENT CULINARY STYLES! IT MAY SEEM AS THOUGH ADDING 8 CUPS OF CORN KERNELS TO THE BASIC MASA DOUGH RECIPE IS EXCESSIVE, BUT THE VOLUME OF THE CORN DIMINISHES TO LITTLE OVER 1 CUP IN THE ROASTING PROCESS, LEAVING THE MASA DELICIOUSLY MOIST AND GIVING IT AN INTRIGUING CORN PUDDING–LIKE TEXTURE.

FOR THE TAMALES

8 cups fresh corn kernels
Masa Seca Tamale Dough (page 2)
$1/3$ cup pure maple syrup
Salt
2 large banana leaves, about 12 inches by 36 inches

FOR THE PINEAPPLE MOLE

2 cups Chicken Stock (page 160)
3 ounces ($3/4$ cup) dried pineapple
$1/2$ yellow tomato, cored and chopped
$1/4$ pineapple, peeled, cored, and chopped
$1/4$ cup sherry
$1/2$ stick cinnamon
$1 1/2$ tablespoons golden raisins
$1/4$ teaspoon ground cumin
$1/2$ teaspoon pure red chile powder
$1/2$ small onion, chopped
2 cloves garlic, chopped
1 small serrano chile, seeded and chopped
1 dried ancho chile, seeded
$2 1/2$ tablespoons sliced almonds
2 tablespoons white sesame seeds

Preheat the oven to 350°F. Place the corn in the bowl of a food processor and process for 3 minutes, until smooth. Transfer to a baking pan and bake in the oven for $1 1/2$ hours, stirring every 15 minutes, until the mixture is dry. Remove from the oven and refrigerate until cooled completely.

Meanwhile, prepare the masa dough. Add the cooled corn and the maple syrup and season with salt to taste. Soften the banana leaves over an open flame for 10 seconds on each side, being careful not to burn them. Cut each leaf crosswise into 4 even pieces, about 8 inches by 10 inches, and lay out on a flat work surface. Divide the masa into 8 even portions and place a portion in the center of each leaf. Spread into a 4-inch square, leaving at least a $1 1/2$-inch border at the ends and $3/4$ inch on the long sides. To fold the tamales, pick up the two long sides of the banana leaf and bring them together. Tuck one side under the other and fold the flaps on each end underneath the tamale.

Fill the bottom of a steamer or saucepan fitted with a strainer or vegetable basket with 2 to 3 inches of water. Bring the water to a boil and place the tamales in the steamer. Cover tightly with a lid or foil (it is important that little or no steam escapes while cooking). Steam the tamales for 45 to 50 minutes over lightly boiling water, adding more boiling water as needed. The tamales are done when they feel firm to the touch but not are hard and the dough comes away easily from the leaves. Let rest for at least 5 minutes before serving.

While the tamales are steaming, prepare the pineapple mole. Preheat the oven to 350°F. In a large saucepan, combine the stock, dried pineapple, tomato, pineapple, sherry, cinnamon, raisins, cumin, and chile powder and bring to a boil. Turn down the heat and simmer for 10 minutes. Meanwhile, combine the onion, garlic, serrano, ancho, almonds, sesame seeds, and tortilla on a baking sheet

(continues)

1 large corn tortilla, quartered
Pinch of ground clove
Pinch of ground nutmeg
$^1/_8$ teaspoon ground allspice
1 tablespoon chopped white chocolate
1 tablespoon vegetable oil
Salt

TO FINISH THE DISH

2 corn tortillas
1 stick canela, or $^1/_2$ stick cinnamon
1 pound foie gras
Salt

and toast in the oven for about 10 minutes, until the tortilla is crisp and dark. Remove from the oven and add to the saucepan. (Keep the oven heated.) Add the spices and chocolate and transfer to a blender. Puree, in batches if necessary, until smooth. Heat the vegetable oil in a clean, large saucepan until just smoking. Add the pureed sauce, being careful to avoid the splattering, and fry until thickened, stirring frequently, about 15 minutes. Remove from the heat and strain into a clean pan through a fine mesh strainer. Season with salt to taste and keep warm.

Place the tortillas on a cookie sheet and bake in the oven for 10 minutes, until dry and crisp. Break up and place the pieces in a spice grinder with the canela, in batches if necessary. Grind to a fine powder and set aside.

Slice the foie gras into 8 even portions and lightly season with salt on both sides. Heat a large, dry sauté pan over high heat for 5 minutes. Add the foie gras slices and sear for 2 minutes on each side. Remove and drain on paper towels.

Unwrap the tamales and, leaving the masa lying on the leaves, place each in the center of a large serving plate. Place a slice of foie gras on top of each tamale and spoon the mole around the tamales, over the leaves. Sprinkle the canela dust around the tamales.

SERVES 8

Caesar Salad with Turkey Tamales

(J O H N   S E D L A R)

THIS DISH, WITH THE CRISP, CHILLED ROMAINE LEAVES, PUNGENT GARLIC-ANCHOVY DRESSING, AND TURKEY TAMALES,

IS HEARTY, TEXTURALLY INTERESTING, QUICK, AND DELICIOUS.

Sweet Corn Tamale Mixture (page 2)

2$^1/_2$ pounds bone-in turkey leg

Salt and freshly ground black pepper

$^1/_2$ cup chopped carrot

$^1/_2$ cup chopped celery

$^1/_2$ cup chopped onion

2 bay leaves

2 sprigs fresh thyme

4 cups water

4 tablespoons pure red chile powder
  (preferably New Mexico)

6 large dried corn husks, soaked in warm water
  for 30 minutes

Olive oil, for brushing

FOR THE CAESAR SALAD

2 egg yolks

5 canned anchovies

$^1/_2$ cup freshly grated Parmesan cheese

$^1/_2$ tablespoon chopped garlic

$^1/_2$ cup sherry vinegar

1$^1/_2$ cups olive oil

1 teaspoon salt

1 teaspoon freshly ground white pepper

6 large heads romaine lettuce, outer leaves discarded, cut lengthwise into quarters, chilled

FOR THE GARNISH

3 Roma tomatoes, seeded and chopped

$^1/_2$ cup freshly shaved Parmesan cheese

Prepare the tamale mixture. Preheat the oven to 375°F.

To prepare the filling, season the turkey with salt and pepper and place in a small roasting pan. Add the carrot, celery, onion, bay leaves, and thyme to the pan, pour in the water, and cover the pan tightly with foil. Roast in the oven for about 1$^1/4$ hours, or until the meat is very tender and falls off the bone.

Transfer the turkey to a cutting board and strain the juice into a clean saucepan; discard the vegetables or use for soup. When the turkey is cool enough, remove the skin and bones from the turkey meat and shred the meat with your fingers. Set aside.

When the cooking liquid in the saucepan has cooled, skim the fat. Cook over high heat for 10 to 12 minutes, until the liquid is reduced to 1 cup. Turn down the heat, add the chile powder, about 1 teaspoon of salt, and the shredded turkey meat. Stir to mix well and set aside.

Drain the corn husks and shake dry. Lay out the husks on a flat work surface. Brush the inside of each husk with the olive oil and divide the masa evenly among them. Evenly spread it out, leaving about 1$^1/2$ inches of exposed corn husk at each end and $^3/4$ inch at each side. Top each portion of the dough with the turkey filling and spread out evenly. Bring the sides of the corn husks together tightly

around the dough; tuck one side of the husk under the other and then fold the ends over to form a neat envelope package. Repeat for the remaining tamales.

Fill the bottom of a steamer or saucepan fitted with a strainer or vegetable basket with 2 to 3 inches of water. Bring the water to a boil and place the tamales in the steamer. Cover tightly with a lid or foil (it is important that little or no steam escapes while cooking). Steam the tamales for 45 to 50 minutes over lightly boiling water, adding more boiling water as needed. The tamales are done when they feel firm to the touch but are not hard and the dough comes away easily from the husk.

While the tamales are steaming, prepare the salad. Mix the egg yolks, anchovies, Parmesan, garlic, and $^1/4$ cup of the vinegar for about 5 minutes in a blender or food processor. With the machine running, slowly add the oil in a thin, steady stream. Add the remaining $^1/4$ cup of vinegar, the salt, and pepper and blend for 5 minutes longer. Place the chilled romaine in a large bowl. Pour the dressing over and gently toss to coat well.

Arrange the salad on each serving plate. Unwrap each tamale and, leaving the dough lying on the husks, place in the center of each serving plate, next to the salad. Pour the sauce over the tamales and garnish with the chopped tomatoes and shaved Parmesan.

SERVES 6

Smoked Duck and Wild Cherry Tamales
with Ancho Sauce

(M A R K   M I L L E R)

CHILES, BOTANICALLY SPEAKING, ARE BERRIES, AND THEIR FLAVOR AND HEAT MAKE THEM NATURAL PARTNERS WITH OTHER TYPES OF FRUIT. LIKE WINE,

MOST CHILES CONTAIN SUBTLE, COMPLEX, FRUITY FLAVOR TONES, AND THIS IS PARTICULARLY TRUE FOR ANCHO CHILES, WHICH ARE DRIED POBLANO

CHILES. THE FLAVOR PROFILE OF ANCHOS INCLUDES MILD TONES OF DRIED PLUM, RAISIN, AND CHERRY, WITH SUBTLE HINTS OF COFFEE, LICORICE,

AND TOBACCO, SO THAT PAIRING ANCHOS WITH DRIED CHERRIES OR PRUNES ENHANCES THE FLAVORS OF EACH, CREATING A PERFECT MARRIAGE OF TASTE.

Fresh and Dried Corn Tamale Masa Dough
  (page 3)
¹/₂ cup dried cherries
12 ounces smoked duck meat or chicken,
  shredded
10 large dried corn husks, soaked in
  warm water for 30 minutes

FOR THE ANCHO SAUCE

1 teaspoon olive oil
2 tablespoons chopped onion
8 ounces dried ancho chile, seeded, toasted,
  and rehydrated (page 165)
2 dried chipotle chiles, seeded, toasted,
  and rehydrated (page 165), optional
2 Roma tomatoes, blackened and chopped
  (page 164)
1 tablespoon roasted garlic (page 165)
¹/₄ teaspoon salt
1 tablespoon peanut oil

Prepare the masa dough.

To prepare the filling, soak the cherries in a large bowl of warm water and let rehydrate for 20 minutes. Drain the water and mix half the cherries with the duck meat; reserve the remaining half of the rehydrated cherries for the sauce.

Drain the corn husks and shake dry. Tear 16 thin strips (about ¹/₈ inch wide) from 2 of the husks and set aside for tying the tamales. Lay out the remaining 8 corn husks on a flat work surface. Take a 2-ounce (¹/₄-cup) portion of masa dough and, using a tortilla press or heavy pan, flatten to a thickness of about ¹/₄ inch. Place the masa dough inside each husk, leaving about 1¹/₂ inches of exposed corn husk at each end and ³/₄ inch at each side. Spread about 2 heaping tablespoons of the filling on top of the masa. Bring the sides of the corn husk together, folding the dough; tuck one side of the husk under the other and roll up the tamale so the dough is completely enclosed inside the husk. Twist each end and tie with the reserved strips of corn husk. Repeat for the remaining tamales.

Fill the bottom of a steamer or saucepan fitted with a strainer or vegetable basket with 2 to 3 inches of water. Bring the water to a boil and place the tamales in the steamer. Cover tightly with a lid or foil (it is important that little or no steam escapes while cooking). Steam the tamales for 30 to 35 minutes over lightly boiling water, adding more boiling water as needed. The tamales are done when they feel firm to the touch but are not hard and the dough comes away easily from the husk. Let rest for at least 5 minutes before serving.

Meanwhile, prepare the sauce. Heat the olive oil in a small skillet and sauté the onion over medium heat for about 20 minutes, until browned. Transfer the onion to a blender and add the rehydrated chiles, the remaining rehydrated cherries, and 1¹/₂ cups of the water in which the chiles rehydrated (or use plain water). Add the tomatoes, garlic, and salt; puree. Heat the peanut oil in a large, heavy, high-sided skillet until just smoking. Strain the puree into the skillet through a fine mesh strainer and fry at a sizzle for 2 to 3 minutes, stirring continuously.

With a knife, slice open the tamales from end to end. Ladle the sauce on serving plates and arrange the tamales on the sauce.

SERVES 8

Duck Tamales with Pineapple and Chipotle

(M A R K   M I L L E R)

THE FLAVOR OF DUCK, LIKE PORK, COMPLEMENTS THAT OF FRUIT, AND PINEAPPLE MAKES A PARTICULARLY GOOD MATCH. THE SMOKY, COMPLEX,

FRUITY TONES OF THE CHIPOTLE CHILE LIKEWISE PAIR WELL WITH THESE INGREDIENTS AND ROUND OUT THE WHOLE DISH IN A NICELY BALANCED MANNER.

THIS RECIPE CAN BE PREPARED WITH ANOTHER RICH POULTRY OR FOWL MEAT, SUCH AS SQUAB OR FREE-RANGE CHICKEN. IF YOU'D LIKE TO ADD

A LITTLE MORE KICK TO THE MASA DOUGH, ADD A TABLESPOON OF CHIPOTLE CHILE PUREE AND REDUCE THE WATER BY THE SAME AMOUNT.

Fresh and Dried Corn Tamale Masa Dough
    (page 3)
1 slice (about 3/4 inch thick) fresh peeled
    and cored pineapple
10 ounces roasted or grilled duck meat, shredded
    into long thin strips, at room temperature
3 tablespoons chipotle chile puree (page 165)
1/4 cup roasted, peeled, seeded and
    diced red bell pepper (page 164)
10 large dried corn husks, soaked in warm water
    for 30 minutes
One recipe Manchamantel Sauce (page 163),
    optional

Prepare the masa dough.

To prepare the filling, heat a dry nonstick sauté pan or skillet and sauté the pineapple over medium heat until browned and caramelized, 10 to 15 minutes on each side. Slice the pineapple into pieces and then finely dice. Transfer the pineapple to a mixing bowl and add the duck meat, chipotle puree, and red bell pepper.

Drain the corn husks and shake dry. Tear 16 thin strips (about 1/8 inch wide) from 2 of the husks and set aside for tying the tamales. Lay out the remaining 8 corn husks on a flat work surface. Take a 2-ounce (1/4-cup) portion of masa dough and, using a tortilla press or heavy pan, flatten to a thickness of about 1/4 inch. Place the masa dough inside each husk, leaving about 1 1/2 inches of exposed corn husk at each end and 3/4 inch at each side. Spread about 2 heaping tablespoons of the filling on top of the masa. Bring the sides of the corn husk together, folding the dough; tuck one

side of the husk under the other and roll up the tamale so the dough is completely enclosed inside the husk. Twist each end and tie with the reserved strips of corn husk. Repeat for the remaining tamales.

Fill the bottom of a steamer or saucepan fitted with a strainer or vegetable basket with 2 to 3 inches of water. Bring the water to a boil and place the tamales in the steamer. Cover tightly with a lid or foil (it is important that little or no steam escapes while cooking). Steam the tamales for 30 to 35 minutes over lightly boiling water, adding more boiling water as needed. The tamales are done when they feel firm to the touch but are not hard and the dough comes away easily from the husk. Let rest for at least 5 minutes before serving.

While the tamales are steaming, prepare the Manchamantel sauce, if desired. Ladle about 1/4 cup of the sauce onto each serving plate. With a knife, slice open the tamales from end to end and serve on the sauce.

SERVES 8

Duck Confit–Black Olive *Humitas*

(S T E P H A N   P Y L E S)

THESE TAMALES ARE A GREAT EXAMPLE OF BRINGING TOGETHER TWO OF MY FAVORITE CULTURES—FRENCH AND SOUTH AMERICAN. CONFIT IS A CLASSICAL SOUTHWESTERN FRENCH TECHNIQUE FOR PRESERVING THE MEAT OF POULTRY AND FOWL (ESPECIALLY DUCK AND GOOSE) BY SLOWLY COOKING IT IN ITS OWN FAT AND THEN LETTING THE FAT SOLIDIFY SO THAT IT COVERS AND SEALS THE MEAT FROM THE AIR. IN THESE DAYS OF REFRIGERATION, THE METHOD IS USED MORE TO PROVIDE FLAVOR AND TEXTURE TO MEAT RATHER THAN OUT OF NECESSITY, AND THE CONFIT CAN BE USED IN ANY NUMBER OF WAYS, INCLUDING IN SALADS AND PASTA. *HUMITAS* ARE A STYLE OF TAMALE INDIGENOUS TO ARGENTINA, BOLIVIA, AND CHILE, TYPICALLY WRAPPED IN FRESH CORN LEAVES (RATHER THAN DRIED HUSKS). WHILE MOST ARE SAVORY, SOME OF THE MOST DELICIOUS ONES I'VE TASTED (IN THE MARKETS OF PERU) WERE SWEET TAMALES. IDEALLY, THE CONFIT NEEDS TO BE PREPARED SEVERAL DAYS IN ADVANCE.

1 fresh duck (about 4 pounds)
3 tablespoons coarse salt (preferably kosher)
1 teaspoon freshly ground black pepper
3 sprigs fresh thyme
2 bay leaves, crumbled
4 cups olive oil, or more if needed
Masa Seca Tamale Dough (page 2)
2 ears fresh sweet corn
1/2 cup golden raisins
1/2 cup dark raisins
1 cup finely chopped kalamata olives,
  or other large black olives
1/4 cup masa harina

To prepare the confit, cut the duck into 8 pieces (2 legs, 2 thighs, and each breast cut in half). Remove the backbone, trim off the neck and wings, and reserve for stock. Rub the duck with the salt and place in a baking dish just large enough to hold the meat in a single layer, fitting snugly. Sprinkle with the pepper and add the thyme and bay leaves. Cover the dish with plastic wrap and refrigerate for 6 to 12 hours, turning the duck occasionally.

Preheat the oven to 300°F.

Remove the duck from the baking dish and wipe off the excess salt. Return the duck, skin-side down, to the baking dish and cook on the stovetop over low heat for 15 to 20 minutes, or until the fat runs and the duck browns lightly. Add enough of the olive oil to cover the duck, cover the baking dish, and cook in the oven for 2 hours, or until the duck is very tender. Remove the dish from the oven and let the duck cool to room temperature. Cover the dish with plastic wrap and refrigerate for at least 1 week for the flavors to mellow.

When you are ready to make the tamales, prepare the masa dough.

Carefully remove the husks from the ears of corn, reserving 10 of the younger untorn leaves. Tear 16 thin strips (about 1/8 inch wide) from 2 of the leaves and set aside for tying the tamales. Cut the corn kernels from the cobs and transfer to a food processor (there should be about 1 1/2 cups). Puree and set aside. Combine the golden and dark raisins, olives, and masa harina in a large mixing bowl. Thoroughly mix in the masa dough and pureed corn with a large spoon and set aside.

Preheat the oven to 200°F. Uncover the baking dish containing the duck and heat in the oven for about 15 minutes, until the fat is melted and the duck is warm. Remove the duck, pull the meat from the bones, and set aside.

Lay out the 8 corn leaves on a flat working surface. Divide the dough into 8 even portions and place 1 portion on each leaf. Evenly

(continues)

spread out the masa mixture, leaving about $1^1/_2$ inches of exposed leaf at each end and $^3/_4$ inch at each side. Place the shredded duck confit on top of the masa, spreading it out evenly. To fold the *humitas*, bring the sides of the corn leaves together, folding the dough; tuck one side of the leaf under the other and roll up the tamale so that the dough is completely enclosed inside the leaf. Twist each end and tie with the reserved strips of corn leaf. Repeat for the remaining tamales.

Fill the bottom of a steamer or saucepan fitted with a strainer or vegetable basket with 2 to 3 inches of water. Bring the water to a boil and place the tamales in the steamer. Cover tightly with a lid or foil (it is important that little or no steam escapes while cooking). Steam the tamales for 30 to 35 minutes over lightly boiling water, adding more boiling water as needed. The tamales are done when they feel firm to the touch but are not hard and the dough comes away easily from the leaf. Let rest for at least 5 minutes before serving.

Transfer the tamales to serving plates and with a knife, slice open the top of the leaves from end to end.

SERVES 8

Shanghai Duck Tamales with Bok Choy and Sake Sauce

(J O H N  S E D L A R)

NOT LONG AGO, I WAS INVITED TO COOK IN HONG KONG AT THE PENINSULA HOTEL, TO PREPARE SOUTHWESTERN FOOD FOR THE CHINESE PRESS. ONE OF MY VIVID MEMORIES IS OF STROLLING THROUGH THE STREETS AND ADMIRING THE MARKET STALLS WITH AIR-DRIED DUCKS PERFUMING THE BUSTLING AND EXOTIC SETTING WITH THEIR COATING OF AROMATIC SPICES. SOME OF THE CHINESE COOKS IN THE PENINSULA'S KITCHEN SHOWED ME HOW TO PREPARE THE DUCKS, AND WE ACTUALLY MADE WHAT I AM SURE WERE THE FIRST EVER CHINESE DUCK TACOS! THE RICHNESS OF THE BARBECUED DUCK MAKES A WONDERFUL MATCH FOR THE EARTHINESS OF CORN MASA, AS THESE TAMALES PROVE. BUY THE DUCK IN YOUR NEAREST CHINATOWN, OR USE A RECIPE FROM A GOOD CHINESE COOKBOOK SUCH AS BARBARA TROPP'S *CHINA MOON* (WORKMAN PUBLISHING).

Masa Seca Tamale Dough (page 2)
1 store-bought Chinese barbecued duck,
    or 3 smoked duck breasts
6 large dried corn husks, soaked in warm water
    for 30 minutes
Olive oil, for brushing
6 baby bok choy, outer leaves trimmed
    (or 2 regular bok choy)
1 package enoki mushrooms

FOR THE SAKE SAUCE

1 tablespoon minced fresh ginger
1 tablespoon minced fresh chives
1 tablespoon minced garlic
3 cups sake
2 tablespoons red wine vinegar
Pinch of sugar
1 tablespoon soy sauce

Prepare the masa dough.

Remove the meat from the duck breast and legs and slice thinly, reserving the rest of the duck for another use.

Drain the corn husks and shake dry. Lay out the husks on a flat work surface. Brush the inside of each husk with the olive oil and then divide the masa dough evenly among them. Evenly spread out the masa, leaving about 1¹/₂ inches of exposed corn husk at each end and ³/₄ inch at each side. Bring the sides of the corn husks together tightly around the dough; tuck one side of the husk under the other and then fold the ends over to form a neat envelope package. Repeat for the remaining tamales.

Fill the bottom of a steamer or saucepan fitted with a strainer or vegetable basket with 2 to 3 inches of water. Bring the water to a boil and place the tamales in the steamer. Cover tightly with a lid or foil (it is important that little or no steam escapes while cooking). Steam the tamales for about 45 minutes over lightly boiling water, adding more boiling water as needed. The tamales are done when they feel firm to the touch but are not hard and the dough comes away easily from the husk.

While the tamales are steaming, preheat the oven to 200°F. Wrap the reserved duck meat in foil and place in the oven just to warm through, about 10 minutes. Thinly slice the meat, cover again in foil, and keep warm.

Fill the bottom of a steamer or saucepan fitted with a strainer or vegetable basket with 2 to 3 inches of water. Bring the water to a boil and place the bok choy in the steamer. Cover tightly with a lid or foil and steam until tender, 8 to 12 minutes. Divide the enoki mushrooms into 6 servings.

To prepare the sauce, combine all the sauce ingredients in a saucepan over medium heat. Simmer for 1 minute and remove from the heat.

Unwrap each tamale and, leaving the dough lying on the husks, place in the center of each serving plate. Place the sliced duck meat leaning against each tamale and arrange the enokis on top of the duck. Place one baby bok choy on each plate and drizzle the sauce over the tamales.

SERVES 6

Roasted Pheasant–Polenta Tamales with Gorgonzola and Dried Fruit Compote

(S T E P H A N   P Y L E S)

POLENTA IS THE GRITSLIKE DISH POPULAR IN NORTHERN ITALY MADE FROM CORNMEAL, AND IT MAKES A FINE SUBSTITUTE FOR TRADITIONAL CORN MASA

DOUGH, AS THIS RECIPE PROVES. ITS CREAMINESS AND LIGHTNESS PROVIDE BOTH A FLAVOR AND TEXTURAL COUNTERPOINT TO THE PEPPERED AND

ROASTED PHEASANT. PHEASANT IS NOW MORE WIDELY AVAILABLE ACROSS THE COUNTRY IN FROZEN FORM, AND BECAUSE IT IS SO LEAN IT IS IMPORTANT

TO COOK IT SLOWLY TO PREVENT IT FROM BECOMING STRINGY AND TOUGH. THIS DISH IS THE ESSENCE OF AUTUMN AND THE COMBINATION OF POLENTA,

GORGONZOLA, AND FRUIT IS A CLASSIC.

1 pheasant, $2^1/_2$ to 3 pounds
Salt
1 small onion, diced
2 carrots, chopped
2 stalks celery, chopped
2 cups port
1 bay leaf
2 sprigs fresh rosemary
3 cups Chicken Stock (page 160)
1 cup cornmeal
Pinch of cayenne powder
$^1/_2$ cup heavy cream
2 poblano chiles, roasted, peeled, seeded,
    and chopped (page 164)
Salt
10 large dried corn husks, soaked in warm water
    for 30 minutes
2 tablespoons crumbled gorgonzola cheese

Preheat the oven to 350°F. Rinse the pheasant inside and out with water and pat dry. Season liberally with salt. Spread the onion, carrots, and celery in a roasting pan and place the pheasant on top. Pour the port over the pheasant and add the bay leaf and rosemary to the port in the pan. Loosely cover the pan with foil and roast in the oven for 1 to $1^1/_2$ hours, until the juices run clear when the leg is pricked with the tip of a knife. Let rest briefly and, just before serving, carve slices of breast and leg meat.

Meanwhile, to prepare the polenta, place the stock in a saucepan and bring to a boil. Slowly whisk in the cornmeal and cayenne and, while stirring constantly, cook over medium heat for 3 minutes. Remove from the heat and let cool for 10 minutes. Stir in the cream and poblanos, season with salt to taste, and set aside.

Drain the corn husks and shake dry. Tear 16 strips (about $^1/_8$ inch wide) from 2 of the husks and set aside for tying the tamales. Lay out the remaining 8 corn husks on a flat work surface. Divide the polenta into 8 even portions and place 1 portion on each husk. Evenly spread out the polenta, leaving about $1^1/_2$ inches of exposed corn husk at each end and $^3/_4$ inch at each side. Sprinkle the gorgonzola evenly on top of the polenta. Bring the sides of the corn husk together, folding the polenta; tuck one side of the husk under the other and roll up the tamale so that the polenta and filling are completely enclosed inside the husk. Twist each end and tie with the reserved strips of corn husk. Repeat for the remaining tamales.

Fill the bottom of a steamer or saucepan fitted with a strainer or vegetable basket with 2 to 3 inches of water. Bring the water to a boil and place the tamales in the steamer. Cover tightly with a lid or foil (it is important that little or no steam escapes while cooking). Steam the tamales for 10 minutes over lightly boiling water, adding more boiling water as needed. The tamales are done when they feel firm to the touch but are not hard and the polenta comes away easily from the husk.

(continues)

FOR THE DRIED FRUIT COMPOTE

¹/₄ cup chopped walnuts
Juice of 3 large oranges
Juice of ¹/₂ lime
2 tablespoons port
¹/₄ cup sugar
¹/₂ cup dried cherries
¹/₄ cup diced dried apricot
¹/₄ cup diced dried pineapple
Zest of 1 orange
Pinch of cayenne powder
Pinch of ground cumin
1 tablespoon snipped chives
1 tablespoon chopped cilantro
1 tablespoon chopped fresh mint

While the tamales are steaming, prepare the fruit compote. Place the walnuts in a hot, dry skillet and toast over medium heat for about 5 minutes, stirring occasionally, until fragrant. Set aside. Place the citrus juices, port, and sugar in a saucepan and bring to a boil. Add the cherries, apricots, pineapple, and orange zest, turn down the heat, and simmer for 5 to 7 minutes, until the fruit is soft. Remove from the heat and stir in the toasted walnuts and the remaining ingredients. Keep warm or serve at room temperature.

Transfer the tamales to serving plates and, with a knife, slice open the top of the tamale wrappers from end to end. Gently push the ends together, as for a baked potato. Lean slices of pheasant against the tamales and spoon the dried fruit compote on top of, or next to, the pheasant.

SERVES 8

Port-Poached Pear Tamales with Molasses Grilled Quail

(S T E P H A N   P Y L E S)

I HAVE HAD A PARTICULAR FONDNESS FOR QUAIL FOR AS LONG AS I CAN REMEMBER, SINCE I GREW UP IN WEST TEXAS AND LEARNED TO HUNT BOBWHITE

AT AN EARLY AGE. TO ME, QUAIL IS THE PERFECT FOWL, AND IN THIS RECIPE IT EXHIBITS JUST ENOUGH GAMINESS TO BALANCE THE PORT AND PEARS,

MAKING THIS COMBINATION AN ABSOLUTE CLASSIC. THE EAST-MEETS-WEST MARINADE GIVES THE QUAIL A WONDERFUL FLAVOR; EVEN WITHOUT THE QUAIL,

THESE TAMALES WOULD MAKE A GREAT DESSERT, ESPECIALLY WITH THE ADDITION OF SOME CANDIED PECANS.

FOR THE QUAIL MOLASSES MARINADE

1/2 cup soy sauce
1/4 cup dark beer
2 tablespoons dark molasses
Zest of 1 lemon, minced
Zest of 1 orange, minced
1 tablespoon chopped fresh lemon verbena
*   or lemon thyme*
1/4 cup finely diced fresh ginger
2 cloves garlic, crushed
8 boneless quail, 4 to 5 ounces each

FOR THE POACHED PEARS

2 cups dry red wine
1/2 cup port
2 cloves
1 stick cinnamon
1/2 cup sugar
4 Anjou or Bartlett pears, peeled, cored,
*   and cut in half*

To prepare the marinade, place all the marinade ingredients except the quail in a mixing bowl and combine thoroughly. Add the quail and let marinate in the refrigerator for at least 1 hour and up to 3 hours, turning occasionally.

Meanwhile, to prepare the pears, combine the wine, port, cloves, cinnamon, and sugar in a saucepan just large enough to hold the pears in a single layer and bring to a boil. Reduce the heat to low and add the pears, cut side down. Let simmer for 10 to 15 minutes, until the pears are tender when pierced with a knife. Remove the pears, place in a dish, and set aside. Strain $1^{1}/_{2}$ cups of the poaching liquid through a fine sieve into a bowl. Reserve $1/4$ cup of the liquid in the bowl in the refrigerator, transfer the remaining $1^{1}/_{4}$ cups of the liquid to a clean saucepan, bring to a boil, and set aside.

To prepare the masa dough, place the masa harina and cinnamon in the bowl of an electric mixer fitted with a paddle attachment. With the machine on low speed, add the $1^{1}/_{4}$ cups of boiled poaching liquid in a slow steady stream and mix until the dough forms a ball. Continue mixing for 5 minutes, then transfer the dough to a clean bowl. Refrigerate for 1 hour.

Return the dough to the bowl of the electric mixer and beat for 5 minutes on high speed. With the machine running, slowly add the butter 2 tablespoons at a time. Continue mixing for about 5 minutes, until the dough is smooth and light. Turn off the machine to scrape down the sides of the bowl with a spatula and return to low speed. While the dough is mixing, combine the salt, baking powder, and the reserved $1/4$ cup of poaching liquid in a small mixing bowl. Add this mixture to the dough in a slow steady stream and continue mixing until thoroughly combined. Increase the speed to high and mix for 5 minutes longer.

Drain the corn husks and shake dry. Tear 16 thin strips (about $1/8$ inch wide) from 2 of the husks and set aside for tying the tamales. Lay out the remaining 8 corn husks on a flat work surface. Divide the masa dough into 8

(continues)

FOR THE MASA DOUGH AND TAMALES

1³/₄ cups masa harina
³/₄ teaspoon ground cinnamon
¹/₂ cup plus 2 tablespoons chilled
    unsalted butter, diced
1¹/₂ teaspoons salt
1 teaspoon baking powder
10 large dried corn husks, soaked in
    warm water for 30 minutes

FOR THE SPICED WALNUTS

1 tablespoon unsalted butter
1¹/₂ cups walnut halves, soaked in water
    overnight and drained
¹/₄ cup light brown sugar
¹/₂ teaspoon sweet paprika
1 teaspoon pure red chile powder
¹/₂ tablespoon ground cumin
2 tablespoons cider vinegar
Salt

even portions and place 1 portion on each husk. Evenly spread out the masa mixture, leaving about 1¹/₂ inches of exposed corn husk at each end and ³/₄ inch at each side. Bring the sides of the corn husk together, folding the dough; tuck one side of the husk under the other and roll up the tamale so that the dough is completely enclosed inside the husk. Twist each end and tie with the reserved strips of corn husk. Repeat for the remaining tamales.

Fill the bottom of a steamer or saucepan fitted with a strainer or vegetable basket with 2 to 3 inches of water. Bring the water to a boil and place the tamales in the steamer. Cover tightly with a lid or foil (it is important that little or no steam escapes while cooking). Steam the tamales for 30 to 35 minutes over lightly boiling water, adding more boiling water as needed. The tamales are done when they feel firm to the touch but are not hard and the dough comes away easily from the husk. Let rest for at least 5 minutes before serving.

While the tamales are steaming, prepare the grill (alternatively, the quail can be broiled). Remove the quail from the marinade; reserve the marinade. Season the quail with salt to taste and grill for 2 to 3 minutes on each side, brushing with the marinade (the molasses may caramelize and look burned, but the flavor is very pleasant).

To prepare the spiced walnuts, preheat the oven to 300°F. Melt the butter in a large skillet, add the walnuts, and sauté over medium heat until lightly browned, about 3 minutes. Add the brown sugar and cook until lightly caramelized. Stir in the paprika, chile powder, and cumin. Add the vinegar and cook until all the liquid has evaporated. Season with salt to taste. Spread the walnuts on a cookie sheet and bake in the oven for 3 to 5 minutes, until crisp.

Transfer the tamales to serving plates and, with a knife, slice open the top of the tamale wrappers from end to end. Gently push the ends together, as for a baked potato. Slice each pear half decoratively and arrange in a fan shape next to the tamales. Cut each quail in half lengthwise and place on top of the tamales. Garnish each plate with 5 to 6 spiced walnuts.

SERVES 8

Smoked Quail Tamales with Canela, Apple, and Apple–Green Chile Salsa

(M A R K   M I L L E R)

SMOKING ADDS AN EXTRA DIMENSION OF FLAVOR TO GAME BIRDS AND OTHER MEAT, ALLOWING THEIR NATURAL SWEETNESS TO EMERGE, ESPECIALLY IF FRUIT WOOD SUCH AS APPLE OR CHERRY IS USED. COLD-SMOKING DELICATE BIRDS IS A VALUABLE TECHNIQUE BECAUSE IT PREVENTS THE MEAT FROM DRYING OUT AND BECOMING TOUGH. BY ALL MEANS SMOKE YOUR OWN QUAIL, BUT BUYING IT PRESMOKED PROVIDES A MAJOR SHORTCUT. CANELA IS A MILD, SWEETER FORM OF CINNAMON THAT IS FAVORED IN MEXICAN COOKING, AND CANELA STICKS HAVE A SOFTER, ALMOST PAPERY TEXTURE. LIKE CINNAMON, CANELA MAKES A WONDERFUL FLAVOR PARTNER WITH APPLES.

Canela Tamale Masa Dough (page 12)

FOR THE FILLING AND TAMALES

2 tablespoons unsalted butter
1 large green apple, peeled, cored, and finely diced (about 1 cup)
2 teaspoons sugar
10 ounces smoked quail meat, or smoked chicken, diced
10 large dried corn husks, soaked in warm water for 30 minutes

FOR THE APPLE–GREEN CHILE SALSA

1/2 cup fresh apple cider
1 green apple, peeled, cored, and diced
1 teaspoon olive oil
2 tablespoons diced onion
1/4 teaspoon dried oregano, toasted and crumbled (page 165)
1 New Mexico green chile, roasted, peeled, seeded, and diced (page 164)
1/2 teaspoon sugar
1/2 teaspoon freshly squeezed lemon juice
1/2 teaspoon balsamic vinegar

Prepare the masa dough.

To prepare the filling, heat the butter in a sauté pan and add the apple and sugar. Sauté over medium heat for about 10 minutes, until cooked but still firm. Transfer to a bowl and combine thoroughly with the quail meat.

Drain the corn husks and shake dry. Tear 16 thin strips (about 1/8 inch wide) from 2 of the husks and set aside for tying the tamales. Lay out the remaining 8 corn husks on a flat work surface. Take a 2-ounce (1/4-cup) portion of masa dough and, using a tortilla press or heavy pan, flatten to a thickness of about 1/4 inch. Place the masa dough inside each husk, leaving about 1 1/2 inches of exposed corn husk at each end and 3/4 inch at each side. Spread about 2 heaping tablespoons of the filling on top of the masa. Bring the sides of the corn husk together, folding the dough; tuck one side of the husk under the other and roll up the tamale so the dough is completely enclosed inside the husk. Twist each end and tie with the reserved strips of corn husk. Repeat for the remaining tamales.

Fill the bottom of a steamer or saucepan fitted with a strainer or vegetable basket with 2 to 3 inches of water. Bring the water to a boil and place the tamales in the steamer. Cover tightly with a lid or foil (it is important that little or no steam escapes while cooking). Steam the tamales for 30 to 35 minutes over lightly boiling water, adding more boiling water as needed. The tamales are done when they feel firm to the touch but are not hard and the dough comes away easily from the husk. Let rest for at least 5 minutes before serving.

While the tamales are steaming, prepare the salsa. Place the cider in a saucepan and reduce by half over high heat. Turn down the heat to medium, add the apple, and cook for 5 minutes, until soft. Transfer to a mixing bowl. Heat the olive oil in a small skillet and sauté the onion over medium heat for 5 minutes. Add to the bowl. Add the remaining salsa ingredients and stir together.

With a knife, slice open the top of the tamale wrappers from end to end. Serve with the salsa.

SERVES 8

Squab Tamales with Château d'Yquem and Rosemary

(J O H N  S E D L A R)

One evening in Bel Air, Los Angeles, I had the pleasure of dining with the Count and Countess de Lur Saluce, the owners of the famed Château d'Yquem winery in the Sauternes region of France. The dinner party was hosted during their trip to promote their new book, Yquem, and that evening we blind-tasted a number of wines. I was most impressed by the palates of our guests of honor, especially when they correctly identified a 1954 vintage of their wine. Château d'Yquem is a wonderful complement to the richness of squab, which has the character to stand up to such strong flavors as black pepper and rosemary.

Rice Tamale Mixture (page 7)
6 sprigs fresh rosemary, chopped
1/4 cup olive oil
Zest of 1 orange, minced
6 star anise
1 tablespoon peppercorns
3 tablespoons honey
6 squabs (deboned by the butcher),
  trimmed of excess fat
1 large banana leaf, about 12 inches by 36 inches
1 1/2 cups Château d'Yquem wine,
  or other sweet Sauternes
6 tablespoons unsalted butter
1 tablespoon coarsely cracked black pepper
6 sprigs fresh rosemary, for garnish

Prepare the rice tamale mixture.

To prepare the marinade, combine the rosemary, olive oil, orange zest, star anise, peppercorns, and honey in a mixing bowl. Lay the squabs in a shallow dish and pour the marinade over them, coating all sides of the birds. Cover and marinate in the refrigerator overnight.

Soften the banana leaf over an open flame for 10 seconds on each side, being careful not to burn it. Cut into 6 squares, about 6 inches by 6 inches, and lay out on a flat work surface. Place a 1/2-cup scoop of rice on each square. Bring the two opposite sides of the banana leaf together over the rice and then, holding the ends, fold the ends down, tucking them under the rice filling to form a neat envelope package. Repeat for the remaining tamales.

Prepare the grill (alternatively, the squab can be broiled). To prepare the sauce, heat the wine in a small saucepan over medium heat until reduced by half, about 15 minutes. Whisk in the butter 1 tablespoon at a time, and add the pepper. Keep warm.

Remove the squab from the marinade and grill (or broil) over very high heat for about 6 minutes on each side, until the skin is cooked and golden but the breast meat is medium rare.

Arrange the tamales on the serving plates. Serve the squab next to the tamales, drizzle the sauce over the top, and garnish with a sprig of rosemary.

SERVES 6

Squab-Chestnut Tamales with Red Cabbage Chow Chow

(S T E P H A N   P Y L E S)

SQUAB, OR YOUNG DOMESTICATED PIGEON, HAS THE RICHEST, GAMIEST FLAVOR OF ANY COMMERCIALLY AVAILABLE FOWL. ITS ASSERTIVE YET DELICATE FLAVORS REMIND ME OF GOOSE AND ALSO OF VEAL LIVER. TOGETHER WITH THE RICH CHESTNUTS IN THE MASA DOUGH, THIS MAKES AN IDEAL FALL OR WINTER DISH, WHICH IS CHESTNUT SEASON. CHESTNUTS HAVE ALWAYS BEEN POPULAR IN FRANCE FOR STUFFING POULTRY, AND CANDIED CHESTNUTS—*MARRONS GLACÉS*—ARE TRADITIONAL TREATS DURING THE HOLIDAY SEASON. BEFORE THE POTATO WAS BROUGHT TO FRANCE FROM THE NEW WORLD, CHESTNUTS (AND FLOUR GROUND FROM THEM) WERE A STAPLE OF THE POOR. THE MILD ACIDITY OF THE CABBAGE CHOW CHOW CUTS THE RICHNESS OF THE REST OF THE DISH AND GIVES AN ATTRACTIVE VISUAL TWIST.

FOR THE RED CABBAGE CHOW CHOW

1/2 head red cabbage, cored and thinly sliced
1/2 onion, finely diced
1 small serrano chile, seeded and minced
1 tablespoon whole-grain mustard
1 teaspoon prepared horseradish
Pinch of ground cloves
Pinch of ground cinnamon
Pinch of ground allspice
1 cup cider vinegar
1/2 cup sugar
1/2 tablespoon salt
1/2 cup water

FOR THE ROASTED SQUAB

4 boneless squab
Salt
3 tablespoons olive oil

To prepare the chow chow, combine all the chow chow ingredients in a saucepan over high heat. Bring to a boil, turn down the heat, and simmer until the cabbage is tender, about 1 hour, stirring occasionally. Let cool and refrigerate until ready to serve.

To prepare the squab, separate the breast meat from the legs and reserve the legs for soup, stock, or another purpose. Season the 8 squab breasts on both sides with salt to taste. Heat the olive oil in a large sauté pan until just smoking. Add the squab breasts and sear over high heat for 1 minute per side, until lightly browned. Remove from the pan and reserve.

Preheat the oven to 400°F. Prepare the masa dough.

Make a slice against the grain on both sides of each chestnut. Place on a baking sheet and roast in the oven for 20 minutes, shaking the pan occasionally. Peel and finely dice the chestnuts and add to the masa dough in a mixing bowl. Add the maple syrup and thoroughly mix together.

Drain the corn husks and shake dry. Tear 16 thin strips (about 1/8 inch wide) from 2 of the husks and set aside for tying the tamales. Lay out the remaining 8 corn husks on a flat work surface and divide the masa mixture evenly among them. Evenly spread out the masa, leaving about 1 1/2 inches of exposed corn husk at each end and 3/4 inch at each side. Place one portion of squab breast on top of each portion of dough. Bring the sides of the corn husk together, folding the dough and enclosing the squab breast; tuck one side of the husk under the other and roll up the tamale so that the dough is completely enclosed inside the husk. Twist each end and tie with the reserved strips of corn husk. Repeat for the remaining tamales.

Fill the bottom of a steamer or saucepan fitted with a strainer or vegetable basket with 2 to 3 inches of water. Bring the water to a boil and place the tamales in the steamer. Cover tightly with a lid or foil (it is important that

(continues)

FOR THE MASA DOUGH AND TAMALES

Masa Seca Tamale Dough (page 2)

1¹/₂ cups chestnuts

3 tablespoons maple syrup

10 large dried corn husks, soaked in warm
*   water for 30 minutes*

little or no steam escapes while cooking). Steam the tamales for 25 to 30 minutes over lightly boiling water, adding more boiling water as needed. The tamales are done when they feel firm to the touch but are not hard and the dough comes away easily from the husks.

Transfer the tamales to serving plates and remove the tie from one end of each husk. Open up the tamale to expose the dough and squab filling. Serve with the chow chow.

SERVES 8

Meat and Game Tamales

Cabernet Tamales with Beef and Black Pepper

Barbecued Brisket Tamales with Jicama Coleslaw

Coney Island Corned Beef and
Cabbage Tamales with Mustard Sauce

Coriander-Cured Beef Tamales
with Barbecue-Onion Marmalade

Veal Tamales Milanese with Basil and Arugula

Beef Wellington Tamales with
Chanterelles and Madeira Sauce

Pork *Carnitas* Tamales with Manchamantel Sauce

Carnitas Tamales with Pineapple
and Tomato-Habanero Sauce

Lamb Tamales with Mint, Black Beans,
and Blackened Tomato and Mint Salsa

Lamb *Adobado* Tamales with
Eggplant–Black Olive Ragout

Greek Tamales with Lamb and Feta Cheese

Venison Chorizo Tamales with
Cranberry-Chipotle Salsa

Red Chile Rabbit Tamales in
Green Chile–Posole Broth

Blue Corn Rabbit Tamales with
Sage and Salsa Verde

Escargot Forestière Tamales

Cabernet Tamales with Beef and Black Pepper

(M A R K M I L L E R)

THE COMPLEX, SATISFYING FLAVORS OF RICH, FRUITY CABERNET SAUVIGNON WINE AND ROBUST PEPPERED BEEF WERE MADE FOR EACH OTHER. CABERNETS ARE OFTEN DESCRIBED AS "PEPPERY," WHICH IS WHY THIS COMBINATION WORKS SO WELL. USE A YOUNG, NONTANNIC CALIFORNIA CABERNET FOR THIS RECIPE. FOR THE MOST DRAMATIC PRESENTATION, I LIKE TO SERVE THESE TAMALES IN DRIED RED CORN HUSKS, BUT AS OUR SUPPLY OF RED CORN IS GROWN SPECIALLY FOR US AT COYOTE CAFE AND IT IS HARD TO FIND OTHERWISE, YOU SHOULD PLAN ON USING YELLOW CORN HUSKS, OR DYE THEM WITH HIBISCUS TEA (SEE PAGE XIII). EITHER WAY, THE RESULTS WILL BE STRIKING.

FOR THE BRAISED BEEF

1 tablespoon olive oil
1 pound chuck steak, diced
Salt and freshly ground black pepper
2 cups water
1 cup Cabernet Sauvignon wine, or more water
1 bay leaf

FOR THE CABERNET SAUCE

2 cups Cabernet Sauvignon wine

FOR THE TAMALES

Fresh and Dried Corn Tamale Dough (page 3)
6 large dried corn husks, soaked in warm water for 30 minutes
2 tablespoons coarsely cracked black pepper

Preheat the oven to 325°F. Heat the olive oil in a sauté pan. Season the steak with salt and pepper to taste and sear over medium-high heat, while stirring, for about 5 minutes, until browned. Transfer to a casserole or oven-proof dish, add the water, wine, and bay leaf (add more water if necessary to cover the steak). Cover the casserole and braise in the oven for about 2 hours, until the meat is perfectly tender. Remove from the oven, strain the meat, and set aside.

While the beef is cooking, pour the wine into a saucepan and bring to a boil. Reduce over high heat until $3/4$ cup remains. Let cool.

Prepare the dough, substituting $1/2$ cup of the reduced Cabernet for an equal amount of water (reserve the remaining reduced Cabernet).

Drain the corn husks and shake dry. Tear 16 thin strips (about $1/8$ inch wide) from 2 of the husks and set aside for tying the tamales. Lay out the remaining 8 corn husks on a flat work surface. Take a 2-ounce ($1/4$-cup) portion of masa dough and, using a tortilla press or heavy pan, flatten to a thickness of about $1/4$ inch. Place the masa dough inside each husk, leaving about $1 1/2$ inches of exposed corn husk at each end and $3/4$ inch at each side. Spread

about 2 heaping tablespoons of the braised beef on top of the masa. Bring the sides of the corn husk together, folding the dough; before securing the husk, press the cracked pepper on top of the dough so that it adheres. Tuck one side of the husk under the other and roll up the tamale so the dough is completely enclosed inside the husk. Twist each end and tie with the reserved strips of corn husk. Repeat for the remaining tamales.

Fill the bottom of a steamer or saucepan fitted with a strainer or vegetable basket with 2 to 3 inches of water. Bring the water to a boil and place the tamales in the steamer. Cover tightly with a lid or foil. Steam the tamales for 30 to 35 minutes over lightly boiling water, adding more boiling water as needed. The tamales are done when they feel firm to the touch but are not hard and the dough comes away easily from the husk. Let rest for at least 5 minutes before serving.

Warm the reserved Cabernet. Place the tamales on serving plates and, with a knife, slice open the wrappers from end to end. Spoon or drizzle the warmed Cabernet around the tamales.

SERVES 8

Barbecued Brisket Tamales with Jicama Coleslaw

(S T E P H A N   P Y L E S)

I CALL THESE MY FOURTH OF JULY TAMALES BECAUSE THEY INCORPORATE ALL THE FLAVORS OF THAT REVERED EVENT. IN TEXAS, BARBECUE IS NOT SIMPLY A TYPE OF FOOD OR A WAY OF COOKING IT; IT IS MORE A WAY OF LIFE AND A STATE OF MIND. DURING HIS PRESIDENCY IN THE 1960S, LYNDON B. JOHNSON DID MORE TO EDUCATE AMERICA ABOUT THE HEDONISTIC PLEASURES OF THE BARBECUE THAN ANYONE BEFORE OR SINCE. THE COOKING METHOD FOR THE BRISKET IN THIS RECIPE IS THE AUTHENTIC TEXAS PREPARATION. YOU CAN BUY A GOOD, INEXPENSIVE HOME SMOKER AT SPECIALTY HARDWARE OR GOURMET STORES, AND IT'S WELL WORTH THE INVESTMENT. YOU CAN ALSO USE A BARBECUE GRILL BY ADDING A PAN OF WATER IN THE BOTTOM, SEALING ALL BUT ONE VENT, AND FOLLOWING THE DIRECTIONS BELOW FOR THE SMOKER. IF YOU DON'T HAVE A SMOKER, OR IF YOU DON'T HAVE THE TIME IT TAKES TO TEND THE FIRE, YOU MAY SIMPLY ROAST THE BRISKET IN A PREHEATED 325°F OVEN FOR 2^1/$_2$ TO 3 HOURS. SEAR THE BRISKET WELL ON BOTH SIDES IN A LIGHTLY OILED HOT SKILLET FIRST. NOTE THAT THE BRISKET SHOULD BE MARINATED DRY IN THE REFRIGERATOR FOR AT LEAST 24 HOURS BEFORE BEING COOKED.

FOR THE BRISKET

^{1}/$_4$ cup salt
2 tablespoons freshly ground black pepper
2 tablespoons sweet paprika
1 teaspoon cayenne powder
1 untrimmed beef brisket, about 4 pounds
Salt

FOR THE BARBECUE SAUCE

1 tablespoon olive oil
2 onions, diced
3 small jalapeño chiles, seeded and minced
^{1}/$_2$ cup dark brown sugar
^{1}/$_2$ cup white vinegar
^{1}/$_4$ cup Worcestershire sauce
1 tablespoon dried mustard
2 cups tomato ketchup

To prepare the brisket, combine the salt, pepper, paprika, and cayenne in a bowl. Trim all but a ^{1}/$_8$-inch layer of fat from the brisket and place in a large glass or ceramic dish. Sprinkle the spice mixture over the meat and roll to coat completely. Marinate in the refrigerator, covered, for at least 24 hours.

Prepare the smoker. Soak 6 to 8 chunks of aromatic hardwood (such as hickory or mesquite) in water for 20 minutes. Place a pan of water in the bottom of the smoker. Build a fire in the smoker with charcoal and let it burn down until covered uniformly with a white-gray ash, 20 to 30 minutes. Spread the coals out, add the soaked hardwood chunks, and let burn for 5 minutes. Place the brisket on the grill over the water pan, place a shallow pan underneath the meat to catch the drippings, and cover the smoker. Stoke the fire every 30 minutes, adding more charcoal and soaked wood chunks as necessary. After about 2 hours,

remove the meat and stoke the fire, adding more soaked wood. Add more water to the pan as needed. Return the meat and smoke the brisket for 5 to 6 more hours, or until fork-tender, maintaining a temperature of 190°F to 225°F. When the brisket is cooked, place on a carving board and slice as thinly as possible. Transfer to a clean, nonreactive saucepan, add the barbecue sauce and salt to taste, and set aside.

Meanwhile, prepare the barbecue sauce. Heat the olive oil in a large saucepan and sauté the onions and jalapeños over medium-high heat for 3 minutes. Add the remaining barbecue sauce ingredients and, stirring frequently, bring to a boil. Turn down the heat and simmer for 15 minutes. Strain the sauce through a medium-fine mesh strainer into a clean saucepan.

Prepare the masa dough.

(continues)

FOR THE TAMALES

Masa Seca Tamale Dough (page 2)
10 large dried corn husks, soaked in
warm water for 30 minutes

FOR THE JICAMA COLESLAW

3 cups shredded red cabbage
3/4 cup grated carrot
1 1/2 medium jicamas, peeled and julienned
(about 4 cups)
1 red bell pepper, seeded and finely diced
1 yellow bell pepper, seeded and finely diced
2 jalapeño chiles, seeded and finely diced
3/4 cup mayonnaise
1 1/2 tablespoons honey
1 1/2 tablespoons raspberry vinegar
1 1/2 tablespoons freshly squeezed lemon juice
Salt and freshly ground black pepper

To prepare the slaw, thoroughly combine all the slaw ingredients with 2/3 cup of the barbecue sauce in a large mixing bowl. Season with salt and pepper to taste and keep refrigerated.

Prepare the tamale wrappers. Drain the corn husks and shake dry. Tear 16 thin strips (about 1/8 inch wide) from 2 of the husks and set aside for tying the tamales. Lay out the remaining 8 corn husks on a flat work surface. Divide the masa into 16 even portions. Take 8 of the portions and place 1 on each husk. Evenly spread out the masa mixture, leaving about 1 1/2 inches of exposed corn husk at each end and 3/4 inch at each side. Divide the brisket evenly and place in the center of the tamale dough. Top with the remaining 8 dough portions to make a "sandwich." Bring the sides of the corn husks together, folding the dough; tuck one side of the husk under the other and roll up the tamales so that the dough is completely enclosed inside the husk. Twist each end and tie with the reserved strips of corn husk.

Fill the bottom of a steamer or saucepan fitted with a strainer or vegetable basket with 2 to 3 inches of water. Bring the water to a boil and place the tamales in the steamer. Cover tightly with a lid or foil (it is important that little or no steam escapes while cooking). Steam the tamales for 20 minutes over lightly boiling water, adding more boiling water as needed. The tamales are done when they feel firm to the touch but are not hard and the dough comes away easily from the husk. Let rest for at least 5 minutes before serving.

Place the tamales on serving plates and, with a knife, slice open the top of the wrappers from end to end. Gently push the ends together as for a baked potato. Serve with the jicama coleslaw and additional barbecue sauce if desired.

SERVES 8

Coney Island Corned Beef and Cabbage Tamales with Mustard Sauce

(J O H N   S E D L A R)

CONEY ISLAND IN BROOKLYN USUALLY CONJURES UP TWO IMAGES—ONE OF AN AMUSEMENT PARK AND THE OTHER OF MUSTARDY HOT DOGS AND CORNED BEEF. NO HOT DOG BUNS HERE; RATHER, EARTHY MASA HOLDS THE JUICY CORNED BEEF AND SETS OFF THE DRESSED COLESLAW AND PUNGENT MUSTARD. BE SURE NOT TO TRIM THE CORNED BEEF TOO MUCH; EVEN IF THE NUTRITION SQUAD WOULD NOT APPROVE, IT SHOULD NOT BE TOO LEAN, SO THE ENHANCED FLAVOR IS EVIDENT. I PREFER TO USE THE ELEGANT NAPA CABBAGE FOR THE COLESLAW BECAUSE OF ITS DISTINCTIVE SOFT TEXTURE; I ALSO FIND IT TO BE LESS INDIGESTIBLE AND "GASSY," BUT YOU CAN USE REGULAR GREEN CABBAGE INSTEAD IF YOU WISH.

$^1/_4$ cup white wine vinegar

1 tablespoon whole-grain Dijon mustard

Pinch of sugar

$^1/_2$ teaspoon freshly ground black pepper

Pinch of salt

2 tablespoons safflower oil

$^1/_3$ cup extra-virgin olive oil

1 head napa cabbage, finely shredded

1 teaspoon caraway seeds

1 carrot, grated

Masa Seca Tamale Dough (page 2)

1 cup heavy cream

$^1/_2$ cup Veal Stock (page 161)

5 tablespoons whole-grain Dijon mustard

2 shallots, chopped

8 ounces corned beef, sliced

6 large dried corn husks, soaked in warm water for 30 minutes

Olive oil, for brushing

6 teaspoons whole-grain Dijon mustard, for garnish

6 teaspoons American mustard, for garnish

Make the vinaigrette. Combine the vinegar, mustard, sugar, pepper and salt, and oils in a glass jar with a tight-fitting lid and shake well. Toss together the cabbage, seeds, and carrot for the coleslaw in a large mixing bowl. Drizzle the vinaigrette over the coleslaw and toss to coat well. Chill for at least 2 hours. Toss again just before serving.

Prepare the masa dough.

To prepare the filling, place the cream, stock, mustard, and shallots in a small saucepan. Bring to a boil, turn down the heat to low, and cook, stirring frequently, until the mixture is reduced by half and has a saucelike consistency, about 10 minutes. Transfer to a mixing bowl and mix thoroughly with the corned beef.

Drain the corn husks and shake dry. Lay out the husks on a flat work surface. Brush the inside of each husk with the olive oil and divide the tamale masa evenly among them. Evenly spread out the masa, leaving about 1$^1/_2$ inches of exposed corn husk at each end and $^3/_4$ inch at each side. Top each portion of the dough with the filling mixture and spread out evenly. Bring the sides of the corn husks together tightly around the dough; tuck one side of the husk under the other and then fold over the ends to form a neat envelope package. Repeat for the remaining tamales.

Fill the bottom of a steamer or saucepan fitted with a strainer or vegetable basket with 2 to 3 inches of water. Bring the water to a boil and place the tamales in the steamer. Cover tightly with a lid or foil (it is important that little or no steam escapes while cooking). Steam the tamales for about 45 minutes over lightly boiling water, adding more boiling water as needed. The tamales are done when they feel firm to the touch but are not hard and the dough comes away easily from the husk. Let rest for at least 5 minutes before serving.

Unwrap each tamale and, leaving the dough lying on the husks, place in the center of each serving plate. With a slotted spoon, serve a scoop of coleslaw on each plate and garnish with a teaspoon of each mustard.

SERVES 6

Coriander-Cured Beef Tamales with Barbecue-Onion Marmalade

(S T E P H A N   P Y L E S)

IN TEXAS AND THE SOUTHWEST, WE REFER TO THE GREEN PARSLEYLIKE LEAF OF THE CORIANDER PLANT AS CILANTRO AND THE SEEDS AS CORIANDER. THE SEEDS HAVE AN AROMATIC FLAVOR WITH OVERTONES OF LEMON, SAGE, ALLSPICE, AND CARAWAY AND SHARE NONE OF THE DELICIOUSLY PUNGENT FLAVOR CHARACTERISTICS OF THE FRESH HERB. THE CORIANDER CURE CAN BE USED FOR ANY NUMBER OF OTHER MEATS, BUT IT REALLY WORKS BEST WITH BEEF AND VENISON. THE BARBECUE-ONION MARMALADE CAN BE USED AS A GARNISH ON ALMOST ANY SAVORY TAMALE.

Masa Seca Tamale Dough (page 2)
$1/4$ cup coriander seeds
$1/4$ cup black peppercorns
4 shallots, minced
4 cloves garlic, minced
$3/4$ cup kosher salt
6 tablespoons dark brown sugar
4 beef tenderloin fillets, 5 ounces each
2 tablespoons olive oil
3 onions, thinly sliced
1 cup barbecue sauce (see Barbecued Brisket Tamales with Jicama Coleslaw, page 108)
$1 1/2$ cups Chicken Stock (page 160), or water
10 large dried corn husks, soaked in warm water for 30 minutes
1 tablespoon olive oil

Prepare the masa dough.

Pulse the coriander seeds and peppercorns in the bowl of a food processor for about 1 minute, until coarsely ground. Add the shallots, garlic, salt, and brown sugar. Pulse to make a thick paste. Transfer to a mixing bowl, add the beef, and let cure for at least 1 hour, turning occasionally.

Meanwhile, heat the olive oil in a large sauté pan until lightly smoking. Add the onions and sauté over high heat, stirring occasionally, until dark brown, about 12 minutes. Add the barbecue sauce and stock to deglaze the pan. Bring the mixture to a boil and reduce until syrupy. Remove from the heat and let the onion marmalade cool to room temperature.

Combine half the marmalade with the tamale dough in a mixing bowl and mix thoroughly with a large spoon.

Drain the corn husks and shake dry. Tear 16 thin strips (about $1/8$ inch wide) from 2 of the husks and set aside for tying the tamales. Lay out the remaining 8 corn husks and divide the dough into 8 even portions. Place 1 portion on each husk. Evenly spread out the masa mixture, leaving about $1 1/2$ inches of exposed corn husk at each end and $3/4$ inch at each side. Bring the sides of the corn husks together, folding the dough; tuck one side of the husk under the other and roll up the tamales so that the dough is completely enclosed inside the husk. Twist each end and tie with the reserved strips of corn husk.

Preheat the oven to 400°F.

Steam the tamales (see page 110 for method) for 30 to 35 minutes over lightly boiling water, adding more boiling water as needed. The tamales are done when they feel firm to the touch but are not hard and the dough comes away easily from the husk. Let rest for at least 5 minutes before serving.

Meanwhile, heat the olive oil in a large sauté pan over high heat, until lightly smoking. Add the tenderloins and sear on all sides. Transfer to a roasting pan and cook in the oven for about 8 minutes for medium rare. Remove from the oven and let the beef rest for 5 to 10 minutes; then cut into $1/2$-inch slices.

To serve, slice open the top of the wrappers from end to end. Gently push the ends together, as for a baked potato. Lean the sliced beef against the tamales and serve the remaining onion marmalade on the side.

SERVES 8

Veal Tamales Milanese with Basil and Arugula

(J O H N   S E D L A R)

"MILANESE," OR "À LA MILANAISE"—IN THE STYLE OF MILAN—TYPICALLY INVOLVES FRYING BREADED INGREDIENTS IN CLARIFIED BUTTER, AND HERE THE CLASSIC METHOD IS ADAPTED FOR THE VEAL. I LIKE TO WRAP AND COOK THESE TAMALES IN DIFFERENT COLORED CORN HUSK WRAPPERS AND BANANA LEAVES AND PRESENT THE MULTIHUED PACKAGES UNWRAPPED AT THE TABLE. HOWEVER, IT CAN BE HARD TO FIND THE BRILLIANT RED CORN HUSKS, AND FOR THE SAKE OF SIMPLICITY, THE RECIPE BELOW OPTS JUST FOR THE REGULAR DRIED CORN HUSKS. "SIMPLY ELEGANT" IS HOW I WOULD DESCRIBE THESE VERSATILE TAMALES, WHICH CAN BE SERVED BUFFET OR HORS D'OEUVRE STYLE OR AS SATISFYING APPETIZERS.

FOR THE VEAL FILLING

1/4 cup olive oil
1 large veal shank
Salt and freshly ground black pepper
1 cup flour
2 carrots, sliced
2 stalks celery, sliced
1 small onion, chopped
1 teaspoon dried thyme leaves
1 bay leaf

FOR THE BASIL-ARUGULA FILLING

1 bunch arugula, cut into thin strips
    (about 1 1/2 cups)
6 large fresh basil leaves, cut into thin strips
1/2 cup seeded and chopped tomato
1 large clove garlic, minced
2 tablespoons extra-virgin olive oil
1 tablespoon balsamic vinegar
1/2 teaspoon salt
1/2 teaspoon freshly ground black pepper

FOR THE TAMALES

Masa Seca Tamale Dough (page 2)
6 large dried corn husks, soaked in warm water
    for 30 minutes
Extra-virgin olive oil, for brushing

Preheat the oven to 375°F. To prepare the veal, heat the olive oil in an ovenproof casserole or large dish. Season the veal shank with salt and pepper to taste and dredge in the flour. Sear the veal in the casserole over high heat until browned, about 6 minutes on each side. Add the carrots, celery, onion, thyme, and bay leaf to the pan and add enough water to cover the veal halfway. Cover the casserole with a lid or foil and transfer to the oven. Cook for 1 1/2 hours, until the veal meat falls off the bone. Remove the veal shank from the casserole and let cool (use the vegetables and liquid for soup or stock). When cool enough, shred the meat and set aside.

Place all the filling ingredients in a mixing bowl, add the shredded veal, and combine thoroughly.

Prepare the masa dough.

Drain the corn husks and shake dry. Lay out the husks on a flat work surface. Brush the inside of each husk with the olive oil, then divide the masa dough evenly among them. Evenly spread out the masa, leaving about 1 1/2 inches of exposed corn husk at each end and 3/4 inch at each side. Top each portion of the dough with the filling mixture and spread out evenly. Bring the sides of the corn husk together tightly around the dough; tuck one side of the husk under the other and then fold the ends over to form a neat envelope package. Repeat for the remaining tamales.

Fill the bottom of a steamer or saucepan fitted with a strainer or vegetable basket with 2 to 3 inches of water. Bring the water to a boil and place the tamales in the steamer. Cover tightly with a lid or foil (it is important that little or no steam escapes while cooking). Steam the tamales for about 30 minutes over lightly boiling water, adding more boiling water as needed. The tamales are done when they feel firm to the touch but are not hard and the dough comes away easily from the husk. Let rest for at least 5 minutes before serving.

Unwrap each tamale and, leaving the dough lying on the husks, place in the center of each serving plate.

SERVES 6

Beef Wellington Tamales with Chanterelles and Madeira Sauce

(J O H N  S E D L A R)

BEEF WELLINGTON IS A TRUE CELEBRATORY DISH—FILET MIGNON SMOTHERED IN FOIE GRAS AND/OR SEASONED MUSHROOMS AND THEN BAKED INSIDE PASTRY. TRADITIONALLY, IT IS A DISH FOR SPECIAL OCCASIONS WHEN NOTHING LESS THAN A GRAND CULINARY TASTE TREAT OF THE HIGHEST SPECIFICATIONS IS CALLED FOR. THE PROBLEM WITH BEEF WELLINGTON, HOWEVER, IS THAT, UNLESS IT IS PREPARED BY EXPERT HANDS, THE CRUST UNDER THE FILET IS INVARIABLY DOUGHY AND MUSHY. BY ADAPTING THE RECIPE TO THE EASIER TAMALE FORMAT AND MATCHING THE INGREDIENTS WITH THE EARTHINESS OF THE MUSHROOM MASA, IT REALLY DOES BECOME MORE APPROACHABLE, LIGHTER, AND ALMOST AN "EVERYDAY" DISH.

FOR THE TAMALES
Mushroom Tamale Dough (page 12)
6 large dried corn husks, soaked in warm water
*   for 30 minutes*
Olive oil, for brushing

FOR THE MADEIRA SAUCE
3 cups Veal Stock (page 161)
2 cups Madeira wine
3 tablespoons unsalted butter, softened
Salt and freshly ground white pepper

FOR THE FILET MIGNON
6 medallions filet mignon, 5 ounces each
Salt and freshly ground black pepper
2 tablespoons clarified unsalted butter

FOR THE GARNISH
2 tablespoons unsalted butter, softened
1 pound chanterelle mushrooms, thinly sliced
Salt and freshly ground white pepper
1 can (6 ounces) foie gras with truffle, cut into
*   6 even slices and held at room temperature*
6 sprigs watercress

Prepare the tamale dough.

Drain the corn husks and shake dry. Lay out the husks on a flat work surface. Brush the inside of each husk with the olive oil, then divide the tamale dough evenly among them. Evenly spread it out, leaving about 1 1/2 inches of exposed corn husk at each end and 3/4 inch at each side. Bring the sides of the corn husk together tightly around the dough; tuck one side of the husk under the other and fold the ends over to form a neat envelope package. Repeat for the remaining tamales.

Fill the bottom of a steamer or saucepan fitted with a strainer or vegetable basket with 2 to 3 inches of water. Bring the water to a boil and place the tamales in the steamer. Cover tightly with a lid or foil. Steam the tamales for about 45 minutes over lightly boiling water, adding more boiling water as needed. The tamales are done when they feel firm to the touch but are not hard and the dough comes away easily from the husk.

Meanwhile, combine the stock and Madeira in a saucepan and bring to a boil. Turn down the heat to a simmer and reduce the liquid by half. Add the butter 1 tablespoon at a time and stir until melted. Season the sauce with salt and white pepper to taste. Keep warm.

Preheat the oven to 400°F. Season the filet mignon with salt and pepper to taste. Heat the clarified butter in a cast-iron skillet or oven-proof sauté pan. Add the steaks and sear on one side over medium heat for about 1 1/2 minutes. Turn and sear on the other side for about 1 minute. Transfer the pan to the oven and cook for about 6 minutes for medium rare. Remove from the oven, drain the fat from the pan, and keep warm.

Heat the butter in a sauté pan. Add the mushrooms and cook over medium-high heat until tender, about 5 minutes. Lightly season with salt and white pepper to taste.

Unwrap each tamale and place in the center of each serving plate. Lean the filets against the tamales, then sprinkle the tamales with the mushrooms. Top the tamales with a portion of the foie gras, spoon the sauce over all, and garnish with the watercress.

SERVES 6

Pork *Carnitas* Tamales with Manchamantel Sauce

(M A R K   M I L L E R)

CARNITAS, OR SMALL PIECES OF REFRIED SEASONED PORK, GIVE THESE TAMALES A FLAVOR-INTENSE FILLING THAT IS PERFECTLY MATCHED BY THE SWEET AND HOT MANCHAMANTEL SAUCE. *CARNITAS* ALSO MAKE A WONDERFUL FILLING FOR BURRITOS, TACOS, AND RAVIOLIS, AND EVEN PIZZA. IT'S IMPORTANT TO USE PORK BUTT FOR THE *CARNITAS* RATHER THAN PORK LOIN, FOR EXAMPLE, WHICH WOULD DRY OUT TOO MUCH DURING THE COOKING PROCESS. *MANCHAMANTEL* TRANSLATES AS "TABLECLOTH STAINER," AND IT'S A CLASSIC SAUCE FROM CENTRAL MEXICO THAT I LOVE TO PAIR WITH PORK BECAUSE OF ITS FRUITINESS. IF YOU DON'T HAVE AN OVERRIPE BANANA ON HAND, YOU CAN DEVELOP THE FLAVORS OF A YELLOW BANANA BY ROASTING IT IN ITS SKIN IN A 400°F OVEN FOR 15 MINUTES. YOU CAN SUBSTITUTE OTHER RIPE FRUIT, SUCH AS PEACHES OR APRICOTS, FOR THE PINEAPPLE OR BANANA.

$1^1/_4$ *pounds pork butt, cut into* $^1/_2$*-inch dice*
4 cups water
$^1/_2$ *teaspoon ground allspice*
1 teaspoon anise seeds
1 teaspoon cayenne powder
1 tablespoon salt
2 teaspoons freshly ground black pepper
2 canned chipotle chiles in adobo sauce, chopped
3 cloves garlic, minced
Roasted Corn Tamale Masa Dough (page 2)
10 large dried corn husks, soaked in warm water
*   for 30 minutes*
One recipe Manchamantel Sauce (page 163)

Place all the *carnitas* ingredients except the dough and corn husks in a large heavy-bottomed, high-sided saucepan and cook slowly over medium-low heat for about 1 hour, until the pork is very tender and the liquid has almost evaporated. The fat of the pork will be liquefied. Transfer the cooked-off fat to a sauté pan and fry the cooked pork and spices, while stirring, over medium-high heat for 5 to 7 minutes, until browned. Set aside and let cool.

Prepare the masa dough.

Drain the corn husks and shake dry. Tear 16 thin strips (about $^1/_8$ inch wide) from 2 of the husks and set aside for tying the tamales. Lay out the remaining 8 corn husks on a flat work surface. Take a 2-ounce ($^1/_4$-cup) portion of masa dough and, using a tortilla press or heavy pan, flatten to a thickness of about $^1/_4$ inch. Place the masa dough inside each husk, leaving about $1^1/_2$ inches of exposed corn husk at each end and $^3/_4$ inch at each side. Spread about 2 heaping tablespoons of the pork *carnitas* on top of the masa. Bring the sides of the corn husk together, folding the dough; tuck one side of the husk under the other and roll up the tamale so the dough is completely enclosed inside the husk. Twist each end and tie with the reserved strips of corn husk. Repeat for the remaining tamales.

Fill the bottom of a steamer or saucepan fitted with a strainer or vegetable basket with 2 to 3 inches of water. Bring the water to a boil and place the tamales in the steamer. Cover tightly with a lid or foil (it is important that little or no steam escapes while cooking). Steam the tamales for 30 to 35 minutes over lightly boiling water, adding more boiling water as needed. The tamales are done when they feel firm to the touch but are not hard and the dough comes away easily from the husk. Let rest for at least 5 minutes before serving.

While the tamales are steaming, prepare the Manchamantel sauce. Ladle the sauce onto serving plates and place the tamales on top of the sauce. With a knife, slice open the top of the tamale wrappers from end to end.

SERVES 8

Carnitas Tamales with Pineapple and Tomato-Habanero Sauce

(M A R K   M I L L E R)

THESE TAMALES ARE INSPIRED BY THE TROPICAL CUISINE OF MEXICO'S YUCATÁN PENINSULA, WHICH FEATURES PLANTAINS, PINEAPPLE, AND THE FIERY
HABANERO, THE HOTTEST CHILE OF THEM ALL. THE FLAVOR COMBINATION IS SIMILAR TO A SPECIALTY OF THE BIG FOOD MARKET IN MÉRIDA—COCHINITA
PIBIL—SUCKLING PIG COOKED IN A SPICY PIBIL SAUCE, SERVED IN TACOS WITH HABANERO SALSA. PLANTAINS ARE STARCHY MEMBERS OF THE BANANA
FAMILY THAT ARE USED AS A STAPLE VEGETABLE IN MUCH OF CENTRAL AND SOUTH AMERICA. THEY ARE HARD TO PEEL; THE BEST METHOD IS TO CUT
BOTH ENDS OFF THE PLANTAIN AND MAKE 4 OR 5 LENGTHWISE SCORES THROUGH THE SKIN WITH A KNIFE. LET IT SOAK IN A BOWL OF SALTED WATER FOR
10 MINUTES OR SO AND THEN RUN YOUR FINGERS UNDER THE SKIN TO PEEL. FOR BEST RESULTS, SLICE THE PLANTAINS ON A MANDOLINE SLICER.

Pork carnitas (see Pork Carnitas Tamales
　with Manchamantel Sauce, page 117)
$1/4$ fresh pineapple, peeled, cored,
　and sliced into $1/2$-inch rings (about 3 rings)
1 tablespoon chopped cilantro
$1/2$ cup pickled pearl onions
Habanero–Blackened Tomato Tamale Masa
　Dough (page 13)
10 large dried corn husks, soaked in warm water
　for 30 minutes

FOR THE TOMATO-HABANERO SAUCE

3 habanero chiles
6 Roma tomatoes
1 large clove garlic
1 teaspoon salt
Juice of 1 lime

Prepare the *carnitas* and transfer to a mixing bowl. Heat a dry cast-iron skillet and dry-sauté the pineapple slices over medium heat for about 8 minutes per side, until caramelized and golden brown. Dice the pineapple and add to the pork together with the cilantro and pearl onions and mix well.

Prepare the masa dough.

Drain the corn husks and shake dry. Tear 16 thin strips (about $1/8$ inch wide) from 2 of the husks and set aside for tying the tamales. Lay out the remaining 8 corn husks on a flat work surface. Take a 2-ounce ($1/4$-cup) portion of masa dough and, using a tortilla press or heavy pan, flatten to a thickness of about $1/4$ inch. Place the masa dough inside each husk, leaving about $1^1/2$ inches of exposed corn husk at each end and $3/4$ inch at each side. Spread about 2 heaping tablespoons of the *carnitas* mixture on top of the masa. Bring the sides of the corn husk together, folding the dough; tuck one side of the husk under the other and roll up the tamale so the dough is completely enclosed inside the husk. Twist each end and tie with the reserved strips of corn husk. Repeat for the remaining tamales.

Fill the bottom of a steamer or saucepan fitted with a strainer or vegetable basket with 2 to 3 inches of water. Bring the water to a boil and place the tamales in the steamer. Cover tightly with a lid or foil (it is important that little or no steam escapes while cooking). Steam the tamales for 30 to 35 minutes over lightly boiling water, adding more boiling water as needed. The tamales are done when they feel firm to the touch but are not hard and the dough comes away easily from the husk. Let rest for at least 5 minutes before serving.

While the tamales are steaming, prepare the sauce. Heat a dry cast-iron skillet and, when hot, add the habaneros, tomatoes, and garlic. Blacken over medium heat, turning frequently, for 25 to 30 minutes. Place the salt in a mortar (or on a cutting board), add the habaneros and garlic, and mash with a pestle

(continues)

FOR THE PLANTAINS

4 cups vegetable oil

*2 green plantains, peeled and finely sliced
lengthwise*

Salt and pure red chile powder

(or with the flat side of a large knife if using the board) to form a puree. Dice the tomatoes and put through a food mill or pulse in a food processor to form a rough puree. Transfer to a mixing bowl, add the mashed habanero mixture and the lime juice and thoroughly combine.

To prepare the plantains, heat the oil in a deep fryer to 350°F. Add the plantain slices one at a time (fry in 2 batches). Deep-fry for 3 to 4 minutes, until golden brown. Remove with tongs, drain on paper towels, and season with salt and chile powder to taste.

Ladle the sauce onto serving plates and place the tamales on top of the sauce. With a knife, slice open the top of the tamale wrappers from end to end. Garnish with the plantain slices.

SERVES 8

Lamb Tamales with Mint, Black Beans, and Blackened Tomato and Mint Salsa

(M A R K   M I L L E R)

THESE TAMALES COMBINE THE FLAVORS OF NATIVE AMERICAN COOKING WITH THOSE FROM MEXICO. LAMB AND MINT ARE NATURAL PARTNERS, OF COURSE, AS ARE MINT AND BLACK BEANS, AND THE FRUIT AND MINT IN THE SALSA DRAW THE WHOLE DISH TOGETHER. LAMB IS RARELY SERVED WITH BLACK BEANS—IT'S NOT A MARRIAGE THAT AUTOMATICALLY COMES TO MIND—BUT THEIR FLAVORS AND TEXTURES WORK TOGETHER WELL IN THIS RECIPE.

2 tablespoons olive oil

1 1/4 pounds lamb shoulder, diced

Salt and freshly ground black pepper

1/2 cup sliced onion

2 cloves garlic, minced

1 bay leaf

1/2 teaspoon dried thyme

1 dried chile de arbol or chipotle, minced

Black Bean–Mint Tamale Masa Dough
(page 13)

10 large dried corn husks, soaked in warm water
for 30 minutes

FOR THE BLACKENED TOMATO AND MINT SALSA

6 Roma tomatoes, blackened (page 164)

1 small serrano chile, blackened and finely minced
(page 164)

1 small orange, peeled, seeded, and sectioned

2 tablespoons finely minced fresh mint

2 teaspoons extra-virgin olive oil

1 tablespoon freshly squeezed orange juice

2 teaspoons minced orange zest

1/4 teaspoon salt

To prepare the filling, heat the olive oil in a large saucepan. Season the lamb with salt and pepper and sear over high heat for 5 minutes, stirring frequently. Add the onion, garlic, bay leaf, thyme, and chile; stir together well; and cook for 2 or 3 minutes. Deglaze the pan with enough water to cover the lamb, turn down the heat to a simmer, and cook gently, uncovered, for 1 1/2 hours, until the liquid is almost evaporated; add a little more water as necessary.

Remove the vegetables and transfer the cooked-off fat to a sauté pan. Fry the cooked lamb, while stirring, over medium-high heat for 5 to 7 minutes, until browned. Set aside and let cool.

Prepare the masa dough.

Drain the corn husks and shake dry. Tear 16 thin strips (about 1/8 inch wide) from 2 of the husks and set aside for tying the tamales. Lay out the remaining 8 corn husks on a flat work surface. Take a 2-ounce (1/4-cup) portion of masa dough and, using a tortilla press or heavy pan, flatten to a thickness of about 1/4 inch. Place the masa dough inside each husk, leaving about 1 1/2 inches of exposed corn husk at each end and 3/4 inch at each side. Spread about 2 heaping tablespoons of the lamb fill-

ing on top of the masa. Bring the sides of the corn husk together, folding the dough; tuck one side of the husk under the other and roll up the tamale so the dough is completely enclosed inside the husk. Twist each end and tie with the reserved strips of corn husk. Repeat for the remaining tamales.

Fill the bottom of a steamer or saucepan fitted with a strainer or vegetable basket with 2 to 3 inches of water. Bring the water to a boil and place the tamales in the steamer. Cover tightly with a lid or foil (it is important that little or no steam escapes while cooking). Steam the tamales for 30 to 35 minutes over lightly boiling water, adding more boiling water as needed. The tamales are done when they feel firm to the touch but are not hard and the dough comes away easily from the husk. Let rest for at least 5 minutes before serving.

While the tamales are steaming, prepare the salsa. Cut the tomatoes in half, remove the seeds, and dice the flesh. Transfer to a mixing bowl and add the remaining salsa ingredients.

Transfer the steamed tamales to serving plates and, with a knife, slice open the top of the tamale wrappers from end to end. Serve with the salsa.

SERVES 8

Lamb *Adobado* Tamales with Eggplant–Black Olive Ragout

(S T E P H  N   P Y L E S)

ADOBO AND *ADOBADO* COOKING TERMS DERIVED FROM THE SPANISH VERB *ADOBAR*, WHICH MEANS TO MARINATE OR SEASON. IN MEXICAN AND SOUTHWESTERN COOKING, IT REFERS TO A PASTE OR THICK STEW MADE FROM GROUND CHILES, HERBS, SPICES, AND VINEGAR (THE SPANISH ALSO INTRODUCED THIS SAUCE TO THE PHILIPPINES, WHERE IT REMAINS A COMMON FEATURE OF THE CUISINE). ADOBO SAUCE IS TYPICALLY USED FOR PICKLING MEAT, FISH, AND, ESPECIALLY IN THE CASE OF THE DRIED CHIPOTLE, CHILES. I ADD ORANGE JUICE TO ADD A SUBTLE FRUITY SWEETNESS TO THE MARINADE.

Masa Seca Tamale Dough (page 2)

FOR THE ADOBO SAUCE

$^1/_2$ cup ancho chile puree (page 165)
2 serrano chiles, halved
6 cloves garlic, minced
$1^1/_2$ cups Chicken Stock (page 160)
$^1/_2$ onion, chopped
2 teaspoons sugar
$^1/_4$ cup red wine vinegar
$^1/_2$ cup freshly squeezed orange juice
1 tablespoon freshly squeezed lime juice
$^1/_2$ teaspoon ground cumin
$^1/_2$ teaspoon chopped fresh thyme
1 teaspoon chopped fresh oregano
2 bay leaves
Salt

FOR THE LAMB FILLING

1 pound boned lamb shoulder
Salt
1 tablespoon olive oil
1 carrot, chopped
1 stalk celery, chopped
1 onion, chopped

Prepare the masa dough.

To prepare the adobo sauce, place the ancho puree, serranos, garlic, stock, onion, sugar, vinegar, citrus juices, cumin, thyme, and oregano in a blender and blend together until smooth. Strain through a medium sieve into a saucepan and add the bay leaves. Bring just to a boil, season with salt to taste, and remove from the heat (do not overseason, as the liquid will be reduced later).

Preheat the oven to 350°F.

To prepare the filling, thoroughly season the lamb shoulder with salt. In a large ovenproof casserole with a lid, add the olive oil and heat on the stovetop until lightly smoking. Add the lamb shoulder and sear over high heat until golden brown, about 3 minutes on each side. Add the carrot, celery, onion, jalapeños, garlic, and tomato and sauté for about 5 minutes, until the onion becomes translucent. Add the wine and deglaze the pan. Add the peppercorns and cumin. Reduce the liquid until it becomes syrupy. Add the chicken stock and bring to a rapid boil. Cover the casserole dish with a lid and transfer to the oven.

Roast the lamb in the oven for $2^1/_2$ to 3 hours. The lamb is done when the meat pulls apart easily. Remove the meat from the liquid, reserving the liquid, and let cool. Shred the lamb with your fingers and reserve.

Strain the liquid through a fine mesh strainer into the saucepan with the adobo sauce and bring to a boil. Turn down the heat to a simmer and cook until the sauce is thick enough to coat the back of a spoon, about 15 minutes. Strain through a fine sieve into a mixing bowl; add the lamb meat and season with salt.

Prepare the tamale wrappers. Drain the corn husks and shake dry. Tear 16 thin strips (about $^1/_8$ inch wide) from 2 of the husks and set aside for tying the tamales. Lay out the remaining 8 corn husks on a flat work surface. Divide the dough into 8 even portions and place 1 portion on each husk. Evenly spread out the masa, leaving about $1^1/_2$ inches of exposed corn husk at each end and $^3/_4$ inch at each side. Place the lamb mixture in the center of the masa and spread it out evenly. Bring the

(continues)

2 jalapeño chiles, seeded and chopped

3 cloves garlic, chopped

1 large ripe tomato, chopped

$1/2$ cup red wine

4 black peppercorns

$1/2$ tablespoon ground cumin

6 cups *Chicken Stock (page 160)*

FOR THE TAMALES

10 large dried corn husks, soaked in warm water
for 30 minutes

FOR THE EGGPLANT–BLACK OLIVE
RAGOUT

4 tablespoons olive oil

$1/2$ cup peeled and diced eggplant

Salt

$1/2$ cup diced onion

$1/2$ cup diced zucchini

5 tomatoes, blanched, peeled, seeded, and diced

2 tablespoons finely minced garlic

1 tablespoon chopped fresh thyme

1 tablespoon chopped fresh oregano

2 tablespoons tomato paste

2 tablespoons chopped fresh basil

1 tablespoon chopped fresh parsley

1 cup black olives, pitted and chopped

Freshly ground black pepper

$1/2$ cup finely sliced jicama, for garnish

$1/2$ cup finely sliced radish, for garnish

1 tablespoon chopped cilantro

2 tablespoons freshly squeezed lime juice

sides of the corn husks together, folding the dough; tuck one side of the husk under the other and roll up the tamales so that the dough is completely enclosed inside the husk. Twist each end and tie with the reserved strips of corn husk.

Fill the bottom of a steamer or saucepan fitted with a strainer or vegetable basket with 2 to 3 inches of water. Bring the water to a boil and place the tamales in the steamer. Cover tightly with a lid or foil (it is important that little or no steam escapes while cooking). Steam the tamales for 30 to 35 minutes over lightly boiling water, adding more boiling water as needed. The tamales are done when the dough comes away easily from the husk. Let rest for at least 5 minutes before serving.

While the tamales are steaming, prepare the ragout. Heat 2 tablespoons of the olive oil in a large skillet until lightly smoking. Add the eggplant, salt lightly, and sauté over medium-high heat for 5 minutes, until translucent, stirring frequently. Transfer the eggplant to a colander and weight with a plate to extract the bitter juices. In the same skillet, heat the remaining 2 tablespoons olive oil until lightly smoking. Add the onion and zucchini and sauté for 2 minutes. Add the tomatoes, garlic, thyme, oregano, and tomato paste. Cook until the liquid has evaporated, 10 to 15 minutes. Add the basil, parsley, and drained eggplant and continue cooking for 2 minutes. Add the chopped olives and season with salt and pepper to taste. Keep warm.

In a mixing bowl, combine the jicama, radish, cilantro, and lime juice and season with salt to taste. Place the tamales on serving plates and, with a knife, slice open the top of the wrappers from end to end. Gently push the ends together, as for a baked potato. Serve with the ragout and sprinkle the jicama-radish garnish over the tamales and around the plate.

SERVES 8

Greek Tamales with Lamb and Feta Cheese

(J O H N   S E D L A R)

THE FLAVORS OF THE GREEK PALATE HAVEN'T CHANGED OVER THE CENTURIES, AND THE CUISINE IS ONE OF MY FAVORITES. OLIVES, FETA, AND LAMB ARE A CLASSIC COMBINATION, AND THEY BLEND WONDERFULLY WITH THE CORN MASA DOUGH IN THESE TAMALES. THIS IS THE ONLY TAMALE IN THE BOOK WRAPPED IN GRAPE LEAVES, AND ALSO THE ONLY ONE WHOSE WRAPPER IS EDIBLE. USING GRAPE LEAVES TO ENCLOSE FOODS IS A TRADITION IN GREEK CUISINE—DOLMAS ARE A GOOD EXAMPLE—AND THE LEAVES ARE AVAILABLE IN SPECIALTY STORES OR MIDDLE EASTERN MARKETS.

FOR THE LAMB FILLING

3 lamb shanks, about 1 1/4 pounds each
1 cup flour
Salt and freshly ground black pepper
1 tablespoon olive oil
1/2 cup chopped carrot
1/2 cup chopped celery
1/2 cup chopped onion
2 bay leaves
2 sprigs fresh thyme
2 cups water
1 pound feta cheese, drained and crumbled
1 cup pitted and coarsely chopped kalamata olives

FOR THE TAMALES

Masa Seca Tamale Dough (page 2)
12 large grape leaves, washed

FOR THE BASIL–PINE NUT SAUCE

4 ounces fresh basil leaves, chopped
1/2 cup pine nuts
1 1/2 cups Veal Stock (page 161)
1/4 cup freshly squeezed lime juice
1 cup olive oil
12 pitted black kalamata olives, for garnish
2 tablespoons oregano leaves, for garnish

Preheat the oven to 350°F. To prepare the lamb, dust the shanks with the flour and season with salt and pepper to taste. Heat the olive oil in a large ovenproof skillet. Add the lamb shanks and sear on all sides over high heat until brown, about 5 minutes on each side. Add the carrot, celery, onion, bay leaves, and thyme and cook for 10 minutes longer. Add the water and bring to a boil. Turn off the heat, cover the pan tightly with a lid or foil, and transfer to the oven. Cook for 1 1/2 hours, until the meat falls off the bone. Let cool; discard the vegetables or use for soup. Shred the meat with your fingers, roughly chop into 1-inch lengths, and place in a mixing bowl. Add all but 3 tablespoons of the feta cheese and all the chopped olives to the lamb and toss to mix well. Season with pepper to taste and set aside.

Prepare the masa dough.

Lay out 2 grape leaves on a flat work surface, overlapping each other and forming a rectangular shape. Repeat for the remaining grape leaves. Divide the masa dough evenly among the 6 wrappers. Evenly spread out the masa, leaving about 1 1/2 inches of exposed grape leaf at each end and 3/4 inch at each side. Top each portion of the dough with the lamb mixture and spread out evenly. Bring the sides of

the grape leaves together tightly around the dough; tuck one side of the leaf under the other and fold the ends over to form a neat envelope package. Repeat for the remaining tamales.

Fill the bottom of a steamer or saucepan fitted with a strainer or vegetable basket with 2 to 3 inches of water. Bring the water to a boil and place the tamales in the steamer. Cover tightly with a lid or foil. Steam the tamales for about 45 minutes over lightly boiling water, adding more boiling water as needed. The tamales are done when they feel firm to the touch but are not hard and the dough comes away easily from the husk. Let rest for at least 5 minutes before serving.

While the tamales are steaming, prepare the sauce. Combine the basil, pine nuts, stock, and lime juice in a blender or food processor and puree. With the machine running, add the olive oil a few drops at a time until incorporated; then add the oil in a thin but steady stream until thoroughly combined.

Place the tamales in the center of large shallow serving bowls and spoon the sauce over the top. Sprinkle the remaining 3 tablespoons of feta cheese over the tamales and garnish with the olives and oregano leaves.

SERVES 6

Venison Chorizo Tamales with Cranberry-Chipotle Salsa

(STEPHAN PYLES)

CHORIZO, THE PICANTE MEXICAN SAUSAGE FOUND IN LATIN MARKETS EVERYWHERE, IS TYPICALLY MADE WITH PORK. I THINK VENISON IS THE

PERFECT SUBSTITUTE—AND ACTUALLY AN IMPROVEMENT—BECAUSE IT WORKS WELL WITH THE FRAGRANT SPICES THAT MAKE CHORIZO SO SPECIAL.

THE TART, SPICY, AND SMOKY-FLAVORED SALSA MAKES THIS A CONSUMMATE FALL HOLIDAY DISH.

Masa Seca Tamale Dough (page 2)

FOR THE CRANBERRY-CHIPOTLE SALSA

2 large oranges
1 cup sugar
1 pound cranberries
1 tablespoon chipotle puree (page 165)
$^1/_2$ cup toasted pecans (page 165)
1 tablespoon chopped fresh mint
2 tablespoons Triple Sec

FOR THE FILLING AND TAMALES

$^1/_4$ cup vegetable shortening
1 small onion, finely diced
1 clove garlic, minced
8 ounces ground venison
$^3/_4$ teaspoon salt
$^1/_4$ teaspoon freshly ground black pepper
$1^1/_2$ teaspoons white wine vinegar
$1^1/_2$ teaspoons pure red chile powder
$^1/_2$ teaspoon sweet paprika
Pinch of cayenne powder
Pinch of ground cinnamon
Pinch of ground cumin
Pinch of ground cloves
10 large dried corn husks, soaked in warm water
*   for 30 minutes*

Prepare the masa dough.

To prepare the salsa, zest 1 orange, mince the zest, and set aside. Juice both oranges, place the juice in a saucepan, add the sugar, and bring to a boil. Add the cranberries, reserved orange zest, and chipotle puree, turn down the heat, and simmer for about 5 minutes, until the cranberries burst their skins. Remove from the heat and stir in the pecans, mint, and Triple Sec. Set aside, and reheat just before you are ready to serve.

To prepare the filling, heat the shortening in a sauté pan until just smoking. Add the onion and garlic and sauté over medium-high heat for about 3 minutes, until they turn translucent. Add the venison and cook for 5 minutes, stirring frequently and crumbling with a fork. Add the remaining filling ingredients and cook for 5 minutes, continuing to stir and crumble. Season with additional salt to taste and remove from the heat. Allow the chorizo to cool to room temperature. When cool, combine the chorizo and the masa dough in a large mixing bowl.

Drain the corn husks and shake dry. Tear 16 thin strips (about $^1/_8$ inch wide) from 2 of the husks and set aside for tying the tamales. Lay out the remaining 8 corn husks on a flat work surface. Divide the dough into 8 even portions and place 1 portion on each husk. Evenly spread out the masa dough, leaving about $1^1/_2$ inches of exposed corn husk at each end and $^3/_4$ inch at each side. Bring the sides of the corn husks together, folding the dough; tuck one side of the husk under the other and roll up the tamales so that the dough is completely enclosed inside the husk. Twist each end and tie with the reserved strips of corn husk.

Fill the bottom of a steamer or saucepan fitted with a strainer or vegetable basket with 2 to 3 inches of water. Bring the water to a boil and place the tamales in the steamer. Cover tightly with a lid or foil. Steam the tamales for 30 to 35 minutes over lightly boiling water, adding more boiling water as needed. The tamales are done when they feel firm to the touch but are not hard and the dough comes away easily from the husk. Let rest for at least 5 minutes before serving.

Place the tamales on serving plates and, with a knife, slice open the top of the wrappers from end to end. Gently push the ends together, as for a baked potato. Spoon some of the salsa over each tamale and pass the remainder separately in a sauceboat.

SERVES 8

Red Chile Rabbit Tamales in Green Chile–Posole Broth

(S T E P H A N   P Y L E S)

WHEN I WAS GROWING UP IN BIG SPRING, IN WEST TEXAS, A DISHWASHER NAMED YOLANDA WORKED AT ONE OF MY FATHER'S CAFES. EVERY SATURDAY, YOLANDA WOULD BRING FRESHLY STEAMED TAMALES FROM HER KITCHEN TO WORK WITH HER TO SHARE WITH THE ENTIRE STAFF. THE TAMALES WERE DIFFERENT EACH WEEK, AND SINCE HER HUSBAND LIKED TO HUNT JACKRABBITS, SHE WOULD OCCASIONALLY BRING THE MOST EXTRAORDINARY, SPICY RABBIT TAMALES. THE WILD JACKRABBITS OF WEST TEXAS AND NEW MEXICO HAVE A MUCH DARKER MEAT THAN THE DOMESTIC ONES THAT ARE MOST READILY AVAILABLE TODAY, BUT THE FLAVOR IS SIMILAR. OF COURSE, CHICKEN CAN BE SUBSTITUTED. POSOLE ORIGINATED IN THE MEXICAN STATE OF JALISCO AND IS USUALLY A THICK AND HEARTY STEW OF PORK AND HOMINY. IN THIS RECIPE, THE POSOLE IS SERVED AS A BROTH SCENTED WITH GARLIC AND CUMIN AND STUDDED WITH ROASTED GREEN CHILES.

FOR THE RABBIT AND MASA DOUGH

1 rabbit, about 3 pounds, cut into 8 pieces
Salt
1 cup red wine
1/2 cup Chicken Stock (page 160)
8 sprigs fresh thyme
1 tablespoon chopped fresh oregano
8 cloves garlic, coarsely chopped
Red Chile–Cilantro Tamale Masa Dough
    (page 13)

FOR THE GREEN CHILE–POSOLE BROTH

8 cups Chicken Stock (page 160)
1/2 cup posole, soaked in water overnight
1 tablespoon olive oil
1 onion, julienned
2 cloves garlic, minced
1/3 cup white wine
1/2 teaspoon ground cumin

Preheat the oven to 350°F. Generously season the rabbit with salt. Place the wine, stock, thyme, oregano, and garlic in a large ovenproof casserole or pan. Add the rabbit, cover, and roast in the oven for 45 minutes. Remove the rabbit, let cool, and then shred the meat with your fingers. Set aside.

Prepare the masa dough.

To prepare the broth, pour 4 cups of the stock into a saucepan and bring to a boil. Drain the posole, add to the stock, and turn down the heat to a simmer. Cook until the posole is tender, about 2 hours, adding more stock as needed to keep the posole covered. Meanwhile, in a separate pan, heat the olive oil over high heat until just smoking. Turn down the heat to medium high, add the onion, and sauté for 2 minutes, until it begins to soften. Add the garlic and cook for 1 minute longer. Add the wine, deglaze the pan, and cook for 1 minute until syrupy. Add the

remaining stock, cumin, and poblanos and bring to a boil. Reduce the heat and simmer for 10 minutes. Add the tomatoes to the pan with the cooked posole, add the cilantro, and season with salt to taste.

While the broth is cooking, drain the corn husks and shake dry. Tear 16 thin strips (about 1/8 inch wide) from 2 of the husks and set aside for tying the tamales. Lay out the remaining 8 corn husks on a flat work surface. Divide the dough into 8 even portions and place 1 portion on each husk. Evenly spread out the masa mixture, leaving about 1 1/2 inches of exposed corn husk at each end and 3/4 inch at each side. Place 2 to 3 tablespoons of the reserved shredded rabbit in the center. Bring the sides of the corn husks together, folding the dough; tuck one side of the husk under the other and roll up the tamales so that the dough is completely enclosed inside the husk.

(continues)

2 poblano chiles, roasted, peeled, seeded,
   and julienned (page 164)
2 Roma tomatoes, outer flesh only with skin,
   julienned
1/2 cup cilantro leaves
Salt
10 large dried corn husks, soaked in warm water
   for 30 minutes

Twist each end and tie with the reserved strips of corn husk.

Fill the bottom of a steamer or saucepan fitted with a strainer or vegetable basket with 2 to 3 inches of water. Bring the water to a boil and place the tamales in the steamer. Cover tightly with a lid or foil (it is important that little or no steam escapes while cooking). Steam the tamales for 30 to 35 minutes over lightly boiling water, adding more boiling water as needed. The tamales are done when they feel firm to the touch but are not hard and the dough comes away easily from the husk. Let rest for at least 5 minutes before serving.

Place the tamales in decorative serving bowls and, with a knife, slice open the top of the wrappers from end to end. Gently push the ends together, as for a baked potato, and ladle the broth into the bowls.

SERVES 8

Blue Corn Rabbit Tamales with Sage and Salsa Verde

(M A R K   M I L L E R)

STORE-BOUGHT RABBIT IS EXCLUSIVELY FARM-RAISED—THESE DAYS, WILD RABBIT IS CONSIDERED RISKY BECAUSE OF ENDEMIC DISEASES, SO HUNTING FOR RABBIT IS A THING OF THE PAST. RABBIT HAS A MILD AND DELICATE FLAVOR, SO THE CHILE IN THE FILLING, THE AROMATICALLY HERBAL QUALITY OF THE SAGE, AND THE INTENSELY FLAVORED BLUE CORN SHOWCASE THE MEAT WITHOUT OVERPOWERING IT. NOTE THAT WHEN MAKING THE BLUE CORN TAMALE DOUGH, YOU CAN SUBSTITUTE THE BRAISING LIQUID IN WHICH THE RABBIT COOKS FOR THE CHICKEN STOCK.

FOR THE FILLING

1 tablespoon unsalted butter

3 cloves garlic, minced

1 pound rabbit meat

Salt and freshly ground black pepper

1 teaspoon pure red chile powder

3 cups Chicken Stock (page 160)

1 tablespoon red pepper flakes

1/2 teaspoon ground dried oregano

1/2 cup fresh roasted corn kernels (page 164)

FOR THE TAMALES

Blue Corn Masa Seca Tamale Dough (page 8)

3/4 teaspoon ground dried sage

10 large dried corn husks, soaked in warm water for 30 minutes

FOR THE TOMATILLO SALSA

12 tomatillos (about 12 ounces), husked and rinsed

2 serrano chiles, chopped

1/2 cup chopped cilantro leaves

1 1/2 tablespoons freshly squeezed lime juice

3/4 teaspoon sugar

1/2 teaspoon salt

To prepare the filling, melt the butter in a saucepan and sauté the garlic over medium-high heat for 2 minutes. Season the rabbit with salt and pepper to taste, and the chile powder and sear in the pan for 3 to 4 minutes, stirring frequently. Add the stock, red pepper flakes, and oregano and bring to a boil. Turn down the heat to medium low and simmer for 15 minutes, until the rabbit is cooked through. Let the rabbit cool in the braising liquid (this will make it more tender). When cool enough, shred the rabbit with 2 forks or your fingers and transfer to a mixing bowl. Add the corn to the rabbit, mixing well.

Prepare the masa dough, adding the sage to the masa harina and blue cornmeal before mixing with the water.

Drain the corn husks and shake dry. Tear 16 thin strips (about 1/8 inch wide) from 2 of the husks and set aside for tying the tamales. Lay out the remaining 8 corn husks on a flat work surface. Take a 2-ounce (1/4-cup) portion of masa dough and, using a tortilla press or heavy pan, flatten to a thickness of about 1/4 inch. Place the masa dough inside each husk, leaving about 1 1/2 inches of exposed corn husk at each end and 3/4 inch at each side. Spread about 2 heaping tablespoons of the rabbit fill-ing on top of the masa. Bring the sides of the corn husk together, folding the dough; tuck one side of the husk under the other and roll up the tamale so the dough is completely enclosed inside the husk. Twist each end and tie with the reserved strips of corn husk. Repeat for the remaining tamales.

Fill the bottom of a steamer or saucepan fitted with a strainer or vegetable basket with 2 to 3 inches of water. Bring the water to a boil and place the tamales in the steamer. Cover tightly with a lid or foil (it is important that little or no steam escapes while cooking). Steam the tamales for 30 to 35 minutes over lightly boiling water, adding more boiling water as needed. The tamales are done when they feel firm to the touch but are not hard and the dough comes away easily from the husk. Let rest for at least 5 minutes before serving.

While the tamales are steaming, prepare the salsa. Blanch the tomatillos in a saucepan of boiling water for 1 minute. Remove, let cool, and chop. Transfer to a food processor or blender, add the remaining salsa ingredients, and puree. Keep refrigerated.

Place the tamales on serving plates and, with a knife, slice open the top of the wrappers from end to end. Serve with the salsa.

SERVES 8

Escargot Forestière Tamales

(J O H N   S E D L A R)

TWO RECENT DEVELOPMENTS TO NOTE REGARDING THIS CLASSIC DISH: ONE, PEOPLE ARE STARTING TO DISCOVER THE DELICIOUS *PETIT GRIS*, OR SMALL GRAY SNAILS, WHICH ARE MORE TENDER THAN THE LARGER BURGUNDY SNAILS IMPORTED FROM FRANCE. WHEN FRESH *PETIT GRIS* ARE UNAVAILABLE, HOWEVER, THE BURGUNDY VARIETY FOUND IN SMALL CANS IN GOURMET GROCERY STORES ARE STILL VERY GOOD. ANOTHER RECENT TREND IS THE GROWING DISCOVERY AND APPRECIATION OF ESCARGOT ROE, THE CAVIAR OF THE SNAIL. I DON'T USE IT IN THIS RECIPE, BUT IF YOU SEE SOME, BUY IT! IT'S WONDERFUL TO TASTE. JUST AS STURGEON CAVIAR TASTES LIKE THE ESSENCE OF THE OCEAN AND THE BRININESS OF THE SEA, SO ESCARGOT ROE IS REDOLENT OF ITS HABITAT: THE SOIL AND THE EARTHINESS OF THE FOREST AND GARDEN. IT MAKES A WONDERFULLY FRAGRANT, HERBACEOUS ACCOMPANIMENT TO ESCARGOT DISHES OR JUST SERVED AU NATUREL ON A PLAIN TAMALE.

Mushroom Tamale Dough (page 12)

6 large dried corn husks, soaked in warm water for 30 minutes

Olive oil, for brushing

$1/4$ cup unsalted butter, at room temperature

$1/2$ teaspoon salt

$1/4$ teaspoon freshly ground white pepper

$1/2$ tablespoon minced garlic

$1/2$ tablespoon minced fresh Italian parsley

1 tablespoon unsalted butter

2 tablespoons minced shallot

$1/4$ cup diced smoked Black Forest ham, or other smoked ham

2 tablespoons chopped shiitake mushrooms caps

2 tablespoons diced portobello mushrooms

2 tablespoons diced chanterelle mushrooms

2 cups dry full-bodied red wine, such as Merlot or Zinfandel

2 cups Veal Stock (page 161)

48 petit gris or Burgundy snails, washed

2 tablespoons snipped chives

3 tablespoons minced fresh Italian parsley

6 ounces thinly sliced smoked ham, julienned

6 sprigs fresh dill

Prepare the tamale dough.

Drain the corn husks and shake dry. Lay out the husks on a flat work surface. Brush the inside of each husk with the olive oil, then divide the tamale dough evenly among them. Evenly spread out the dough, leaving about $1^1/2$ inches of exposed corn husk at each end and $3/4$ inch at each side. Bring the sides of the corn husk together tightly around the dough; tuck one side of the husk under the other and then fold the ends over to form a neat envelope package. Repeat for the remaining tamales.

Fill the bottom of a steamer or saucepan fitted with a strainer or vegetable basket with 2 to 3 inches of water. Bring the water to a boil and place the tamales in the steamer. Cover tightly with a lid or foil (it is important that little or no steam escapes while cooking). Steam the tamales for about 45 minutes over lightly boiling water, adding more boiling water as needed. The tamales are done when they feel firm to the touch but are not hard and the dough comes away easily from the husk.

While the tamales are steaming, prepare the garlic butter. In a bowl, mix the butter with the salt, pepper, garlic, and parsley with a wooden spoon. Set aside.

To prepare the stew, melt the butter in a sauté pan. Add the shallot, ham, and mushrooms and sauté over medium heat until the shallot is translucent, 3 to 4 minutes. Add the red wine and stock and cook for about 5 minutes, until the liquid is reduced by about one-quarter. Add the *petit gris* and the garlic butter and stir to mix well. Continue cooking until the butter melts and the snails are heated through. Stir in the chives and parsley.

Unwrap each tamale and, leaving the dough lying on the husks, place in the center of a large pasta bowl. Spoon 8 snails and some of the stew over the top of each tamale and garnish with the ham and dill.

SERVES 6

Dessert Tamales

Arborio Rice–Dried Fruit Pudding Tamales with Rum Cream

(STEPHAN PYLES)

THESE TAMALES COMBINE CLASSIC RICE PUDDING WITH DRIED FRUIT, WHITE CHOCOLATE, AND RUM, MAKING A DELICIOUS DESSERT.

THIS IS ANOTHER RECIPE THAT CAN BE GIVEN A DRAMATIC APPEARANCE BY SOAKING THE CORN HUSKS IN HIBISCUS TEA FOR AN HOUR

OR TWO TO DYE THEM A DEEP RED (SEE PAGE XIII).

FOR THE FILLING

$1/4$ cup golden raisins

$1/2$ cup dark rum

$1/2$ cup Arborio rice

1 cup water

3 tablespoons sugar

2 large eggs, lightly beaten

1 cup heavy cream

$1/4$ cup milk

$1/2$ teaspoon pure vanilla extract

$1/2$ teaspoon ground cinnamon

$1/4$ teaspoon freshly grated nutmeg

$1/4$ cup dried cherries

$3/4$ cup grated white chocolate

FOR THE RUM CREAM

1 egg yolk

$1/4$ cup sugar

1 cup heavy cream

1 tablespoon dark rum

FOR THE TAMALES

10 large dried corn husks, soaked in warm water
for at least 30 minutes

To prepare the filling, place the raisins in a bowl with the rum and soak for 2 hours. Preheat the oven to 300°F. Place the rice, water, and 2 tablespoons of the sugar in a small saucepan and cook for 20 minutes over medium heat. Spoon the rice into a mixing bowl and add the remaining 1 tablespoon of sugar, the eggs, cream, milk, vanilla, cinnamon, nutmeg, raisins, and dried cherries. Mix thoroughly and pour the mixture into a 9-inch by 12-inch baking dish or pan. Cover with foil and bake in the oven for 20 minutes. Remove from the oven, mix thoroughly, and let cool. Stir in the white chocolate.

While the filling is cooling, make the rum cream. Beat the egg yolk and sugar together in a mixing bowl until the yolk has lightened in color. Set aside. In a small saucepan, bring the cream and rum to a boil over medium-high heat. Remove the pan from the heat and pour half into the yolk mixture while stirring. Whisking vigorously, return the saucepan to the heat. Slowly pour the egg mixture back into the saucepan, still whisking vigorously, until incorporated. Cook the mixture until it thickens and coats the back of a spoon, about 5 minutes. Strain and cool.

Drain the corn husks and shake dry. Tear 16 thin strips (about $1/8$ inch wide) from 2 of the husks and set aside for tying the tamales. Lay out the remaining 8 corn husks on a flat work surface. Divide the filling mixture into 8 even portions and place 1 portion on each husk. Evenly spread out the filling, leaving about $1^1/2$ inches of exposed corn husk at each end and $3/4$ inch at each side. Bring the sides of the corn husk together, folding the filling; tuck one side of the husk under the other and roll up the tamale so the filling is completely enclosed inside the husk. Twist each end and tie with the reserved strips of corn husk. Repeat for the remaining tamales.

Fill the bottom of a steamer or saucepan fitted with a strainer or vegetable basket with 2 to 3 inches of water. Bring the water to a boil and place the tamales in the steamer. Cover tightly with a lid or foil (it is important that little or no steam escapes while cooking). Steam the tamales for 5 to 7 minutes over lightly boiling water until they are warmed through.

Place the tamales on serving plates and, with a knife, slice open the top of the wrappers from end to end. Gently push the ends together, as for a baked potato. Pour the cooled rum cream over each tamale.

SERVES 8

Day of the Dead Sweet Tamales

(M A R K   M I L L E R)

ONE OF THE GREAT LANDMARKS OF THE MEXICAN CALENDAR IS EL DIA DE LOS MUERTOS—THE DAY OF THE DEAD. ON OCTOBER 31 AND NOVEMBER 1 EVERY YEAR, THE SOULS OF THE DEAD ARE WELCOMED BACK ONTO THE EARTHLY PLANE, AND ALTARS GROANING WITH TYPICAL OFFERINGS OF MARIGOLDS, OTHER FLOWERS, BREAD, AND CANDIES ARE SET UP IN HOMES AND IN CEMETERIES ACROSS THE COUNTRY. THIS PUBLIC HOLIDAY COMBINES THE CATHOLIC TRADITION OF ALL SOUL'S DAY WITH PRE-HISPANIC BELIEFS RELATING TO THE CYCLICAL NATURE OF LIFE AND DEATH, AND THE SPIRIT OF REBIRTH IS CELEBRATED BY THE LIVING WITH ELABORATE FEASTS OF SPECIAL DISHES THAT OFTEN INCLUDE THOSE PARTICULARLY ENJOYED BY THE DEPARTED. THIS RECIPE IS BASED ON DELICIOUS SWEET TAMALES THAT I HAVE ENJOYED IN OAXACA, PROBABLY THE REGION OF MEXICO THAT TAKES THE COLORFUL AND SPIRITUAL TRADITIONS OF THE DAY OF THE DEAD THE MOST SERIOUSLY.

$^1/_2$ cup cajeta sauce (see *Sweet Potato Tamales with Spicy Pecans and Cajeta, page 140*)

2 tablespoons pine nuts

$^3/_4$ cup unsalted butter

1 teaspoon baking powder

$^1/_2$ teaspoon salt

2 tablespoons honey

1 tablespoon dark brown sugar

$1^1/_4$ cups masa harina

$^1/_2$ cup milk

1 tablespoon ground canela

2 tablespoons raisins

$^1/_4$ cup dried cherries

$^1/_4$ cup dried apricots

2 tablespoons finely diced candied papaya

1 tablespoon minced orange zest

10 large dried corn husks, soaked in warm water for 30 minutes

1 cup blackberries

2 tablespoons sugar

1 tablespoon brandy (optional)

1 tablespoon raisins

1 tablespoon dried cherries

1 tablespoon finely diced candied papaya

Prepare the *cajeta*.

To prepare the filling, place the pine nuts in a hot, dry skillet and toast over medium heat for 4 to 5 minutes, stirring occasionally, until lightly browned. Set aside. Meanwhile, place the butter, baking powder, salt, honey, and brown sugar in the bowl of an electric mixer fitted with a paddle attachment. Cream on high speed until light and smooth, about 5 minutes. Add the masa harina and turn down the speed to low. Add the milk, canela, raisins, dried cherries, dried apricots, candied papaya, orange zest, and toasted pine nuts and mix until a firm dough forms. Work the dough by hand for about 1 minute, until the dough is thoroughly mixed and gathered together. Divide the dough into 8 equal pieces.

Drain the corn husks and shake dry. Tear 16 thin strips (about $^1/_8$ inch wide) from 2 of the husks and set aside for tying the tamales. Lay out the remaining 8 corn husks. Take a portion of the dough, place in a corn husk, and spread out evenly, leaving about $1^1/_2$ inches of exposed corn husk at each end and $^3/_4$ inch

at each side. Bring the sides of the corn husk together, folding the dough; tuck one side of the husk under the other and roll up the tamale so the dough is completely enclosed inside the husk. Twist each end and tie with the reserved strips of corn husk. Repeat for the remaining tamales.

Steam the tamales (see page 136 for method) for 30 to 35 minutes over lightly boiling water, adding more boiling water as needed. The tamales are done when they feel firm to the touch but are not hard and the dough comes away easily from the husk.

Meanwhile, prepare the blackberry sauce. Place the blackberries, sugar, and brandy in a blender and puree until smooth. Strain and reserve.

Ladle the blackberry sauce onto serving plates. Place the tamales on top of the sauce and, with a knife, slice open the top of the wrappers from end to end. Spoon small dollops of the *cajeta* on top of the blackberry sauce and garnish with the raisins, dried cherries, and candied papaya.

SERVES 8

Sweet Potato Tamales with Spicy Pecans and *Cajeta*

(S T E P H  N   P Y L E S)

IS THERE A BETTER COMBINATION OF FLAVORS THAN SWEET POTATOES AND PECANS? PROBABLY NOT TO A SOUTHERNER. THE ADDITION OF A LITTLE

CAJETA—MEXICAN GOAT MILK CARAMEL—CLEARS AWAY ANY DOUBT! CARAMELIZING SWEET POTATOES IN THE OVEN AND ADDING MAPLE SYRUP, RAISINS,

NUTMEG, AND CINNAMON GIVE THIS DESSERT A HOMEY YET DISTINGUISHED QUALITY. YOU WILL HAVE ABOUT HALF A CUP OF CANDIED PECANS LEFT OVER

FROM THIS RECIPE, BUT NOT TO WORRY! THEY MAKE GREAT SNACKS AND GIFTS, ESPECIALLY DURING THE HOLIDAY SEASON, SO YOU MAY

WANT TO DOUBLE THE RECIPE.

FOR THE CAJETA

1¹/₂ cups sugar
2 cups goat's milk
2 cups cow's milk
1 teaspoon cornstarch
Pinch of baking soda

FOR THE CANDIED PECANS

1 tablespoon unsalted butter
1¹/₂ cups pecan halves
¹/₄ cup light brown sugar
¹/₈ teaspoon cayenne pepper
2 tablespoons Calvados
Salt

FOR THE TAMALES

1 sweet potato, about 12 ounces
Masa Seca Tamale Dough (page 2)
¹/₄ teaspoon ground cinnamon
¹/₄ teaspoon ground allspice
Pinch of ground nutmeg
1 cup raisins
3 tablespoons maple syrup
¹/₂ cup light brown sugar
10 large dried corn husks, soaked in
*   warm water for 30 minutes*

To prepare the *cajeta*, place ³/₄ cup of the sugar in a small skillet and melt over medium heat for about 7 minutes, stirring constantly, until golden brown and free of lumps. Remove from the heat. Combine the two milks in a mixing bowl. Pour 1 cup of this mixture into another bowl, add the cornstarch and baking soda, and set aside. Place the remaining ³/₄ cup of the sugar in a separate saucepan and add the remaining 3 cups of combined milk. Bring to a boil over medium heat, stirring occasionally, and add the caramelized sugar, stirring vigorously. Add the reserved milk-cornstarch mixture and combine well. Reduce the heat to low and simmer for 50 to 60 minutes, stirring occasionally. The *cajeta* will begin to thicken during the last 15 minutes of cooking, so be sure to stir more frequently to prevent sticking. Keep warm.

Preheat the oven to 350°F. To prepare the candied pecans, melt the butter in a large skillet. Add the pecans and sauté over medium heat until lightly browned, about 3 minutes. Add the brown sugar and cook until lightly caramelized, about 3 minutes longer. Stir in the cayenne, add the Calvados, and reduce

until all the liquid has evaporated, about 2 minutes. Season with salt to taste and spread out the pecans on a cookie sheet. Transfer to the oven and bake until crisped, 4 to 5 minutes. Let cool.

To prepare the filling, bake the sweet potato in the oven (at 350°F) for 45 minutes, until it is very soft. Remove from the oven and let cool completely.

While the potato is baking, prepare the masa dough.

Peel the potato, discarding the skin, and transfer to the bowl of an electric mixer fitted with a paddle attachment. Add the cinnamon, allspice, nutmeg, raisins, maple syrup, brown sugar, and candied pecans and thoroughly combine. Add the tamale dough and beat on medium speed for 5 minutes until the mixture is light and fluffy.

Drain the corn husks and shake dry. Tear 16 thin strips (about ¹/₈ inch wide) from 2 of the husks and set aside for tying the tamales. Lay out the remaining 8 corn husks on a flat work surface. Divide the filling mixture into 8 even portions and place 1 portion on each

(continues)

husk. Evenly spread out the filling, leaving about $1^1/_2$ inches of exposed corn husk at each end and $^3/_4$ inch at each side. Bring the sides of the corn husk together, folding the filling; tuck one side of the husk under the other and roll up the tamale so the filling is completely enclosed inside the husk. Twist each end and tie with the reserved strips of corn husk. Repeat for the remaining tamales.

Fill the bottom of a steamer or saucepan fitted with a strainer or vegetable basket with 2 to 3 inches of water. Bring the water to a boil and place the tamales in the steamer. Cover tightly with a lid or foil (it is important that little or no steam escapes while cooking). Steam the tamales for 40 to 45 minutes over lightly boiling water, adding more boiling water as needed. The tamales are done when they feel firm to the touch but are not hard and the dough comes away easily from the husk.

Place the tamales on serving plates and, with a knife, slice open the top of the wrappers from end to end. Gently push the ends together, as for a baked potato. Spoon the warm *cajeta* over the tamales.

SERVES 8

West Palm Beach Tamales

(J O H N   S E D L A R)

GROWING UP IN THE ARID SOUTHWEST, WHERE STONEFRUIT WAS ABOUT AS EXOTIC AS LOCAL FRUIT GOT, I WAS ALWAYS INTRIGUED WITH THE LUSCIOUS, AROMATIC, SWEET AND TART FRUITS OF THE TROPICS. VERY OCCASIONALLY, A COCONUT OR FRESH PINEAPPLE WOULD CROSS THE SEDLAR FAMILY THRESHOLD, BUT IT WAS LATER ON IN MY PROFESSIONAL COOKING CAREER THAT I DISCOVERED WHAT A WONDERFUL FLAVOR PARTNERSHIP THEY MADE. (WHEN I WAS STILL SMALL, I WAS CONVINCED THAT COCONUTS GREW ON PALM TREES FROM WEST PALM BEACH!) LATER STILL, AFTER TRAVELING TO MEXICO AND ENJOYING THE SWEET MASA TAMALES THAT THE SEÑORAS WERE MAKING, I DISCOVERED THAT TAMALES HAD A PLACE ON THE DESSERT PLATE IN ADDITION TO THEIR MORE TRADITIONAL ROLE AS APPETIZERS OR MAIN COURSES. FOR A RECIPE SHORTCUT, USE 1 QUART OF HÄAGEN-DAZS® VANILLA ICE CREAM INSTEAD OF THE ICE CREAM FILLING BELOW.

FOR THE ICE CREAM TAMALE FILLING

3 cups toasted unsweetened shredded coconut
2 cans (14 ounces each) sweetened coconut milk
1 cup milk
3 cups heavy cream
10 egg yolks
1/2 cup sugar

FOR THE PINEAPPLE SAUCE

1 ripe pineapple, peeled, cored, and coarsely
    chopped
3/4 cup sugar
1/2 cup water
6 tablespoons white rum
1/4 cup light corn syrup
1/2 cup chopped fresh mint

FOR THE TAMALES

6 large dried corn husks, soaked in warm water
    for 30 minutes

To prepare the ice cream, combine 2 cups of the toasted coconut, the coconut milk, milk, and cream in a large saucepan and bring to a boil over high heat. Turn down the heat and simmer for about 30 minutes. Remove from the heat and let cool slightly. Meanwhile, whisk the egg yolks and sugar together in a mixing bowl. Add a small amount of the hot coconut milk mixture to the eggs and whisk to combine. Add the egg mixture to the coconut mixture and whisk to mix well. Place the saucepan over medium heat, stirring constantly with a wooden spoon, and cook until the mixture coats the back of a spoon, about 20 minutes. Pour through a fine mesh strainer into a mixing bowl, let cool completely, and place in an ice cream machine. Process according to the manufacturer's directions.

To prepare the tamales, cut 6 pieces of plastic wrap measuring about 4 inches by 5 inches each. Lay out each piece of plastic on a flat work surface. Place a 3/4 cup serving of the ice cream on each and pat into a rectangular shape. Fold two of the sides of the plastic wrap over, and then fold over the other two sides to form a tight envelope package. Repeat for the remaining tamales. Place in the freezer until ready to serve.

To prepare the sauce, puree the pineapple in a blender or food processor. In a mixing bowl, dissolve the sugar in the water and, with the machine running, add to the pureed pineapple. Process to mix well. Pour through a fine mesh strainer into a mixing bowl and discard the pulp. Stir in the rum, corn syrup, and mint and refrigerate until chilled.

Prepare the tamale wrappers. Drain the corn husks and shake dry. Lay out each husk in the center of a large serving bowl. Place the remaining 1 cup of shredded coconut on a platter, unwrap the ice cream filling from the plastic wrap, and dredge on all sides in the shredded coconut. Place one ice cream rectangle in the center of each corn husk, and serve the sauce at the base of each tamale.

SERVES 6

Ginger–Sticky Rice Tamales with Mango and Basil

(STEPHAN PYLES)

THIS DESSERT IS CLEARLY ASIAN IN INSPIRATION, AND IT PROVIDES ANOTHER EXAMPLE OF HOW WELL RICE SUITS THE TAMALE FORMAT. GLUTINOUS STICKY RICE IS A SHORT-GRAIN VARIETY WITH A HIGH STARCH CONTENT, AND, WHEN COOKED, ITS TEXTURE MAKES IT EASY TO HANDLE WITH CHOPSTICKS— HENCE ITS POPULARITY IN THE ORIENT. UNLIKE OTHER LONG- AND SHORT-GRAIN RICE, STICKY RICE MUST BE STEAMED, AND ITS RICHNESS MAKES IT A PERFECT FOIL FOR DESSERTS. THIS IS A DISH WITH CLEAR, STRAIGHTFORWARD FLAVORS THAT IS BEST SERVED AFTER A FULL-FLAVORED, HIGHLY SPICED MEAL. MAKE SURE THE MANGOES USED FOR THE SALSA ARE AT THEIR RIPEST.

FOR THE MANGO-BASIL SALSA

6 tablespoons sugar
5 tablespoons water
2 ripe mangoes, peeled, pitted, and diced
2 tablespoons chopped fresh basil
1 tablespoon Sambuca liqueur
Juice of 1 lime

FOR THE GINGER-CUSTARD SAUCE

5 tablespoons grated fresh ginger
1 cup milk
$^1/_2$ vanilla bean, halved lengthwise,
    seeds scraped
3 egg yolks
$^1/_4$ cup sugar
6 tablespoons sour cream or crème
    fraîche, chilled

FOR THE FILLING AND TAMALES

2 cups glutinous rice, soaked overnight
1 can (14 ounces) coconut milk
2 tablespoons minced fresh ginger
$^1/_2$ cup sugar
$^1/_4$ teaspoon salt
2 large banana leaves, about 12 inches
    by 36 inches

To prepare the salsa, combine the sugar and water in a large saucepan. Cook over high heat, stirring with a wooden spoon, until the sugar dissolves, 3 to 4 minutes. Continue cooking until the syrup comes to a full boil. Immediately remove the simple syrup from the heat and set aside to cool completely. Pour the simple syrup into a mixing bowl, add all of the remaining salsa ingredients, and stir to combine well. Keep chilled.

To prepare the sauce, fill a large bowl with ice and set aside. Blanch the ginger in boiling water for 30 seconds and drain well. Combine the milk, ginger, and the vanilla pod and seeds in a saucepan and bring to a boil. Remove from the heat, cover, and let infuse for 15 minutes.

Meanwhile, place the egg yolks in a mixing bowl and whisk in the sugar until the yolks have lightened in color. Reheat the milk mixture and return to a boil. Remove from the heat and pour slowly through a strainer into the yolks, stirring constantly; discard the ginger and vanilla bean. Pour the mixture back into the saucepan and cook over low heat, stirring constantly with a wooden spatula and

scraping down the sides of the pan. Continue to cook until the mixture registers 175°F on a candy thermometer and has thickened considerably, 5 to 10 minutes. Remove from the heat immediately and place the pan over the ice. Stir in the chilled sour cream, transfer to the refrigerator, and chill thoroughly.

To prepare the tamale filling, drain the soaked rice in a strainer and rinse well with cold running water. Line the top of a steamer or a strainer fitted in a saucepan with damp cheesecloth and spread the rice over it (alternatively, the rice can be placed on a heatproof plate). Steam for 30 to 40 minutes; sprinkle the rice with water occasionally throughout the cooking process and check for doneness as you would for pasta. When cooked, transfer to a mixing bowl.

Place the coconut milk, ginger, sugar, and salt in a saucepan and bring to a boil. Turn down the heat and simmer for 20 minutes. Add to the bowl containing the rice and mix thoroughly. Transfer the rice mixture to a baking sheet and spread out evenly in a rectangle or square about 1 inch thick. Cool to room

(continues)

temperature, transfer to the refrigerator, and chill for 1 hour. Divide the chilled rice mixture into 8 equal square portions.

Soften the banana leaves over an open flame for 10 seconds on each side, being careful not to burn them. Cut each leaf crosswise into 4 even pieces, about 8 inches by 10 inches, and lay out on a flat work surface. Place 1 portion of the rice mixture in the center of each leaf. Spread into a 4-inch square, leaving at least a $1^{1}/_{2}$-inch border at the ends and $^{3}/_{4}$ inch on the long sides. To fold the tamales, pick up the 2 long sides of the banana leaf and bring them together. Tuck one side under the other and fold the flaps on each end underneath the tamale.

Fill the bottom of a steamer or saucepan fitted with a strainer or vegetable basket with 2 to 3 inches of water. Bring the water to a boil and place the tamales in the steamer. Cover tightly with a lid or foil (it is important that little or no steam escapes while cooking). Steam the tamales for 15 to 20 minutes over lightly boiling water, adding more boiling water as needed.

Place the tamales on serving plates and, with a knife, slice open the top of the wrappers. Ladle about $^{1}/_{4}$ cup of the sauce to the side of each tamale and spoon the salsa over the rice.

SERVES 8

OAXACAN TAMALES

Adapted from Hilda Jaimes
Time: 2 hours, 15 minutes

1 **pound package of banana leaves (see note)**
3½ **to 4 pounds bone-in chicken breasts, skin removed**
5 **cloves garlic, peeled and halved**
1 **medium onion, peeled and halved**
4 **ounces dried guajillo peppers, stemmed and seeded**
1 **large tomato, quartered**
1 **teaspoon cumin seed**
1 **teaspoon black peppercorns**
1 **teaspoon coriander seeds**
1 **tablespoon oregano**
8 **cloves**
2 **tablespoons corn oil**
3 **bay leaves**
 salt and freshly ground black pepper
1 **cup fresh lard**
½ **cups instant corn masa mix.**

Trim fibrous edges from banana leaves, ～d cut into 14-inch long rectangles. Soak in ～rm water until ready to use. (At least 20 ～ll be needed.)

～Put chicken, 3 garlic cloves and onion in a ～dium stockpot, cover with cold water, ～d bring to boil over high heat. Skim off ～m, reduce heat to medium, and cook for ～ minutes. Put chicken in a bowl to cool; ～ain and reserve 4 cups broth.

～Put 1 cup cold water in a blender. Toast ～jillos in a large, dry pan over medium ～t for one minute, pressing down with a ～tula to soften each side. Submerge pep～s in blender. Add remaining garlic, to～to, cumin, peppercorns, coriander, oreg～ and cloves. Blend until smooth, about 2 ～utes.

～ombine oil, guajillo sauce, bay leaves, 2 ～espoons salt, some black pepper and ～rved broth in a large Dutch oven, and ～e over high heat to boil. Reduce to ～ium low and simmer for 20 minutes.

～hile sauce is simmering, shred chicken

into bite-size strands with your fingers; set aside. Melt lard in a small saucepan over low heat and cool to room temperature. After sauce has simmered for 15 minutes, remove 1 cup and set aside to cool.

6. In a large mixing bowl, whisk 3 cups cold water into 2 cups masa to form a loose paste. Whisk paste into simmering sauce, switch to a spoon, and stir until sauce has thickened, about three minutes. Stir in chicken and remove from heat. Season to taste.

7. In a large mixing bowl, combine reserved guajillo sauce, 1 cup cold water, 2 tablespoons salt, and 5½ cups masa. Mix masa between your fingers, adding lard and 1½ to 2 cups more water. Continue mixing; dough is ready when it no longer sticks to your hands.

8. Drain banana leaves and dry with paper towels; discard leaves with sizeable tears. Place a leaf shiny-side-down on a sturdy work surface. Roll ⅓-½ cup masa dough into a ball, flatten it in the leaf's center, and spread it thinly with the palm of your hand to cover all but 2-inch perimeter. Add more masa, if necessary. Add ⅓-½ cup filling (it will be soupy), then fold tamale into a rectangular package: top edge of leaf to the bottom edge of masa; bottom edge leaf to top of tamale; right and left sides overlapping in the center. Turn over and stack until ready to steam. (Tamales may be frozen now: thaw for two hours before steaming.)

9. Fill stockpot with two inches of water, line pot or steamer insert with leaf, carefully stack tamales, and cover tightly. Steam for 40 minutes; tamales are ready when leaves easily pull away from masa.

Yield: about 20 large tamales (about 6 inches long).
Note: Banana leaves are sold at Asian and Mexican markets.

By JIM ROBBINS

GUSTAVUS, Alaska NOT long ago it would have seemed surprising that anyone would want to set up ocean farms to raise sablefish. Could there really be so much demand for that oily, paprika-flecked smoked fish?

But under the name black cod, sablefish's popularity has grown in American restaurants and stores. It has long been popular in Japan.

So, as the wholesale price for Pacific salmon dropped to 50 cents a pound, those who fish for a living saw opportunities in another denizen of northern waters, the sablefish.

Sablefish, also known as butterfish, has been caught deep in the northern Pacific, mostly off the coast of British Columbia and Alaska.

Now the first sablefish fingerlings have been introduced into two fish farms along the coast of British Columbia, and more than 40 new farms have been permitted in the last year along its Pacific shoreline. The first

fish will
year and

The D
has propo
off the c
state ban
consideri
aquacultu
Sablefish,
wholesale

But the
problems
— disease
tion — wi

"Wild s
spend th
said Eri
director
Associati
fish farm
inlets, wl
of diseas

Some
died off
because
salmon,

John
lumbia
and fish
entific e
caused
he said
protect

Many
also opp
flood th
a staff
Conserv
to prote
"it wou
coastal

But I
tor of t
mosphe
aquacu
would

Seafood Rule Without Jaws

By MARION BURROS

AN interim regulation requiring most seafood to be labeled with its country of origin is scheduled to take effect on Sept. 30, but the Agriculture Department has told the seafood industry it would not enforce the rule for a year.

Julie Quick, a department spokeswoman, said she could not "talk about it because the rule is not public." The department said it would not publish the regulation until the day it goes into effect.

The rule, based on legislation from 2002, is intended to tell consumers whether fish is farmed or wild, fresh or frozen. But it applies only to fish counters in supermarkets or other stores that carry a variety of products. Stand-alone fish stores and restaurants are exempt. It would not apply to smoked fish, canned fish or breaded shrimp; fish substantially reshaped, as in surimi; or fish that is an ingredient in a dish, like clams in garlic sauce.

The original Congressional legislation applied to beef and pork, but implementation for these foods has been delayed.

Linda Candler, a spokeswoman for the National Fisheries Institute, a seafood trade group, said the reason for delay was that the Agriculture Department "is not going to have the manpower to do what they are expected to do," enforce the regulation.

There can be a maximum fine of $10,000 for a violation, but apparently not for at least a year.

Sweet Pumpkin Tamales with Nutmeg Crème Anglaise

(M A R K   M I L L E R)

IN MEXICO, IN THE FALL, AROUND THE TIME OF THE DAY OF THE DEAD (SEE THE HEADNOTE ON PAGE 139), THE MARKETS SELL DARK ORANGEY-BROWN WHOLE CANDIED CALABAZA, OR PUMPKIN, AND IT'S ONE OF THE SWEETEST WAYS IMAGINABLE TO ENJOY THIS SEASONAL SQUASH. IT'S THE SOUTH-OF-THE-BORDER EQUIVALENT OF PUMPKIN PIE, AND THIS RECIPE OFFERS THAT DISTINCTLY AMERICAN CLASSIC IN TAMALE FORM—A TRUE SCRUMPTIOUS HYBRID.

FOR THE TAMALES

$^3/_4$ cup unsalted butter

$1^1/_2$ cups pumpkin puree

1 teaspoon baking powder

$^1/_2$ teaspoon salt

2 tablespoons honey

2 tablespoons dark brown sugar

$^1/_2$ teaspoon ground nutmeg

$^1/_2$ teaspoon ground canela

$^1/_4$ teaspoon ground cloves

$^1/_4$ teaspoon freshly ground black pepper

$1^1/_2$ cups masa harina

$^1/_4$ cup milk

$^1/_4$ cup roughly chopped pecans, toasted (page 165)

FOR THE TAMALES

10 large dried corn husks, soaked in warm water for 30 minutes

FOR THE NUTMEG CRÈME ANGLAISE

6 egg yolks

$^1/_2$ cup sugar

2 cups heavy cream

2 teaspoons ground nutmeg

To prepare the filling, place the butter, pumpkin puree, baking powder, salt, honey, brown sugar, nutmeg, canela, cloves, and pepper in the bowl of an electric mixer fitted with a paddle attachment. Cream on high speed until light and smooth, about 5 minutes. Add the masa harina and turn down the speed to low. Add the milk and toasted pecans and mix until a firm dough forms. Transfer the dough to a work surface and work by hand for about 1 minute, until the dough is thoroughly mixed and gathered together. Divide the dough into 8 equal pieces.

Drain the corn husks and shake dry. Tear 16 thin strips (about $^1/_8$ inch wide) from 2 of the husks and set aside for tying the tamales. Lay out the remaining 8 corn husks on a flat work surface. Take a portion of the dough, place in a corn husk, and spread out evenly, leaving about $1^1/_2$ inches of exposed corn husk at each end and $^3/_4$ inch at each side. Bring the sides of the corn husk together, folding the dough; tuck one side of the husk under the other and roll up the tamale so the dough is completely enclosed inside the husk. Twist each end and tie with the reserved strips of corn husk. Repeat for the remaining tamales.

Fill the bottom of a steamer or saucepan fitted with a strainer or vegetable basket with 2 to 3 inches of water. Bring the water to a boil and place the tamales in the steamer. Cover tightly with a lid or foil (it is important that little or no steam escapes while cooking). Steam the tamales for 30 to 35 minutes over lightly boiling water, adding more boiling water as needed. The tamales are done when they feel firm to the touch but are not hard and the dough comes away easily from the husk.

While the tamales are steaming, prepare the anglaise. Whisk the egg yolks and sugar in a mixing bowl until the yolks have lightened in color. Stir the cream and nutmeg together in a saucepan and bring to a simmer over medium-high heat. Remove the pan from the heat and pour half into the yolk mixture while stirring constantly. Whisking vigorously, return the saucepan to the heat. Slowly pour the egg mixture back into the saucepan, still whisking vigorously, until incorporated. Cook the mixture until it thickens and coats the back of a spoon, about 5 minutes.

Ladle about $^1/_4$ cup of the anglaise onto each serving plate. With a knife, slice open the top of the tamale wrappers from end to end and place on top of the sauce.

SERVES 8

Chocolate–Dried Cherry Tamales with Sambuca–Milk Chocolate Sauce

(S T E P H A N P Y L E S)

THESE TAMALES ARE A REAL CHOCOHOLIC'S DELIGHT. THE RECIPE IS BASED ON THE UBIQUITOUS FLOURLESS CHOCOLATE CAKE THAT CAME INTO VOGUE DURING THE 1980S, AND THE ADDITION OF DRIED CHERRIES, MILK CHOCOLATE AND SAMBUCA—THE ANISE-FLAVORED ITALIAN LIQUEUR—RESOLVES ANY DOUBTS ABOUT ITS RICHNESS. SAMBUCA IS TRADITIONALLY SERVED WITH A GARNISH OF TWO OR THREE ROASTED COFFEE BEANS, SO PAIRING IT WITH COFFEE IN THE SAUCE IS A NATURAL. I RECENTLY SERVED THESE TAMALES AT AN AMBASSADOR'S BALL, EXPOSING DIPLOMATS AND DIGNITARIES FROM COUNTRIES AS DIVERSE AS THE NETHERLANDS AND PARAGUAY TO THE DELIGHTS OF CHOCOLATE TAMALES. IN THIS RECIPE, THE CORN HUSKS ARE STEAMED INSIDE PLASTIC WRAP TO KEEP THE FILLING AIRTIGHT; ANY STEAM OR WATER WILL MAKE IT SOGGY. TO DYE THE CORN HUSKS RED FOR A MORE SPECTACULAR PRESENTATION, SEE THE NOTES ABOUT HIBISCUS TEA ON PAGE XII.

FOR THE DRIED CHERRY SALSA

1 cup dried cherries
1 tablespoon kirsch
1/2 cup chopped pecans
1/2 pint raspberries
2 tablespoons sugar

FOR THE SAMBUCA–MILK CHOCOLATE SAUCE

12 ounces milk chocolate, chopped
6 tablespoons strong brewed coffee
3 tablespoons Sambuca
1/4 cup light corn syrup
1 cup heavy cream

Preheat the oven to 350°F. To prepare the salsa, combine the cherries and kirsch in a small mixing bowl. Cover the cherries with hot water and let soak for 30 minutes. Meanwhile, place the pecans on a cookie sheet and toast in the oven for about 8 minutes. (Keep the oven on for baking the cake filling.) Let cool, chop finely, and set aside. Drain the rehydrated cherries, chop finely, and transfer to a clean bowl. Puree the raspberries with the sugar in a blender. Pass through a fine mesh strainer into the bowl with the cherries. Add the pecans and stir thoroughly to combine. Keep chilled in the refrigerator.

To prepare the sauce, combine all the sauce ingredients in the top of a double boiler set over gently simmering water. Stir frequently until the chocolate has melted and all the ingredients are completely blended. When the mixture is smooth, remove from the heat and let cool completely. Warm slightly before serving.

Place a round of parchment (or waxed) paper in the bottom of a 9-inch cake pan. Butter and flour the pan and paper. To prepare the filling, place the cream in a saucepan, bring to a boil, and remove from the heat. Add both the chopped chocolates and stir to blend. Cover the pan and allow the chocolate to melt, about 5 minutes. Stir again to blend completely and set aside. Place the eggs, sugar, and vanilla in a mixing bowl and set over a saucepan of gently simmering water. Whisk the mixture until warm to the touch, about 1 minute, then remove from the heat. Beat the mixture with an electric mixer at high speed until tripled in volume, 7 to 10 minutes.

Gently whisk one-quarter of the egg mixture into the chocolate and incorporate completely; gently fold in the rest, taking care to deflate the egg mixture as little as possible. Pour the chocolate mixture into the prepared

(continues)

FOR THE CHOCOLATE–DRIED CHERRY TAMALE FILLING

1 cup heavy cream

10 1/2 ounces semisweet baking chocolate, chopped

2 ounces unsweetened chocolate, chopped

5 large eggs

1/3 cup sugar

1 teaspoon pure vanilla extract

1 cup dried cherries, soaked in tequila for 30 minutes, drained, and roughly chopped

10 large dried corn husks, soaked in warm water for 30 minutes

cake pan and place inside a slightly larger pan or bain-marie. Pour enough boiling water into the larger pan so that it comes halfway up the side of the 9-inch cake pan. Transfer to the oven and bake for about 50 minutes, or until an inserted toothpick or skewer comes out clean.

Remove from the oven and let the pan sit in the water for 30 minutes. When cool, invert the cake onto a platter and remove the parchment paper. Crumble the cake into a mixing bowl, add the cherries soaked in tequila, and combine thoroughly. Divide the mixture into 8 even portions and roll each into a ball.

Drain the corn husks and shake dry. Tear 16 strips (about 1/8 inch wide) from 2 of the husks and set aside for tying the tamales. Lay out the remaining 8 corn husks on a flat work surface. Place 1 portion of the filling mixture on each husk. Evenly flatten out the filling, leaving about 1 1/2 inches of exposed corn husk at each end and 3/4 inch at each side. Bring the sides of the corn husk together, folding the

filling; tuck one side of the husk under the other and roll up the tamale so that the filling is completely enclosed inside the husk. Twist each end and tie with the reserved strips of corn husk. Wrap the tamale tightly with plastic wrap. Repeat for the remaining tamales.

Fill the bottom of a steamer or saucepan fitted with a strainer or vegetable basket with 2 to 3 inches of water. Bring the water to a boil and place the tamales in the steamer. Cover tightly with a lid or foil (it is important that little or no steam escapes while cooking). Steam the tamales for about 10 minutes over lightly boiling water until they are warmed through.

Ladle about 1/4 cup of the sauce onto serving plates. Remove the plastic wrap from the tamales and, with a knife, slice open the top of the wrappers from end to end. Gently push the ends together, as for a baked potato, and place the tamales on top of the sauce. Spoon about 1 tablespoon of the salsa over each tamale.

SERVES 8

Mom's Apple Pie Tamales

(J O H N S E D L A R)

THIS RECIPE COMBINES THOSE TWO DISTINCTIVELY AMERICAN ICONS: MOTHERHOOD AND APPLE PIE! ON EVERY MENU, THERE SHOULD ALWAYS

BE A CATEGORY FOR APPLES. AND WHAT BETTER DISH THAN THE OLD STANDBY. NO, NOT MOM. HER PIE!

FOR THE BRIOCHE BASE

2 large eggs plus 1 egg yolk
1/2 cup light brown sugar
3/4 cup heavy cream
1 loaf fresh bakery brioche bread, crust removed,
    cut into 1/2-inch cubes (about 3 cups)

FOR THE APPLE FILLING

4 Granny Smith apples, cored, peeled,
    and cut into 1/4-inch slices
1/4 cup plus 1 tablespoon light brown sugar
1 tablespoon cornstarch
Pinch of ground nutmeg
1 teaspoon ground cinnamon
3 tablespoons sour cream

FOR THE TAMALES

6 large dried corn husks, soaked in warm water
    for 30 minutes
6 scoops Häagen-Dazs® vanilla ice cream
1 to 2 tablespoons confectioners' sugar,
    for garnish

To prepare the brioche base, whisk together the eggs, egg yolk, and brown sugar in a mixing bowl. Whisk in the cream and continue mixing until the sugar is dissolved. Place the brioche cubes in a large mixing bowl, add the egg mixture, and toss gently to coat. Press the bread cubes into the mixture with a wooden spoon to soak up the liquid completely. Set aside.

To prepare the filling, place the apples in a separate mixing bowl and combine with the brown sugar, cornstarch, nutmeg, cinnamon, and sour cream. Toss with a wooden spoon or use your hands to coat the apple slices completely. Set aside.

Preheat the oven to 350°F. Butter a 9-inch square by 2-inch deep baking pan and line the bottom and sides of the pan with parchment paper.

Using half the bread mixture, spread a thin, even layer in the bottom of the baking pan. Top with the apple filling, making an even layer. Finish with a layer of the remaining bread. Transfer to the oven and bake until the top is brown and the center springs back when touched, 50 to 60 minutes. Let cool to warm or room temperature. Cut around the edges of the pan to loosen the apple pie filling and invert onto a flat work surface. Cut into 6 even rectangles and turn them right side up.

Drain the corn husks and shake dry. Lay out each husk in the center of a shallow dessert bowl. Place a rectangle of the apple pie filling in the center of each husk. Serve with a scoop of vanilla ice cream on the side and garnish the tamales with the confectioners' sugar.

SERVES 6

Bittersweet Chocolate Tamales with Anchos, Prunes, and Raisins

(M A R K   M I L L E R)

SOME PEOPLE GIVE ME STRANGE GLANCES WHEN I MENTION THE WORDS *CHILES* AND *DESSERTS* IN THE SAME SENTENCE, BUT SOME CHILES (SUCH AS THE ANCHO) CONTAIN SUBTLE FRUIT FLAVORS THAT MAKE THEM NATURAL INGREDIENTS FOR SWEET DISHES. AND BESIDES, LET US NOT FORGET THAT, BOTANICALLY, CHILES ARE FRUITS! IN THIS RECIPE, THE FLAVORS OF THE PRUNES AND RAISINS WORK WONDERFULLY WELL WITH THE ANCHO, AND TOGETHER THEY COMPLEMENT THE RICHNESS OF THE CHOCOLATE. THIS DISH WITH ITS MILD HEAT MAKES A PERFECT WINTERTIME DESSERT.

FOR THE FILLING AND TAMALES

4 ounces bittersweet chocolate, chopped
1 tablespoon cocoa powder
$^1/_2$ cup milk
$^1/_2$ cup unsalted butter
1 teaspoon baking powder
$^1/_2$ teaspoon salt
2 tablespoons honey
$1^1/_2$ cups masa harina
1 dried ancho chile, toasted, rehydrated,
    and finely chopped (page 165)
10 large dried corn husks, soaked in warm water
    for 30 minutes
8 prunes
$^1/_2$ cup raisins

FOR THE CHOCOLATE SAUCE

4 ounces bittersweet chocolate, finely chopped
$^1/_2$ cup hot water

FOR THE VANILLA ANGLAISE

6 egg yolks
$^1/_2$ cup sugar
2 cups heavy cream
$^1/_2$ teaspoon pure vanilla extract

To prepare the filling, heat the chocolate in a saucepan over low heat and, when melted, add the cocoa and milk. Raise the heat to medium and stir the mixture until it is smooth and well incorporated. Remove from the heat and let cool.

Place the butter, baking powder, salt, and honey in the bowl of an electric mixer fitted with a paddle attachment. Cream on high speed until light and smooth, about 5 minutes. Add the masa harina and turn down the speed to low. Add the chocolate-milk mixture and ancho and mix until a firm dough forms. Transfer the dough to a work surface and work by hand for about 1 minute, until the dough is thoroughly mixed and gathered together. Divide the dough into 8 equal pieces. Using a floured rolling pin, flatten the dough to a thickness of about $^1/_8$ inch, with a diameter of 4 to 5 inches.

Drain the corn husks and shake dry. Tear 16 thin strips (about $^1/_8$ inch wide) from 2 of the husks and set aside for tying the tamales. Lay out the remaining 8 corn husks on a flat work surface. Place the dough inside each husk, leaving about 2 inches of exposed corn husk at each end and 1 inch at each side. Divide the prunes and raisins equally and place on top of the dough.

Bring the sides of the corn husk together, folding the dough; tuck one side of the husk under the other and roll up the tamale so the dough is completely enclosed inside the husk. Twist each end and tie with the reserved strips of corn husk. Repeat for the remaining tamales.

Fill the bottom of a steamer or saucepan fitted with a strainer or vegetable basket with 2 to 3 inches of water. Bring the water to a boil and place the tamales in the steamer. Cover tightly with a lid or foil (it is important that little or no steam escapes while cooking). Steam the tamales for 30 to 35 minutes over lightly boiling water, adding more boiling water as needed. The tamales are done when they feel firm to the touch but are not hard and the dough comes away easily from the husk.

While the tamales are steaming, prepare the chocolate sauce and anglaise. Place the chocolate in a mixing bowl, add the water, and

(continues)

FOR THE GARNISH

1 bar (8 ounces) bittersweet chocolate

whisk until the chocolate has melted and the mixture is smooth. Keep warm.

To prepare the anglaise, whisk the egg yolks and sugar in a mixing bowl until the yolks have lightened in color. Stir the cream and vanilla together in a saucepan and bring to a simmer over medium-high heat. Remove the pan from the heat and pour half into the yolk mixture while stirring constantly. Whisking vigorously, return the saucepan to the heat. Slowly pour the egg mixture back into the saucepan, still whisking vigorously, until incorporated. Cook the mixture until it thickens and coats the back of a spoon, about 5 minutes.

Ladle about $1/2$ cup of the anglaise onto each serving plate. With a knife, slice open the tamale wrappers from end to end and place on top of the anglaise. Place a dollop of the chocolate sauce on top of the tamale and using a potato peeler, grate 7 to 8 shavings from the chocolate bar over each tamale.

SERVES 8

The Gold Tamales
(Don't Leave Home Without Them!)

(J O H N   S E D L A R)

TWO OF THE MOST LUXURIOUS INGREDIENTS KNOWN TO MAN—CHOCOLATE AND GOLD—MAKE THIS ONE OF THE MOST SUMPTUOUS DESSERTS EVER.

COMBINED WITH THE GOOEY CARAMEL SAUCE, THIS IS ONE OF THE RICHEST DISHES AS WELL. FORTUNATELY, THE TART FRESH LIME JUICE IN

THE SAUCE BALANCES AND CUTS THE SWEETNESS. THE FLAVORLESS TISSUE-THIN GOLD LEAF NOT ONLY MAKES FOR AN IMPRESSIVE AND UNIQUE

VISUAL PRESENTATION, BUT IT IS ALSO EDIBLE; IN INDIA, IT HAS BEEN USED AS A CELEBRATORY DESSERT DECORATION FOR CENTURIES. IT IS AVAILABLE

IN SMALL BOOKS OF 24 SHEETS IN CAKE DECORATING SUPPLY STORES OR IN INDIAN MARKETS, WHERE IT IS LABELED "VARAK."

FOR THE CHOCOLATE TAMALES

10 ounces dark semisweet chocolate,
 broken into ¹/₂-inch pieces
1³/₄ cups heavy cream
12 large dried corn husks, soaked in
 warm water for 30 minutes

FOR THE CARAMEL-LIME SAUCE

1 cup sugar
1 tablespoon water
³/₄ cup heavy cream
¹/₂ cup freshly squeezed lime juice
1 sheet gold leaf, for garnish

To prepare the chocolate tamale filling, put the pieces of chocolate in the top of a double boiler and melt over simmering water, stirring constantly. Add the cream and stir until completely blended. Transfer the top half of the double boiler to the refrigerator, stirring from time to time. Chill until the mixture is firm but pliable, 30 to 45 minutes; do not let the mixture coagulate.

To prepare the tamales, cut 6 pieces of plastic wrap, each large enough to completely surround a corn husk. Lay out each piece of plastic on a flat work surface. Drain 6 of the corn husks and shake dry; reserve the remaining husks for serving. Lay out 1 husk on each piece of plastic. Divide the chocolate into 6 even portions and place one inside each husk. Wrap up the husk, shaping the chocolate into a rectangle, and wrap the plastic firmly around the husk, forming a tight envelope package. Transfer immediately to the refrigerator.

Repeat for the remaining tamales. Refrigerate for at least 3 hours. Remove the tamales 1 hour before serving and bring to room temperature.

Meanwhile, to prepare the sauce, combine the sugar and water in a heavy saucepan. Cook over medium heat, stirring frequently, until the sugar turns a medium caramel color, 10 to 15 minutes. Immediately add the cream and stir until fully incorporated. Remove from the heat and stir in the lime juice. Set aside and let cool to room temperature.

Unwrap the chocolate tamales from the corn husks and plastic wrap, discarding the old husks. Drain the remaining corn husks, shake dry, and lay out in the center of dessert plates. Place 1 rectangle of the chocolate filling in the center of each husk. Using a small-tipped dry brush, carefully place flecks of gold leaf on top of the chocolate. Spoon the sauce onto the plate around the base of the husk.

SERVES 6

Chocolate Bread Pudding Tamales

(M A R K   M I L L E R)

SIR WINSTON CHURCHILL, BRITAIN'S HEROIC WARTIME PRIME MINISTER, ONCE DECLINED A DESSERT AT AN OFFICIAL BANQUET, COMMENTING DEFTLY
AND IMPERIOUSLY, "PRAY REMOVE THIS PUDDING. IT HAS NO THEME." WELL, HERE'S A PUDDING FOR A TAMALE FILLING THAT YOU CERTAINLY
WILL NOT WANT TO REMOVE—FOR ONE THING, IT HAS PLENTY OF THEME. THESE CHOCOLATY TAMALES, UNIQUE AMONG THOSE IN THIS BOOK BECAUSE
THEY ARE BAKED RATHER THAN STEAMED, HAVE BEEN ON THE MENU AT COYOTE CAFE FOR YEARS—ALAS, A LITTLE AFTER SIR WINSTON'S TIME.

FOR THE CORNBREAD

1/4 cup unsalted butter, melted
1 cup plus 2 tablespoons milk
2 large eggs, separated
2 tablespoons honey
1 cup all-purpose flour
3/4 cup yellow cornmeal
1/2 tablespoon baking powder
1 teaspoon salt
1/4 cup sugar

FOR THE CUSTARD AND TAMALES

1 teaspoon anise seed
1/4 cup pine nuts
3 large eggs
1 cup heavy cream
6 ounces bittersweet chocolate, melted
2 tablespoons cocoa powder
10 large dried corn husks, soaked in warm water
 for 30 minutes
Nutmeg crème anglaise (see Sweet Pumpkin
 Tamales with Nutmeg Crème Anglaise,
 page 147) or cajeta (see Sweet Potato
 Tamales with Spicy Pecans and Cajeta,
 page 140)

Preheat the oven to 375°F. To prepare the cornbread, place the butter, milk, egg yolks, and honey in a mixing bowl and whisk together. In a separate bowl, stir together the flour, cornmeal, baking powder, salt, and sugar. Stir the dry ingredients into the liquids just until they are combined; do not overmix. Whisk the egg whites in a bowl until they form soft peaks and gently fold into the batter with a spatula. Pour the batter into an oiled 10-inch square baking pan and bake in the oven for 16 to 18 minutes. Remove from the oven and let cool in the pan on a rack.

To prepare the custard, place the anise seed in a hot, dry skillet and toast over medium heat, while shaking the pan, for about 1 minute, until fragrant. Transfer to a spice mill and grind to a powder. Place the pine nuts in the skillet and toast over medium heat for 4 to 5 minutes, stirring occasionally, until lightly browned. Set aside. Whisk the eggs and cream together in the top of a double boiler set over simmering water until warmed to room temperature. Whisk in the chocolate, cocoa, ground anise, and toasted pine nuts.

Break up the cooled cornbread into 1-inch cubes (approximately) and place in a mixing bowl. Pour the custard mixture over the cornbread and let it soak in the refrigerator for 30 minutes.

Reheat the oven to 325°F. Drain the corn husks and shake dry. Tear 16 thin strips (about 1/8 inch wide) from 2 of the husks and set aside for tying the tamales. Lay out the remaining 8 corn husks on a flat work surface. Place the cornbread mixture inside each husk, leaving about 1 inch of exposed corn husk at each end and 3/4 inch at each side. Bring the sides of each corn husk together, folding the filling; tuck one side of the husk under the other and roll up the tamale so the filling is completely enclosed inside the husk. Twist each end and tie with the reserved strips of corn husk. Repeat for the remaining tamales.

Transfer the tamales to a cookie sheet and bake in the oven for 25 to 30 minutes.

While the tamales are baking, prepare the anglaise or *cajeta*. Ladle about 1/4 cup of the anglaise or *cajeta* onto each serving plate. With a knife, slice open the top of the tamale wrappers from end to end and place on top of the sauce.

SERVES 8

Cookies and Cream Tamales with Chocolate Cognac Sauce

(J O H N   S E D L A R)

ONE OF THE NEWCOMERS ON RESTAURANT DESSERT MENUS IS A SIMPLE PLATE OF ASSORTED FLAVORED COOKIES. THESE TAMALES TAKE THEIR CUE FROM THIS HOMEY DEVELOPMENT, BUT DO NOT EXPECT THE MUNDANE; YOU WILL FIND THAT THE RICHEST OF CHOCOLATE COGNAC SAUCES MAKES THESE TAMALES A GRAND FINALE TO ANY MEAL. BUY THE BEST-QUALITY CHOCOLATE CHIP COOKIES YOU CAN FIND FOR THIS RECIPE, AS IT WILL MAKE A DIFFERENCE; EVEN BETTER, MAKE YOUR OWN, OR BUY FOUR OR FIVE OF THOSE LARGE HOMEMADE COOKIES AT SPECIALTY OR NATURAL FOODS STORES. TO SAVE TIME, SUBSTITUTE 1 QUART OF HÄAGEN-DAZS® VANILLA ICE CREAM FOR THE ICE CREAM TAMALE BASE IF YOU PREFER.

Ice Cream Tamale Filling
  (*see West Palm Beach Tamales, page 142*)
4 ounces Valrhona semisweet chocolate, chopped
3 tablespoons unsalted butter
2/3 cup water
2/3 cup sugar
1/4 cup premium cognac
16 chocolate chip cookies, crumbled
6 large dried corn husks, soaked in warm water
  for 30 minutes

Prepare the ice cream tamale filling.

To prepare the chocolate sauce, slowly melt the chocolate and butter together in the top of a double boiler set over simmering water. Meanwhile, in a saucepan, combine the water and sugar and boil for about 10 minutes, until syrupy. Stir the cognac into the chocolate mixture, then add the sugar syrup and stir until well combined. Let the sauce remain in the top of the double boiler over warm water, covered, until ready to serve.

To prepare the tamales, cut 6 pieces of plastic wrap measuring about 4 inches by 5 inches each. Lay out each piece of plastic on a flat work surface. Place the cookie crumbs on a platter. Take a 2/3-cup serving of the ice cream, pat into a rectangular shape, and press into the cookie crumbs to coat on all sides, working quickly so the ice cream doesn't melt on your fingers. Fold two of the sides of the plastic wrap over, then fold over the other two sides to form a tight envelope package. Repeat for the remaining tamales. Place each rectangle in the freezer before proceeding to the next.

Drain the corn husks and shake dry. Lay out each husk in the center of a shallow serving bowl. Unwrap the ice cream tamales from the plastic wrap and place one in the center of each corn husk. Briefly warm the sauce and spoon around the base of the ice cream inside the husk.

SERVES 6

Basic Recipes, Sauces, and Techniques

Chicken Stock

THIS RECIPE IS LOW IN SODIUM; AT AROUND 8 MILLIGRAMS OF SODIUM PER CUP, IT COMPARES VERY FAVORABLY WITH SOME READY-TO-USE CANNED STOCKS, WHICH CONTAIN AS MUCH AS 1500 MILLIGRAMS. YOU CAN USE DRIED HERBS FOR THE BOUQUET GARNI INSTEAD OF FRESH; SUBSTITUTE 1/4 TEASPOON EACH OF DRIED PARSLEY AND DRIED THYME AND 1/8 TEASPOON EACH OF DRIED MARJORAM AND TARRAGON. ADD THE BAY LEAVES, SECURE IN A DOUBLE LAYER OF CHEESECLOTH, AND TIE SECURELY.

4 quarts cold water

4 pounds uncooked chicken bones, and/or raw wings and backs (from 3 large chickens)

1 large onion, chopped

2 carrots, sliced

2 stalks celery, sliced

3 cloves garlic

5 black peppercorns

FOR THE BOUQUET GARNI

2 sprigs fresh parsley

2 sprigs fresh thyme

1 sprig fresh marjoram

1 sprig fresh tarragon

2 bay leaves

Place the water, chicken bones, onion, carrot, celery, garlic, and peppercorns in a stockpot or large saucepan and bring to a boil. For the bouquet garni, tie all the herbs together securely with kitchen twine and add to the pan. Turn down the heat to low, cover partially, and simmer for at least 4 hours and up to 6 hours, occasionally skimming any fat or impurities that rise to the surface. Add water as needed to keep all the ingredients covered.

Strain the stock into a large bowl and let stand for 15 minutes. Carefully skim the fat and then strain again into another bowl. Refrigerate the stock until the fat congeals on the surface; then skim off the fat. Cover and keep stored in the refrigerator for up to 4 days, or freeze for up to 3 months.

YIELD: ABOUT 3 QUARTS

Veal Stock

IF VEAL BONES ARE UNAVAILABLE, USE BEEF SOUP BONES. FOR A RICHER STOCK, REDUCE THE LIQUID BY HALF.

IF YOU LIKE, ADD SOME RED PEPPER FLAKES AND OREGANO SPRIGS.

4 pounds veal bones
4 quarts cold water
1 large onion, chopped
2 carrots, sliced
2 stalks celery, sliced
3 cloves garlic
1 bay leaf
4 sprigs fresh thyme, or $^1/_2$ teaspoon dried
$^1/_2$ cup chopped fresh parsley
5 black peppercorns
$^1/_2$ cup tomato paste or 4 tomatoes, chopped
$^1/_4$ cup coarsely chopped mushroom stems
   (optional)
$^1/_2$ cup white wine

Preheat the oven to 350°F.

Wash the veal bones in cold water and place in a roasting pan in a single layer. Roast in the oven for 30 minutes, stirring occasionally. Transfer the bones to a stockpot, drain off the fat, and reserve. Place a cup or two of the water in the roasting pan and deglaze over medium heat. Add this liquid to the stockpot with the bones.

Add the remaining water to the stockpot and bring to a simmer. Heat the reserved veal fat in a sauté pan and sauté the onion, carrots, celery, and garlic for 7 to 8 minutes over medium heat, until browned. Drain well and add to the stockpot with the bay leaf, thyme, parsley, peppercorns, tomato paste, mushrooms, and wine. Return the stock to a simmer and cook for 6 to 7 hours, occasionally skimming any fat or impurities that rise to the surface. Add water as needed to keep all the ingredients covered.

Strain the stock into a large bowl and let stand for 15 minutes. Carefully skim the fat and then strain again into another bowl. Refrigerate the stock until the fat congeals on the surface; then skim off the fat. Cover and keep stored in the refrigerator for up to 4 days, or freeze for up to 3 months.

YIELD: ABOUT 3 QUARTS

Vegetable Stock

YOU CAN ADD OR SUBSTITUTE INGREDIENTS AS YOU SEE FIT; FOR EXAMPLE, ADD A DICED TURNIP, A FEW RED PEPPER FLAKES, OR SOME CHOPPED SHALLOTS. THIS STOCK WILL KEEP FOR UP TO A WEEK IN THE REFRIGERATOR, OR YOU CAN FREEZE IT.

3 quarts cold water
1 onion, chopped
1 leek, sliced
2 carrots, sliced
2 stalks celery, sliced
2 tomatoes, diced
4 ounces mushrooms, sliced
$^1/_2$ bulb fennel, sliced (optional)
2 cloves garlic, chopped
2 bay leaves
2 sprigs fresh thyme
2 sprigs fresh parsley
2 sprigs cilantro
5 black peppercorns
$^1/_2$ cup white wine

Place all the ingredients in a large stockpot and bring to a boil. Reduce the heat to low, cover partially, and simmer for 30 minutes. Remove from the heat, cover, and let stand for 15 minutes. Strain and discard the solids.

YIELD: ABOUT 3 QUARTS

Manchamantel Sauce

THIS SAUCE IS PAIRED WITH THE PORK CARNITAS TAMALES WITH MANCHAMANTEL SAUCE ON PAGE 117 AND THE DUCK TAMALES WITH PINEAPPLE AND CHIPOTLE ON PAGE 89. *MANCHAMANTEL* TRANSLATES AS "TABLECLOTH STAINER," AND IT'S A CLASSIC SAUCE FROM CENTRAL MEXICO THAT GOES WELL WITH PORK BECAUSE OF ITS FRUITINESS. IF YOU DON'T HAVE AN OVERRIPE BANANA ON HAND, YOU CAN DEVELOP THE FLAVORS OF A YELLOW BANANA BY ROASTING IT IN ITS SKIN IN A 400°F OVEN FOR 15 MINUTES. YOU CAN SUBSTITUE OTHER RIPE FRUIT, SUCH AS PEACHES OR APRICOTS, FOR THE PINEAPPLE OR BANANA.

5 dried ancho chiles, seeded, toasted,
   and rehydrated (page 165)
2 dried red New Mexico chiles, seeded, toasted,
   and rehydrated (page 165)
2 cups hot water
1 Roma tomato, blackened (page 164)
1 clove roasted garlic (page 165)
3/4 cup peeled, cored, and chopped pineapple
1 overripe banana, peeled and chopped
1/2 green apple, peeled, cored, and chopped
1/2 teaspoon ground cinnamon
1 tablespoon cider vinegar
Pinch of ground cloves
1/8 teaspoon ground allspice
1/2 teaspoon salt
1/2 tablespoon brown sugar
1 1/2 cups unsweetened pineapple juice
1 tablespoon peanut oil

Transfer the rehydrated dried chiles to a food processor or blender and add all the remaining ingredients except the peanut oil. Puree until smooth. Heat the peanut oil in a large cast-iron skillet until just smoking. Add the sauce and fry at a sizzle for 3 to 4 minutes, stirring constantly.

Blackening Tomatoes, Tomatillos, Chiles, and Onions

This technique, typical of Southwestern and Mexican cooking, is used to give more robust and complex flavors; the ingredients are used blackened parts and all.

Remove the stems (and peel the onions) and place on a rack over a gas flame (or under a broiler) until the exterior parts blister, crack, and blacken (but do not overly blacken). Chop or process as directed, with the blackened parts.

Roasting Chiles and Bell Peppers

Roasting chiles and bell peppers gives them an attractive smoky and complex flavor and concentrates their natural sugars to bring out their full sweetness. It also makes it possible to peel the tough outer skin, which can sometimes be bitter-tasting.

Preheat the broiler or prepare the grill. (Alternatively, the chiles or peppers can be roasted on a wire rack over a gas flame on top of the stove.) Spray or brush each chile or pepper with a little olive oil. Place under the broiler or on the grill or rack and turn frequently with tongs until the skin is roasted and charred on all sides. Take care not to burn the flesh. Transfer to a bowl, cover the bowl with plastic wrap, and let cool for 10 minutes. Remove the plastic wrap and peel the blackened skin with the tip of a sharp knife. Remove the stems, cut the chiles or peppers open, and remove the seeds, core, and pale internal ribs. Chop, dice, or slice and set aside.

Take care to wash your hands thoroughly after handling chiles, and never touch your face or eyes with your hands until you have done so. If you have sensitive skin, wear rubber gloves when handling chiles.

Roasting Corn

Roasting gives corn a smoky quality that enhances its natural flavor. Cut the kernels from the cob with a sharp knife, taking care not to cut too deeply into the cob. Heat a large, dry skillet or nonstick sauté pan for 3 to 4 minutes over high heat. When hot, add the corn in a single layer. Roast for 3 to 4 minutes, tossing after 2 minutes, until dark.

Roasting Garlic

Roasting garlic gives it a sweet, mellow flavor.

Place unpeeled garlic cloves in a heavy skillet and dry roast over low heat for about 30 minutes, shaking or stirring the skillet occasionally, until the garlic becomes soft. (Alternatively, place the garlic cloves in a roasting pan and roast in a 350°F oven for 25 to 30 minutes.) When the garlic has roasted, you can peel the cloves or squeeze the garlic clove out of the skin.

Toasting, Rehydrating, and Pureeing Dried Chiles

This is the standard technique for preparing dried chiles in Southwestern and Mexican cooking, and it can be done ahead of time.

Stem and seed the chiles, place in a single layer in a dry, heavy skillet, and toast over medium heat for 2 to 3 minutes. Shake the skillet occasionally and do not let the chiles blacken or burn or they will taste bitter. Transfer the chiles to a large bowl and cover with hot water. Let stand for 30 minutes until they are rehydrated and soft. Transfer the chiles to a blender. Taste the water in which the chiles were soaking; if not bitter-tasting, add enough to the blender to make pureeing possible. If the water tastes bitter, use plain water. Puree the chiles and strain.

Toasting Nuts and Seeds

This technique brings out the full flavors of these ingredients. Place nuts in a single layer on a baking sheet and toast them in a 300°F oven for 10 to 15 minutes or until lightly browned, shaking occasionally. (Pine nuts, which burn easily, will take only 7 to 10 minutes.) Seeds can also be toasted in a dry skillet over medium-high heat for 2 to 3 minutes, stirring frequently. Toast pumpkin seeds in this manner over medium heat until lightly browned and popped open, about 5 minutes. (It takes 2 to 3 minutes for them to pop open.) Toast pecans in this manner over medium heat for 5 to 7 minutes, until lightly browned.

Toasting Dried Herbs and Spices

Place the herbs or spices in a dry skillet and toast them over low heat, stirring or tossing constantly, for about 1 minute or until fragrant. Do not scorch them or they will taste burnt and bitter.

Sources

Chiles, spices, herbs, canela, masa harina, dried cherries, barbecue sauce, and other Southwestern ingredients:

COYOTE CAFE GENERAL STORE
132 W. Water St.
Santa Fe, NM 87501
☎ (800) 866-HOWL or (505) 982-2454

Southwestern and Mexican products:

MONTERREY FOODS
3939 Cesar Chavez
Los Angeles, CA 90063
☎ (213) 263-2143

Chiles, pine nuts, spices, and other Southwestern ingredients:

PENDERY'S
304 E. Belknap
Fort Worth, TX 76102
☎ (800) 533-1870

Herbs (including epazote and hoja santa), cactus, and wild mushrooms:

B. RILEY
607A Juan Tabo Blvd. N.E.
Albuquerque, NM 87123
☎ (505) 275-0902

Hoja santa and epazote:

GOLDEN CIRCLE FARMS
1109 N. McKinney
Rice, TX 75155
☎ (903) 326-4263

Chiles:

LOS CHILEROS
PO Box 6215
Santa Fe, NM 87501
☎ (505) 471-6967

CASA LUCAS MARKET
2934 24th St.
San Francisco, CA 94110
☎ (415) 826-4334

Chiles and corn husks:

LA PALMA
2884 24th St.
San Francisco, CA 94110
☎ (415) 647-1500

Huitlacoche:

GLENN BURNS
16158 Hillside Circle
Montverde, FL 34756
☎ (407) 469-4356

Chocolate, oils, vinegars, spices:

PACIFIC GOURMET
PO Box 2071
San Rafael, CA 94912
☎ (415) 641-8400

Dried cherries:

AMERICAN SPOON FOODS
PO Box 566, 1668 Clarion Ave.
Petoskey, MI 49770
☎ (800) 222-5886 or (616) 347-9030

Blue cornmeal/masa harina:

BLUE CORN CONNECTION
3825 Academy Parkway South N.W.
Albuquerque, NM 87109
☎ (505) 344-9768

Meats, including venison, quail, squab, free-range chickens, and naturally raised beef:

D'ARTAGNAN INC.
399-419 St. Paul Ave.
Jersey City, NJ 07306
☎ (201) 792-0748

PREFERRED MEATS
2050 Galvez St.
San Francisco, CA 94124
☎ (415) 285-9299

Venison:

BROKEN ARROW RANCH
PO Box 530
Ingram, TX 78025
☎ (210) 367-5875

Organic seeds, including chiles and corn:

SEEDS OF CHANGE
PO Box 15700
Santa Fe, NM 87506
☎ (800) 762-7333

List of Photographs

Photography and prop styling by: Lois Ellen Frank
Lighting Technican: John Middelkoop
Photographic Assistance: Walter Whitewater & Alberto Ramirez

MARK MILLER:

Wild Mushroom and White Truffle Tamales with Tomatillo-Chipotle Sauce 20
Matate & Mano from prop collection of Lois Ellen Frank

Fresh Corn Tamales with Black Truffles and Black Truffle Butter 33
New Red Salad by Waechterbach Germany; Dinner plate from American Home Furnishings: ☎ (800) 876-4454

Roasted Corn and *Huitlacoche* Tamales 41
Plate from prop collection of Lois Ellen Frank

Goat Cheese Tamales with Black Olive Masa and Lemon-Fig Salsa 47
Aletha Soule Dinner plate from Cookworks of Santa Fe: ☎ (800) 972-3357

Salmon Tamales with Red Pepper Masa and Mole Amarillo 53
Plate from prop collection of Lois Ellen Frank

Shrimp Tamales with Rancho Sauce 62
Aletha Soule Dinner plate from Cookworks of Santa Fe: ☎ (800) 972-3357

Chicken Tamales with Mole Poblano 78
Comalera Dinner plate from American Home Furnishings: ☎ (800) 876-4454

Turkey Tamales Yucatán Style with Black Beans, Chipotle, and Pumpkin Seeds 83

Carnitas Tamales with Pineapple and Tomato-Habanero Sauce 118

Cabernet Tamales with Beef and Black Pepper 107

Day of the Dead Sweet Tamales 138
Dinner plate from American Home Furnishings: ☎ (800) 876-4454

Bittersweet Chocolate Tamales with Anchos, Prunes, and Raisins 152
Dinner plate from Cookworks of Santa Fe: ☎ (800) 972-3357

Index

Page references for photographs are in italics.

171